CENTRAL ITALY:
An Archaeological Guide

Central Italy:
An Archaeological Guide

*The prehistoric, Villanovan, Etruscan,
Samnite, Italic and Roman remains and
the ancient road systems*

R. F. PAGET

NOYES PRESS

Noyes Building

Park Ridge, New Jersey 07656, USA

First U.S. Edition: 1973
Copyright © 1973 by R.F. Paget
Library of Congress Catalog Card No.: 72–85330

ISBN: 0–8155–5009–X

Printed in Great Britain

To my wife ADA IMMACOLATA, in gratitude for fifty-four happy years together

A VOICE FROM THE PAST

'I shall find in antiquity a rewarding study, if only because, whilst I am absorbed in it, I shall be able to turn my eyes from the troubles which so long have tormented the modern world; and to write without any of that over-anxious consideration which may well plague a writer on contemporary life, even if it does not lead him to conceal the truth.'

Livy, *The Ancient History of Rome* (Bk. I, 22-27)

CONTENTS

Acknowledgements page 15

Preface 17

General information 21

Historical note (Prehistory, until 753 B.C., by Graeme Barker) 26

Dates of main Roman Emperors mentioned in the Guide 38

Pottery styles and dates 39

Chronology of Roman roads 40

Alphabetical list of museums 42

PART I PREHISTORY

1 Some Prehistoric Sites in Central Italy (*by Graeme Barker*) 59

PART II ROME AND OSTIA

2 Rome and Ostia 77

PART III ETRURIA

3 Via Aurelia (S.S.1) 109

4 Via Claudia (S.S.493), Via Cassia (S.S.2), Via Amerina 138

5 Via Flaminia (S.S.3) and Via Tiberina (S.S.313) 158

PART IV SAMNIUM AND THE ITALIOTE TRIBES

6 Via Salaria (S.S.4), Via Sabina (S.S.17), Via Caecilia (S.S.80) 179

7 Via Tiburtina, Via Valeria (S.S.5) and Roads 17, 82, 83 186

PART V LATIUM, CAMPANIA AND
ROMAN COLONIZATION

8 Via Prenestina, Via Casilina (S.S.6), Via Tuscolana
(S.S.215), Via Latina (S.S.215)   *page* 207

9 Via Appia (S.S.7)   224

Glossary   241

Addresses of the Superintendents of Antiquities in Central Italy   245

Italian inns, cooking and wines   246

Bibliography   248

Index   250

ILLUSTRATIONS

PLATES

1. Villanovan biconical urns from Tarquinia   *page* 31
2. Tomb contents from Bisenzio from the Iron Age in Lazio   53
3. Grotta di Ortucchio, a prehistoric site near Avezzano   66
4. The 'Warrior of Capestrano'   72
5. The Roman She-Wolf   81
6. The Roman Forum   85
7. Ostia: mosaic showing ships being loaded or unloaded at the port   100
8. Ostia: detail from a mosaic illustrating the trade network around the port   100
9. Ostia: an oil store   101
10. Ostia: the great Capitolium, the Temple of Jupiter, Minerva and Juno   104
11. Cerveteri, the vast Etruscan necropolis   115
12. The sarcophagus of the married couple ('dei Sposi') from Cerveteri   116
13. San Giovenale, showing the impressive Etruscan walls around the acropolis   118
14. The terracotta Winged Horses from Tarquinia   123
15. A Villanovan cinerary hut urn   123
16. The Lady Velcha, from an Etruscan tomb painting at Tarquinia   123
17. Cosa: port works to prevent silting   128
18. Cosa: a second view of the harbour works   128
19. Volterra: the Porta all'Arco. The lower part of the gate is Etruscan   135

20. Orvieto: the necropolis with the tombs laid out in streets *page* 147
21. The François Vase, found at Chiusi 153
22. One of the most famous of Etruscan bronzes: the splendid Chimera 156
23. Narni: the Augustan bridge which carried the original Via Flaminia 162
24. The springs of Clitumnus near Spoleto 164
25. Spello: the Porta Consulare, of Roman construction 166
26. Ancona: the Arch of Trajan 169
27a. Hadrian's villa: the Teatro Marittimo 193
  b. Hadrian's villa: the Canopus 193
28. Horace's villa at Licenza 195
29. Terracotta head of Samnite origin from Triflisco 220
30. Cales: black terracotta oil-lamp 221
31. Portico in the Temple of Jupiter Anxur at Terracina 229
32. Fondi: a splendid example of polygonal walling 232
33. Minturnae: the Augustan aqueduct 234
34. The Pons Auruncus at Sessa Aurunca on the Appian Way 237
35. The Via Appia at Castel Starza in the Ager Falernus 238

FIGURES

1a. Bronze ring with key, from Cales 23
  b. Bronze fibula (brooch) from Cales 23
  c. Terracotta Roman lamp 23
2. Etruscan alphabet engraved on an ivory writing tablet 34
3. The tomb of Cecilia Metella on the Via Appia Antica 94
4. Mithraism: the birth of Mithras from an egg 102
5. Ostia lighthouse, from a mosaic 105
6. A diagrammatic section of a Roman road showing the method of construction 109
7. A diagrammatic section of a 'pozzo' or 'pozzetto' grave 114
8. A diagrammatic section of a 'fossa' grave 114

9. The Ponte dell'Abbadia at Vulci   *page* 125
10. The 'fasces' of Vetulonia: the origin of Roman consular
      'fasces'   131
11. A coin of Populonia showing ironworkers' tools   133
12a and b. Hut urns from Clusium, perhaps models of com-
      mon types of Etruscan villas   154
13. Bronze model of a ploughing scene   156
14. A wooden oil or wine barrel from Gualdo Tadino: dated
      to the sixth century B.C.   171
15. Types of masonry used in the ancient world   211
16. Ancient loom weights   222
17. Model of a gouty foot from Cales, used in magical
      medical cures   222

PLANS

1. Ancient Rome   82–3
2. Ostia   99
3. Tarquinia   120
4. Vulci   125
5. Rusellae   130
6. Volterra   134
7. Faliscan road network   139
8. Veii   141
9. Bolsena   145
10. Florence   149
11. Civita Castellana   159
12. Hadrian's villa at Tivoli   191
13. Alba Fucens   198

MAPS

1. Central Italy: the system of main highways radiating
      from Rome   21

2.   Central Italy: the tribal territories *c.* 350 B.C.   *page* 32
3.   Central Italy: selected prehistoric sites discussed in the
        text   60
4.   Etruria: the Twelve Territories of the Etruscan cities   110
5.   Main modern roads and ancient sites north of
        Rome   112-13
6.   Main modern roads and ancient sites east and south of
        Rome   188-9

ACKNOWLEDGEMENTS

First I must thank the Superintendents of Antiquities for the various areas for permission to work in their territory; then Graeme Barker for kindly supplying the chapter and notes on prehistory; Michael Tyler-Whittle for reading the script and removing many errors; Fred Bullock who made all the draft maps and plans; and my working team of J. Carpenter, T. Failmezger, F. Alexander and T. Ross for much help in the field.

I am grateful to the following for the illustrations: Thames and Hudson Ltd. for allowing me to base my Plans 3, 5, 6, 7, 8, 9 and 11, Figures 2, 10, 12a and b and Map 4 on Figures 7, 16, 19, 13, 11, 15, 12, 3, 25, 5 and 26 respectively in Professor H. H. Scullard's *The Etruscan Cities and Rome*; to Fototeca Unione for Plates 1, 2 (Gabinetto Fotografico Nazionale photograph), 4 (Alinari photograph), 6, 7, 11, 12, 13, 14 (Anderson photograph), 15, 16 (Alinari photograph), 17, 18, 20 (Anderson photograph), 21 (Alinari photograph), 23, 24 (Alinari photograph), 25, 27a, 27b, 28, 29 and 30 (German Archaeological Institute photograph); to the Italian Institute, 39 Belgrave Square, London S.W.1 for Plates 9, 10 and 26; to Graeme Barker for Plate 3 and to T. Failmezger for Plates 31, 32 and 34.

I also have to thank W. Heinemann Ltd. for permission to quote from H. H. Jones's Loeb translation of *The Geography of Strabo* and Penguin Books Ltd., for the quotation from A. de Sélincourt's translation of Livy's *Ancient History of Rome*. Finally I want to thank Professor E. T. Salmon of McMaster University, Canada, for much help derived from reading his books *Samnium and the Samnites* and *Roman Colonization under the Republic*.

PREFACE

Central Italy offers the visitor several quite distinct but complementary attractions: Rome and the Etruscan country, Samnium and the Italian tribes, Latium and the Campania. The student of Roman history can base himself in the city of Rome and within a radius of 30 kilometres can find examples of every period, from the prehistoric necropolis in the Forum to the glories of the Imperial Age.

Beyond the zone of the metropolis, the expansion of Roman power over the mainland of Italy was achieved by a wise policy of alliances and absorption into the Empire, in contrast to the usual practice in antiquity of destroying the conquered towns and enslaving the inhabitants. The scheme of the Guide follows the modern road system, the major part of which has been built upon the former Roman military road system.

It is one of the fascinating aspects of Italy that as soon as the big towns are left behind the visitor is carried back through the centuries. The further he goes into the countryside, the deeper he delves into the past. Farmhouses not only occupy the same position that they did under the Caesars, but paintings from Pompeii and elsewhere show their identical construction. The ancient customs still survive. Along the valley of the Tiber the farmer ploughs his fields with a yoke of great white oxen, the descendants of the wild aurochs that roamed the forests of Europe in the Ice Ages, patient and docile survivors from man's first experiments in tilling the soil. He reaps the first ears of corn to make 'corn dollies', which will be placed on the stooks to protect the corn from damage by earth spirits while it is drying in the sun. Two thousand years of Christianity have not eliminated a wise insurance in the old pagan gods.

The most rewarding way to explore the archaeological treasures of Central Italy is to drive one's own car. The well-known centres, such as Rome, Florence and Naples, can be reached by aeroplane or train, or even by coach, and in these towns the traveller eats and sleeps in maximum comfort in international hotels . . . same old food, no local colour, no romance, just plain utility. But the car owner can roam over the countryside on good roads to seek the less frequented places, step into the past, and above all enjoy the truly enchanting scenery, not forgetting the local food and wine at some ancient inn. In the Etruscan country to the north of Rome, any turning off the great Roman highway soon brings the traveller to the cork forests, olive groves and chestnut scrub of the foothills of the mountains. Alongside the road, every so often, a glimpse of a rock-hewn tomb, half hidden in the undergrowth, gives promise of exciting finds later on. The road winds upwards with many hairpin bends and wonderful views into the valley below. All kinds of strange new flowers carpet the space between the lichen covered rocks making an irresistible appeal to the botanist.

Country women with voluminous bundles on their heads and leading heavily laden donkeys with panniers of fruit and vegetables as they make their way up to the hilltop village for the day's market, give friendly waves and call a cheerful greeting to the visitors.

The long climb is often well worth the effort. The entry to the village, built of the local stone and perched precariously on an impossible crag and so bleached by the sun as to be almost invisible against the rocks, is made through a gateway in the Cyclopean walls of the citadel, built five centuries before the birth of Christ. The ancient church in the main square has adopted into its walls the columns of the temple to the pagan god that it has succeeded. Even today many of the old pagan rites are still performed in honour of the Christian saint who now protects the village. There might also be a small museum, and a local archaeological enthusiast who would guide the visitor to the sites.

If the only restaurant has only half a dozen tables in the shade of a vine-covered pergola, do not be discouraged. The local bank manager and his staff probably feed there every day, and bank managers do not feed rough. I still recall the excellent lunch we had at Allumiere in that lone *trattoria*. There we found genuine home-cooking, with each dish individually prepared by the *padrona*, maybe with a local attraction of fried truffles, or something equally exotic, which is only an expensive dream in London, Paris, Berlin or New York. Even the wine is from grapes grown on the slopes of the hillside, on terraces cut many hundreds of years ago—nectar which has nothing in common with the sophisticated liquor that passes for wine in the northern capitals.

If you have no car, you can make use of the local bus network which links the larger villages with the market towns all over Italy. There are frequent services and a small suitcase can be carried free. The present Guide is arranged so that the traveller can start his explorations from Rome, Florence, Naples or wherever the train or plane deposits him.

Walking tours can also be fun. One of the best to take is the route from Rome to Perugia along the Via Flaminia, an ancient ridgeway dating from Neolithic times and later paved by the Romans. In places one looks down into valleys hundreds of feet below on either hand. The villages along the Via Flaminia have captivating names and are all spaced about 5 kilometres apart, just a nice hour's stroll before resting and recuperating at Quercia (the Oaktree), Nocera (the Walnut Tree), Osteria del Gatto (the Inn of the Cat), and Gualdo (perhaps the old Gallic word for 'forest'). Pliny the Younger often made this journey from Rome to his villa near the headwaters of the Tiber, in the vicinity of Perugia, stopping overnight at farms owned by his mother-in-law of whom he was very fond. He wrote her a 'Thank-you letter' (*Letters*, 1, 4): 'What comfort in your farms at Otriculum, Narnia, Carsulae and Perusia. At Narnia there is even a bath . . . and your servants treated me better than my own.'

It is said that not one thousandth part of the buried treasures of the past has yet been excavated or even discovered. So do not neglect to make friends with the local archaeological enthusiasts, and the village policeman and the farmers. With their goodwill your visit will be a memorable one; you will see a lot that others miss.

I have included all the sites that are marked on Amadeo Mauiri's archaeological map in his book *The Art and Civilisation of Italy*, published by the Touring Club Italiano. Items of special interest have a descriptive note. Many of the smaller sites offer a grand field for research and countless others await discovery. Remember to get permission for serious study from the appropriate Superintendent of Antiquities (see page 245) as clandestine working is illegal and liable to lead to complications.

Take plenty of photographs; you will be surprised how much can be learnt from them long after you get home again. Don't forget to have a good compass, a measuring tape and a wooden rule 20 centimetres long (the first 10 centimetres painted red and the next white for use as a scale when photographing, by laying it alongside the item). Take a notebook, pencils and rubber. You will also need a few simple medicines to deal with headaches from too much sun and tummy troubles from too much exciting food and *vino*, also disinfectant and plaster for small cuts and scratches which should not be neglected.

Do read the pages of General Information, and the Bibliography. You will find it very helpful to have with you a good book on the particular subject that interests you.

GENERAL INFORMATION

As prehistory is a rather special subject, the information has been gathered into Part 1 (Chapter 1) so that its addicts will not have to dig it out from under the material in the subsequent chapters. The

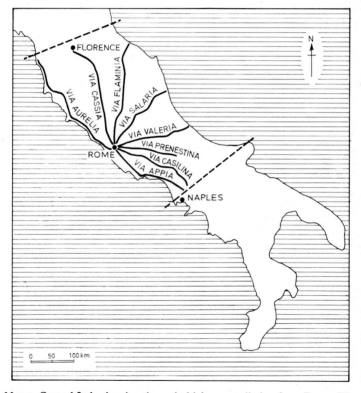

Map 1. Central Italy showing the main highways radiating from Rome. The chapters of the Guide are based upon these roads in a clockwise direction from the west coast.

remaining four Parts are laid out in the form of journeys along those modern roads which are based on the main Roman highways radiating from Rome in a clockwise rotation, from the west coast. (See chronology on pages 40–1.) They are known as S.S. (*Strada Statale*) 1, 2, 3, etc. As distances are measured from Rome, and are marked in kilometre 'milestones' at the side of the roads (which are all numbered), identification of turnings and sites is greatly simplified. Cross-roads and other interesting side turnings are followed to their destination as a 'diversion' before proceeding along the main road.

There are over three hundred known sites and other places of interest, and countless others yet to be discovered or at least eluding identification. Many towns and even some of the larger villages have more or less important museum collections of local material. The larger museums are listed on pages 42–55 and in the chapters the more interesting items have a short note which should make the crumbling ruins live once again in the visitor's imagination.

The maps in the Guide are only intended to be historically informative. Travellers should provide themselves with Sheets 13, 14, 15, 16 and 17 of the series *Carta Automobilistica 1:200,000* of the Touring Club Italiano before leaving for Italy as it is not usually possible to buy maps locally. Maps may be obtained from Edward Stanford Ltd., 12 Long Acre, London W.C.2, the Map House, 67 St James's Street, S.W.1 and the Rizzoli Bookstore, 71 Fifth Avenue, New York, U.S.A. General small-scale road maps are given away by roadside filling stations in Italy. If the visitor is seeking scenery as well as archaeological treasures he is strongly advised to explore the by-roads between the state highways for it is there that the answer to that fascinating question 'How did the people live?' is likely to be found. In these backways of the real countryside nothing changes. If the people spoke Latin and there were no television aerials or motor cars, twenty centuries would just slide away and time stand still. Most of the diversions in the Guide are into this ancient road net.

It has been a difficult problem with the limited space available, to know how to make the Guide both comprehensive and portable. The solution has been achieved by keeping to the rule that the object is to tell the visitor how to reach the sites and where they are situated and what they contain. The Bibliography will provide hints for detailed study. In this manner I have been able to include most of the sites mentioned by Livy and Strabo, and in modern times those marked on Maiuri's map in *The Art and Civilisation of Italy*.

Bus routes, accommodation, etc. All large market towns and the surrounding villages are linked by frequent bus services. Details of coach tours can be obtained from the C.I.T. Travel Service, 10 Charles II Street, London S.W.1, or in the U.S.A. at 11 West 42nd Street, New York. There is ample hotel accommodation everywhere in Italy. A note on the food and wines is on p. 246.

Museums. Consult the list given on pp. 42–55. I have given opening times where I know them but visitors will be well advised to check these anyway with the relevant Superintendent of Antiquities before making a special journey as times are often changed without notice. I have given a brief description of the outstanding items but would remind visitors that it is the little intimate items that really tell the story of someone's life—the little toilet box of make-up, the key ring

Figs. 1*a* and *b*. Domestic bronze work from Cales: the key ring is dated to the third century B.C. and the serpentine fibula, or safety pin brooch, is an early Villanovan form, some 500 years earlier.

Fig 1*c*. A terracotta Roman lamp from Lucerna dated to the first century B.C.

to the jewel case, false teeth, a banqueting scene on a painted vase (see Figs. 1a, b and c). Try to find these in the museums and you will get a better insight into the way of life of the past than you will by admiring the Coliseum or the Pantheon. It is the proper use of museums that brings to life the crumbling wall-footing on a bleak hillside—all that is left of a patrician's luxurious country villa. Permission to inspect special and private collections can usually be obtained by application to the Superintendent of Antiquities for the area. But be sure to make the application well in advance of the proposed visit.

Official Guides to the sites are available at some places at the

booking offices; they are very reasonably priced and are useful as a
record of what is at the site or in the collection. Coloured slides and
photographs are also on sale at the sites. Replicas of the local finds
and copies of learned academic treatises on the area can all be
bought at the larger sites.

Free passes, Italian Museum cards for the State owned sites and
museums can be obtained on application to the headquarters of the
Automobile Association, Fanum House, Leicester Square, London
W.C.2 and the Royal Automobile Club, 83 Pall Mall, London S.W.1
and the Italian Institute at 686 Park Avenue, New York, U.S.A.
Council of Europe Cultural Identity Cards, available to graduates,
teachers, authors, etc., give free passes, and in some cases reduced
terms, to a rather wider selection of museums, libraries, monuments,
etc., in particular the Vatican museums. Apply to the Central
Bureau for Educational Visits and Exchanges, 43 Dorset Street,
London W1H 3FN (Tel. 01-486 5101).

Autostrade. These highways are not specifically mentioned in the
Guide as they are not related in any way to the archaeology of the
countryside. Moreover they are routed to avoid all towns and
villages, access to which is along the approach roads. Much of the
beautiful scenery that exists along the normal roads is lost. It must,
however, be borne in mind that high average speeds can be maintained on the autostrade with much less physical effort over long
distances. Travellers will naturally make use of these roads to reach
specific points.

Measurements. I have used metrication throughout. A metre is
just over 3 feet and a kilometre is equivalent to about $\frac{5}{8}$ of a mile.
Petrol and oil are sold by the litre and there are $4\frac{3}{4}$ litres in an imperial
gallon and 5 litres to an American gallon.

A Note of Caution. Remember you are in a country with very
different customs from those in your homeland. Goods and services
that would be cheap at home may turn out to be very expensive, so
always fix the price before placing an order. Medical services can be
very expensive indeed and the wise visitor will arrange accident and
illness insurance before leaving home.

A Historical Note for the non-specialist follows. It should be remembered that, in this part of Italy, which is near to Rome, most of the historical events that come in are tales of Rome's conquests very early in her history. That is a period whose story, as told by Livy and other ancient authorities, was more legendary than historical, and the appearance of accuracy of detail given by such things as Rome's Samnite wars and the decline of Etruscan power is quite spurious.

HISTORICAL NOTE
(Prehistory, until 753 B.C., by Graeme Barker)

Our earliest prehistory, the *Palaeolithic* or *Old Stone Age*, is thought to coincide approximately with the geological Pleistocene epoch, when during repeated cold periods, each of tens of thousands of years' duration, great ice-caps covered large areas of the surface of the earth. First signs of 'hominization', or the development of man-like activities—such as the assumption of an erect posture and other biological changes marking the divergence of the hominids from the apes—probably appeared long before this, perhaps as much as 20,000,000 years ago; for the archaeologist, however, the main criterion of our evolution has necessarily been the technological development of our *tools*, the material remains of the past, and so far tool-making, in even its crudest forms, does not appear to be earlier than the Pleistocene—that is, of some one or even two million years' duration.

The Palaeolithic therefore represents an immense period of time—one or two million years save for the last 12,000, for the end of the Last Glaciation or Ice Age has been dated to about 10,000 B.C., or 12,000 B.P. (years before the present). For the greater part of this period, the traces of our past consist mainly of the hunters' 'industries', or collections of flint tools, and the bones of the animals they hunted. The total technological evolution of the Palaeolithic can be summarized in three stages which roughly coincide with the principal divisions of the period—Lower, Middle and Upper. Sites of each period have been included in Chapter 1. Our earliest tools seem to have been simple choppers and axes, but during the *Lower Palaeolithic* much finer hand-axes were developed (often called Acheulean after the site of St Acheul in France) shaped by the removal of shallow flakes on both sides of the tool, which were extraordinarily standardized over Africa, southern Europe and parts of Asia. The hunters at Torre in Pietra (see Chapter 1, p. 61) manufactured such tools formed from flint cores, and the flakes taken from

26

them during the making of the axes were probably also used for cutting skins, meat and so on. This first type of standardized tool developed by men was also the sole type used for several hundreds of thousands of years, until 50,000 or 60,000 years ago. In the *Middle Palaeolithic*, however, the prehistoric flint-knapper developed a variety of flake tools instead, and prepared the flint cores so that flakes could be struck from them 'ready-made' in particular shapes. This 'prepared-core technique' is characteristic of Middle Palaeolithic Levallois-Mousterian industries in Europe, including Italy— the term is again taken from sites in France. Mousterian industries containing points and side scrapers made from beach pebbles are found in Italy, especially in caves along the western coast. Radiocarbon dates for Mousterian sites in Europe are spread from about 55,000 B.C. (from an open camp site excavated in the Pontinian plain to the south of Rome) to about 30,000 B.C. Between 35,000 and 40,000 years ago more complex industries were developed in the *Upper Palaeolithic* in Europe, western Asia and northern Africa, consisting of a variety of scrapers, points, knives and a special engraving tool called a burin, made from long narrow blades struck from the core with a wooden or bone punch. Although radiocarbon dates for the Upper Palaeolithic in Europe reach back to 35,000 B.C., there are as yet no dates in central or southern Italy earlier than *c.* 30,000 years ago. Upper Palaeolithic groups produced the fabulous cave paintings of France and Spain; their art in Italy is less spectacular, but a rich series of engraved bone plaques was found in the Grotta Polesini near Rome (see p. 64). Three 'Venus figurines' have also been found in Italy. Upper Palaeolithic hunters in central Italy may well have practised close or loose herding with the game that they killed—in its way a kind of domestication, rather like the relationship between Lapps and reindeer. In Italy at this time in the Last Glaciation the climate on the western coastal plains was dry and fairly cold; large herds of red deer and Steppe horses (as large as the modern donkey) grazed wide steppes here during the winter and moved up into the high Apennines during the summer: as the snows melted each spring the hunters left their winter camps (such as the Grotta Polesini) and followed the herds into the hills to summer camps such as the Fucine caves.

With the end of the Last Ice Age at about 10,000 B.C. the great herds disappeared as the coastal steppes gradually became afforested— first with pine and birch, then the great oak and chestnut forests that were still extensive in Roman times. The peoples of central Italy had to adapt to these fundamental changes in climate, environment and even in food, for the large herds were replaced by the forest animals —red or roe deer, pigs and cattle. As the ice-caps melted, the seas rose and fishing sites have been found on the western coasts of Italy (at Monte Circeo, for example) consisting largely of great heaps or middens of shells. The hunters and fishers of this period are termed *Mesolithic*, or Middle Stone Age, and in many ways their way of life persisted long after the beginning of the Neolithic, or New Stone Age, which has been traditionally defined as the period of the first agriculture. In addition to the coastal settlements, fishing villages also grew up round the Fucine Lake in the high Apennines, which gradually began to shrink after the end of the Pleistocene (see pages 66–7). The rich resources of the lake provided food for many thousands of years, for Mesolithic, Neolithic and Bronze Age settlements at the water's edge.

In addition to an agricultural economy, archaeologists normally *c. 4$.* include certain material attributes, such as pottery and polished *B.C* stone tools, in the *Neolithic* or New Stone Age. The accepted theory is that Neolithic farmers arrived on the eastern shores of Italy with domestic animals and cereals, from a homeland in the eastern Mediterranean. In central Italy, early Neolithic villages on the east coast are dated by radiocarbon to the fifth millennium B.C. The inhabitants used pottery often decorated with the impressions of sea shells—the so-called 'cardial ware'—as well as fine painted pottery; both types were also used by the Neolithic villagers in southern Italy, in Apulia, and possibly derived from impressed and painted wares manufactured at a rather earlier date in Greece. The local painted wares in central Italy are named after the site of Ripoli, near the eastern coast in Abruzzo.

Evidence of domestic animals and cereals has been found, particularly in Neolithic sites around Ripoli. On the other side of the Apennines, however, the local Mesolithic communities seem to have continued their accustomed way of life and only gradually integrated new ways of exploiting their environment into their hunting and gathering economies. The dominant influence on life for tens of thousands of years in central Italy has been the marked difference between winter and summer conditions on the coastal plains and in the high Apennines. Pasture, whether for game or for flocks, was for the most part seasonal. Upper Palaeolithic hunters probably followed their game regularly between the coastal plains and the high summer pastures. In the same way, Neolithic and Bronze Age communities seem to have practised largely *mobile* economies with their flocks and herds, camping on the Tuscan and Roman plains in the winter and moving up with the animals in the spring as the lowlands began to wither under the blazing sun of June. (This seasonal movement between winter and summer grazing areas is called transhumance.) In central Italy, prehistoric economies, whether of the hunter or of the herdsman, had to be adapted to the seasonal pasture too; today large flocks are still taken into the Apennines from the western plains every summer—the way of life of the shepherds reaches back 5,000 or 6,000 years, and really reflects a rhythm of life that is many thousands of years older than the Neolithic. Perhaps this is the main reason why the evolution of prehistoric cultures in central Italy often lags behind cultural developments to the north and south—cultural change had to adapt to that age-old rhythm which had been evolved to overcome the problems created for hunter or herdsman by topography and climate.

Recent excavations in central Italy have shown that cultural developments in the Neolithic and after were often remarkably local. We speak of a Copper Age or *Eneolithic* after the Neolithic, then the full *Bronze Age* and the *Iron Age*, which takes us from the pre-historic to the historic peoples of Italy, the Etruscans and other Italian tribes known to the Romans. These terms are technological, denoting the evolution of ever more advanced metal industries. Until the very end of the Bronze Age, however, central Italy seems to have had a remarkably *limited* copper and bronze industry, which was almost entirely confined to Etruria, the later homeland of the Etruscan civilization.

A large number of Eneolithic burials have been found here with the earliest metalwork amongst the grave goods, such as simple flat axes and daggers of copper, as well as exquisitely worked flint blades and daggers; this Eneolithic culture is named after the 'type-site' of Rinaldone near Montefiascone and probably lasted from the middle of the third millennium into the first centuries of the second millennium B.C. In much of central Italy the inhabitants lived out their lives little if at all affected by the introduction of metallurgy until the *Late Bronze Age* in about 1000 B.C. or a little earlier; yet the earliest copper objects in the Rinaldone graves date to 2500 B.C. or even earlier. In Etruria, too, the full Bronze Age was much richer than in other parts of central Italy. The local metal industry continued around the copper and tin ores of Etruria, yet only a handful of metal objects found their way across the Apennines to Marche and Abruzzo, for most of the second millennium B.C. The Bronze Age culture of central Italy is usually called the 'Apennine' Bronze Age; transhumant flocks were clearly an important part of the economy, and one distinctive pottery type found on many upland and lowland sites has been identified as a 'milk-boiler' or 'strainer', and can be compared directly with the implements used by shepherds today to make 'pecorino' or sheep's cheese. The beginnings of the Apennine culture are usually placed in the first half of the second millennium B.C., perhaps 1800 or 1700 B.C.; by the second half of the millennium in the later phases of the Bronze Age a fairly uniform assemblage appears over central Italy, in even the remoter parts of Marche and Abruzzo.

Apart from some evidence of new population on the eastern seaboard at the start of the Neolithic, between 5000 and 4500 B.C., there is hardly *any* archaeological proof of newcomers on a large scale until possibly in the last centuries of the second millennium B.C., when cremation cemeteries appear first singly then in large numbers down the length of the peninsula. In central Europe similar cemeteries had appeared during the Middle Bronze Age and cremation was the customary burial rite across much of Europe by the Late Bronze Age; the ashes of the dead were buried in ceramic 'biconical' urns (see Plates 1 and 2) together with a few personal ornaments, in a pit which was sometimes lined with stone slabs. What exactly this 'urnfield' culture meant in human terms is one of the fiercest battlegrounds of archaeology. The older theory was that all the cemeteries represent invading peoples, hopefully the Indo-Europeans; certainly the end of the second millennium was a troubled time across Europe, when the Aegean civilizations clearly suffered at the hands of foreign raiders, sometimes catastrophically. In central Italy, however, there is strong evidence of the persistence of the 'Apennine' culture; hence several scholars have concluded in the last few years that a new burial rite may simply have been adopted by the local population, or, if there were newcomers, that they can only have been few in number. Occasional iron implements appear in the later burials and iron does not seem to have replaced bronze as the common metal amongst the population in Italy until *c.* 800 B.C., or even later in the remoter parts.

*c. 1
120
B.0*

Plate 1. Villanovan biconical urns from Tarquinia, dated to the eighth century B.C. Museo Preistorico, Rome.

By this time the Italian tribes known to the Romans must have developed across the central peninsula—the Marsi, Paeligni, Vestini and so on (see Map 2), whose Iron Age culture flourished for several centuries, little if at all affected by developments in Etruria. In Etruria the '*Villanovan*' Iron Age (named after a large cemetery in the Po valley near Bologna) has been divided into three phases; by the beginning of the third period *c.* 700 B.C. we can recognize the formation of Etruscan civilization and the huge Villanovan cremation cemeteries were supplemented with magnificent rock-cut tombs built near the Etruscan cities for the ruling élite. Older theories looked to the eastern Aegean for the origins of the Etruscans; recent excavations, however, particularly in the cemeteries around the Etruscan city of Veii, have shown that hardly any of the material assemblage of the graves can be seen as exotic and foreign: the greater part of the material culture is firmly rooted in the Bronze Age of Etruria. The glories of the civilization fill the museums of Italy; the cities were rich and powerful, linked on the ground by a network of roads that was in some ways the basis of the Roman system, supporting craftsmen whose works were eventually to be traded far into barbarian Celtic Europe. The infant Rome grew up to equal and eventually

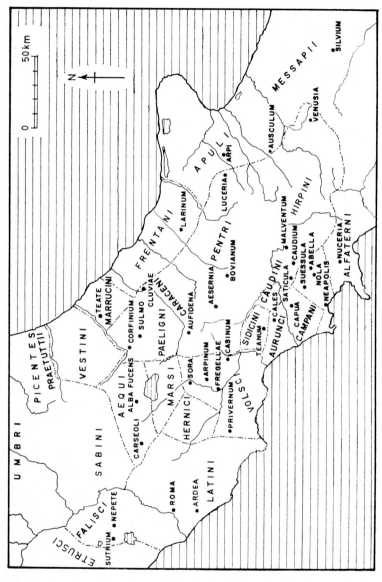

Map 2. Central Italy: the tribal territories c. 350 B.C. showing the regions occupied by the various indigenous tribes.

conquer the great Etruscan cities, whose civilization had dominated most of the western lowlands of central Italy and whose influence had spread up the Rhône into central France, across the Alps to the Celtic hill forts of Germany.

The traditional date for the foundation of the city of Rome. But it was to be another two hundred years before she began to extend her power over the neighbouring cities and to lay the foundations of the Empire.

Inhumation was now replacing cremation in the Villanovan area. Not only had wattle and daub hut villages developed into wealthy cities, but the Etruscan language was being used. The Etruscanization of the Latin area, including Rome, came later (by conquest, not by infiltration and gradual evolution). At some time a bit before or a bit after 600 B.C. Rome became an Etruscan city with an Etruscan King, Tarquinius Priscus.

Inhumation had now entirely replaced cremation. The Etruscan League comprising twelve cities was formed, perhaps Tarquinii, Caere, Clusium, Perusia, Volaterrae, Arretium, Rusellae, Veii, Volsinii, Vulci, Vetulonia and Populonia (see Map 4). Others like Faesulae and Cortona were added later. A period of great prosperity based on agriculture, mining and metal working set in which was to last for at least a century. Bronzework and vases were exported all over Italy and even to Central Europe. At the same time Etruscan influence and culture spread as far south as the right bank of the river Sele, just to the north of Paestum, and northwards into the Po Valley.

Concurrently with political developments, yet in many ways apart, was the evolution of culture and religion and its effect upon the neighbouring peoples, and also upon the succeeding generations and posterity. We know little of the social or cultural life of the Etruscans. No literary works have survived, not even as quotations by later authors; in consequence, although many individual words are understood, the language remains an 'undeciphered' one; most scholars think it is not even Indo-European (see Fig. 2). From frescoes and funerary furniture in the tombs, it has been possible to reconstruct part of their religious beliefs. The Etruscans had inherited the Nature gods of the woods and streams, lakes and mountains, and the fertility divinities of the fields and crops from their Villanovan ancestors. When they came into contact with Magna Graecia (the

Greeks in southern Italy) in the 6th century they adopted Demeter, or more correctly Hera, who became their goddess Uni (Juno), with Tinia (Jupiter), Minerve (Minerva) and others. They passed these three divinities on to Rome, and their statues adorned the principal temple in the forum of every Roman *municipium*. More important still they passed on to Rome their religious rites for prophecy of the future, especially augury, and the symbols of magistracy and government, such as the axe and *fasces*.

Aristodemos of Cumae inflicted a crushing defeat on the Etruscans *524* in the marshes and woods to the north of Cumae. He followed up his *B.C.*

Fig. 2. The Etruscan alphabet engraved on an ivory writing tablet from Marsiliana d'Albegna, dating from the first half of the seventh century B.C.

victory by winning a decisive battle in alliance with the Latins, and routing the Etruscans at Aricia. There followed a naval defeat by the combined forces of Hiero of Syracuse and of Cumae in 474. These events meant the loss of the Etruscans' seapower and overseas trade. The battle at Aricia encouraged Rome to revolt and expel the last Etruscan king in 510 B.C. (according to the traditional chronology). The sack of Veii by Rome virtually marks the end of the Etruscan *396* period of cultural dominance.   *B.C.*

With the liberation of Rome and the Latin League from the domination of the Etruscans, consolidation of her territory and the conquest of the neighbouring cities began. The secret of the Roman success was their Imperial diplomacy, whereby they offered first alliances to their neighbours and ultimately, contrary to the usual practice in antiquity, citizenship. Those who resisted were incorporated or destroyed. Naturally there were opposition and temporary setbacks.

345
C.
A fifty-year war now began against the Samnites, who were linguistically and culturally akin to the Roman people and by far the strongest of the Italic tribes. Their territory extended from the western foothills of the Apennines to the Adriatic coast and from Umbria in the north to Apulia in the south. In 321 B.C. the Roman army surrendered to the Samnites at the Caudine forks, a pass near Beneventum, and the 16,000 prisoners were forced to pass under the yoke, a ceremony of humiliation and degradation.

Rome soon recovered from this disaster during the five years' peace which followed before the renewed outbreak of hostilities. By 290 B.C. all Samnium was incorporated into the Roman Confederacy.
2
C.
In the meantime Rome and Carthage had, as early as 508 B.C., entered into a commercial treaty which defined their spheres of influence. By 264 Rome dominated the whole of Italy south of the river Po, and a clash between Rome and Carthage was inevitable. The First Punic War began in 264 B.C. By a decisive naval battle off the Aegates Islands in 241 B.C., Rome became a naval power for the first time. Tradition has it that the capture of a Carthaginian trireme gave them a model for the construction of a fleet of more than two hundred ships. As a consequence of the First Punic War, Sicily became the first Roman possession overseas.

8
C.
The clash came again, this time in Spain where Hannibal captured and sacked Saguntum, a town which was the ally of Rome. In the spring of 218 Hannibal marched along the south coast of France and crossed the Alps with a large army. As soon as he arrived in Italy he defeated the Roman forces twice before he wintered in the Po Valley. The following year he marched southwards, defeating and killing the Roman consul Gaius Flaminius at the battle of Lake Trasimene. Hannibal now entered Apulia, and in the following year defeated and routed a large Roman army at the battle of Cannae. The road to Rome was now open, but Hannibal missed his opportunity, preferring to winter at Capua to consolidate his gains. He remained, laying

waste with fire and sword in Italy for several years, but was never again able to win a battle. He was unable to capture a port and in consequence reinforcements, led by his brother Hasdrubal, had to come all the way from Spain by the land route over the Alps. When Hasdrubal reached Italy in 207 B.C. he was met by the consuls C. Claudius Nero and M. Livius Salinator. In the battle on the River Metaurus that ensued Hasdrubal was killed, and his death decided the war. Hannibal was able to maintain himself in Italy for a few more years but with no military successes.

Scipio Africanus devised the original Roman intention of attacking the homeland of Carthage in North Africa, thus forcing Hannibal to hurry back to oppose him. At Zama Scipio won a great and decisive victory in 202 B.C. and the Second Punic War was ended. *203 B.C.*

The Third Punic War. Hostilities between Rome and an all-too-easily revived Carthage broke out again, but they were soon over. In 146 B.C. Carthage was razed to the ground and Rome was Mistress of the Mediterranean, having between 200 and 146 also conquered Philip of Macedon and Antiochos the Great of Syria, and ended the age-old freedom of mainland Greece. *149 B.C.*

The next century was a time of great further expansion and colonization. Asia Minor, southern Spain and North Africa all became part of the Roman dominions. But this was not achieved without continuous internal struggles for power by the political leaders such as Marius, Sulla, Pompey and (the greatest of them all) Julius Caesar.

The Social War. Two years of hostilities resulted from the Roman refusal to grant the franchise to her Latin allies. The war was finally ended by the capture of Nola by L. Cornelius Sulla in 88 B.C. *90 B.C.*

The Catiline Plot. An attempt at a *coup d'état* by L. Sergius Catilina and others. They were ill prepared for the venture, and after Cicero had delivered his second oration in the Forum against them they were declared Public Enemies and quickly suppressed. *63 B.C.*

The assassination of Julius Caesar marked the end of republican Rome. For the next fifteen years the Roman state was torn by civil war. First Octavian, Caesar's adopted son, and Antony revenged the death of Julius Caesar by destroying Brutus and Cassius at the battle of Philippi. For eight years Octavian was engaged in a war with Sextus Pompeius in Sicily. Then came the final struggle between Octavian and Antony, who had allied himself with Cleopatra and dominated the eastern Mediterranean. Matters came to a show-down *44 B.C.*

at the naval battle of Actium in 31 B.C. when Cleopatra lost her nerve and fled with all her ships. Antony followed her to Egypt and the next year, hearing a false report of her suicide, he killed himself; as later Cleopatra did too to avoid being led in triumph by Octavian at Rome. Egypt was added to the empire of the Roman people.

B.C. Octavian took the name Augustus Caesar, and to avoid accusations of kingship designated his regime a 'Principate', ushering in a long period of prosperity. Order was restored in political affairs at home and in the provinces of the Empire; further expansion took place—in Gaul, the Rhineland, Britain, the Danube lands and Algeria and Morocco. The wealth and prosperity of the next four hundred years is still visible in the ruins of the triumphal arches, temples, public buildings, palaces, aqueducts, roads, port works, bridges and whole new cities, not only in Italy but all over Europe, Asia Minor, and the North African coast. Trade was carried on by great ships running between Ostia, the port of Rome, via the Aegean and the Levant to Egypt, whence there was a sea route as far as India. Pliny the Elder wrote that the importation of silk, gems and spices from India, China and Arabia was causing a drain on the coinage amounting to more than one hundred million sesterces a year, adding cynically 'That's what luxury and our women cost us' (*N.H.* 12, 84). (Actually it was not a very large sum.)

For the next four hundred years, Rome ruled most of the known world. Many factors contributed to the decline and fall of the Roman Empire, but especially the fact that the homeland became incapable of providing reinforcements and proper defence against the ever increasing pressure of raids by immigrants into the European sphere from the Asiatic steppes. The civilization that was Rome sank into the semi-barbarity of the dark ages. The story of these events can be read elsewhere. Further details on the period covered by the above Historical Note will be found in some of the works quoted in the Bibliography on pages 248-9.

DATES OF MAIN ROMAN EMPERORS
MENTIONED IN THE GUIDE

Augustus	27 B.C.–A.D. 14
Tiberius	A.D. 14–37
Claudius	A.D. 41–54
Nero	A.D. 54–68
Vespasian	A.D. 69–79
Titus	A.D. 79–81
Domitian	A.D. 81–96
Trajan	A.D. 98–117
Hadrian	A.D. 117–38
Septimius Severus	A.D. 193–211
Aurelian	A.D. 270–5
Diocletian	A.D. 284–305
Maxentius	A.D. 306–12
Constantine	A.D. 311–37
Honorius	A.D. 395–423

POTTERY STYLES AND DATES

c. 1000 B.C.	Proto-Geometric period begins
900–c. 700 B.C.	Geometric period
c. 725–575 B.C.	Orientalizing period

Attic

c. 710 B.C.	Proto-Attic
600–c. 474 B.C.	Black-figure period
c. 530–320 B.C.	Red-figure period

Corinthian

Before 630 B.C.	Proto-Corinthian
630 B.C.	Early (Archaic)
600 B.C.	Middle
570 B.C.	Late

Pottery produced in the Greek colonies in South Italy (Italiote)

From 700 B.C.	Copies of Greek types
c. 400 B.C.	Campanian ware (Black-glazed and Red-figure)

Pottery Styles in Etruria

Period I	Coarse, hand-made pottery
Period II	Influences from Greek Geometric pottery
Period III	Orientalizing. This period begins with the importing of Proto-Corinthian pottery

CHRONOLOGY OF ROMAN ROADS (See Maps 1, 5, 6)

This is a chronology of the Roman roads to help the reader. It cannot be taken as wholly accurate because so much research is still going on in this field. Again the Romans often used, and improved, tracks that were there already: when we say a Roman road was 'built' in a certain year it means that the Senate and people authorized a magistrate to mark out a strip of land as public property and make it passable to wheeled traffic and naturally they used what was already there when it went in the direction they wanted. Finally, we can only date the roads that are named after their constructors since it is the name that gives the possible date. For a good general account of the roads near Rome, see T. Ashby, *The Roman Campagna in Classical Times*. For a recent detailed discussion, see T. P. Wiseman, 'Roman Republican Road-building', *Papers of the British School at Rome*, XXXVIII, 1970, 122–52.

Roman name	Modern equivalent in part or whole	Route	Date of building	Purpose
Aurelia Vetus	Aurelia (S.S.1)	Rome–Fregenae–Centum Cellae–Cosa	?241 B.C.	communication with coastal colonies
Aurelia Nova		?Rome–Cosa–Populonia	?119 B.C.	improved communications with port of embarkation for Provence. This route cut out some of the minor coastal sites
		Rome–Pisae and Luca	?107 B.C.	to join the coastal colonies
Clodia	Claudia/Braccianese (S.S.493)	?from the Cassia to Manziana, then through hills to Tuscana and Saturnia	?287 or 285 B.C.	communications for police purposes in newly conquered Etruria
Cassia	Cassia (S.S.2); but today goes to Florence via Siena and the hills, not via Arezzo and the Val di Chiana	Rome–Arretium; eventually to Faesulae and Pisae	?154 B.C.	to link with Bologna (Bononia)–Faesulae–Arretium road built in 187 B.C.
Amerina	—————	Rome–Falerii Novi–Ameria	?about 240 B.C.	communication with new Roman colonies at Nepet and Falerii Novi and with southern

Road	Modern road (S.S.)	Route	Date	Purpose
Tiberina?	Tiberina (S.S.313 and 3 *bis*)	Rome–Tiber crossing south of Ocriculum	?about 350 B.C.	modification of existing track when Romans moved into southern Etruria
Salaria	Salaria (S.S.4)	Rome–Cures–Asculum and Adriatic	extended from Cures to coast in 17–16 B.C. by Augustus	control of Sabine territory and communications with coast
Caecilia	Sabina (S.S.17) and Caecilia (S.S.80)	?extension of Salaria from Cures to Reate, Amiternum and Interamnia (Teramo)	?284 B.C.	to control the newly conquered highland areas–
Valeria	Tiburtina/Valeria (S.S.5)	Rome–Tibur–Alba Fucens	?307 B.C.	control of newly conquered territory
		extended to Aternum (Pescara)	A.D. 47–9 by Claudius	
Praenestina	Prenestina	Rome–Praeneste–Frusino	all based on older tracks or lanes	local communications
Labicana	Casilina (S.S.6)	Rome–Labicum		
Tuscolana	Tuscolana (S.S.215)	from the Latina–Tusculum		
Latina Nova	Latina (S.S.215) and Casilina (S.S.6.)	Rome–Frosino–Aquinum–Casinum to join the Appia just north of Capua	?127 bypassing Anagnia and other towns on hill and keeping to Liris valley	long distance communications
Appia	Appia Antica (S.S.7) for first 20 km; Appia Nuova then takes over route	Rome–Capua	312 B.C.	fast communications with Campania and South Italy
		extended to Beneventum, Venusia, Tarentum	early 3rd century B.C.	
		extended to Brundisium	soon after 248 B.C.	

ALPHABETICAL LIST OF MUSEUMS

In the following pages a list is given of the towns possessing museums containing collections of archaeological interest, with a description of the principal items. In the main text of the Guide I have referred to this list wherever a museum exists. In this way the student or visitor can plan his museum visits according to his general itinerary. Always ask if there is a local museum at the sites or in the villages as there is often a small but valuable civic collection of finds from the surrounding areas.

1. **Agnani** (p. 217). Small museum next to the Cathedral.

2. **Alatri** (p. 214). Small museum in the Palazzo Casgrande. Open every day.

3. **Allumiere** (p. 117). In the Piazza Vittorio Emmanuele II. Open 10.30–12.30, 17–19, Sunday 10–12. Good collection of Etruscan and local material.

4. **Ancona** (p. 169). National Archaeological Museum of the Marche. Palazzo Ferretti. Open summer 9–13, 15–18, Sunday 9–13, winter 10–16, Sunday 10–13, closed Monday. Recently reorganized, it contains collections of great interest from the Iron Age, local Picentine, Greek, Gallic and Roman cultures. Of note is the funerary furniture from the Gallic tombs of the Graeco-Roman necropolis at Ancona of the 3rd to the 1st century, including three reconstructed funerary biers; furniture from the Gallic tombs of Montefortino including three gold Etruscan crowns and some superb torques; magnificent Attic vases from the Hellenistic necropolis of Numana and from San Severino, Marche; material from the Gallic necropolis of Filottrano and of Osimo, and from the Picentine necropolis of Castel Bellino comprising gold, bronzework, ivory and vases; the 6th-century B.C. Tripod of Amendola; Etruscan *situla* from San

Genisto; items from the 9th-century Picentine tombs until the Roman epoch (note the reconstructed war chariot); head of a warrior from Numana; local sculpture of Italic origin; a series of Roman portraits; also Palaeolithic, Neolithic, Eneolithic and Bronze Age collections.

5. **Arezzo** (p. 155). Maecenate Archaeological Museum in the 15th-century building of the Monastery of St Bernard, 10 Via Margaritche. Open 9–16, Sunday 9–12, closed Wednesday. The museum was reconstructed after the last war. On the ground floor are twelve rooms of Etruscan and Roman funerary items (urns, stelae, terracotta statuettes, mosaics, fragments of sarcophagi), and a fine series of Arretine vases with relief decoration from the Roman period. On the upper floor is a collection of prehistoric material, Etruscan and Roman statuettes, tools in bronze, seals for marking terracotta items, looking-glasses, jewellery, coins, ceramics, Greek, Etruscan and Roman vases.

6. **Assisi** (p. 166). In the Palazzo del Comune. Open 9–13, 16–20. Comprises a small collection from local excavations in the town.

7. **Campobasso**. The Samnite Museum at 21 Via Vittorio Veneto. Open 9–1, closed Sunday. Contains a collection of Samnite arms, small bronze items, gold and silver jewellery, terracottas and coins.

8. **Chieti** (p. 200). National Archaeological Museum in the Villa Communale. Open 9–12, Sunday 10–13. Comprises sculpture and inscriptions from the Greek and Roman periods. There is also an antiquarium of Roman products, the 'Pansa' collection of Italiote items, coins, and a prehistoric collection; the latter has been re-organized in recent years and is particularly well displayed. Of particular interest are the *Warrior of Capestrano* (see Plate 4), the Bronze Bed from Amiterno, reliefs from the temple of Lucius Storax and statues from the excavations at Alba Fucens and Scoppito.

9. **Chiusi** (p. 152). Etruscan Museum at the side of the Cathedral. Open summer 8.30–12.30, 15–18, Sunday 9–13, winter 9–12, 14.30–17, Sunday 10–12, closed Monday. One of the best of the smaller museums. Of special note are the urns and sarcophaghi in alabaster (particularly those in Room II and the big sarcophagus with reliefs

of battles), also the portrait of Lars Sentinate. In addition there are Canopic vases, bucchero ware and Attic vases, and some bronzework. In the Roman series, there is a head of Augustus and a mosaic with a hunting scene.

10. **Corfinio** (p. 199). Museum in the annexe in the Basilica di San Pelino. Can be visited only on request. It is a magnificent Roman building containing many antiquities from the excavations at *Corfinium*, including inscriptions, marbles, terracotta objects, bronzes and Italiote and Roman weapons and armour.

11. **Cortona** (p. 155). Museum of the Etruscan Academy, Via Roma. Open summer 9–12, 15–19, winter 9–12, 15–17, Sunday free. Contains a splendid collection of Etruscan material. Of note is a large 5th-century bronze lamp with reliefs of satyrs and sirens, various Egyptian and Roman items, mosaics and coins.

12. **Florence** (p. 148). The National Archaeological Museum, 9 Piazza S. Annunciata. Open 10–16, Sunday 9–13, closed Monday. One of the largest and most interesting museums in Italy, and particularly important for its Etruscan collection. Laid in sections on the three floors of the building as follows:

GROUND FLOOR Rooms I-VI: Graeco-Roman sculpture, with the *Artemis Laphria*, copy of a Greek original of the 5th century B.C., *Apollo Apollini* and *Milani*, Attic sculpture of the 6th to 5th centuries, some sculptured lions in *nenfro* (a local stone) (Etruscan of the 4th to 3rd centuries). Rooms VIII-XLIX contain the extremely important Topographical Etruscan Museum comprising a collection from all the Etruscan peoples subdivided into territories, thus offering a complete picture of the evolution of the Etruscan civilization from the 8th to the 1st centuries; each room or group of rooms is confined to a specific region. Explanatory notices are at the entrance to each section. The Etruscan towns most profusely represented are Tarquinia (Rooms XII-XIV), note the urn covered with a bronze helmet; Tuscania (Rooms XV-XVI), look at the sepulcral lions in *nenfro*; Orvieto (Room XVIII), 5th-century stele with head of warrior; Vulci (Room XIX), lion in *nenfro*; Vetulonia (Rooms XXV-XXVIII), objects from 7th- to 6th-century tombs; Clusium (Chiusi) (Rooms XXXIX-XLVI), 5th-century statue of the *Mother of the Gods on a Throne*; Luni (Room XLIX), 2nd-century B.C. antefixes from the temples in terracotta. In the garden Etruscan monuments and tombs have been reconstructed from original material.

THE FIRST FLOOR contains the Egyptian section and also rooms containing an antiquarium with various Greek, Etruscan and Roman sculptures and the 4th-century B.C. *Sarcophagus of Ramia Uzenai.* Amongst the bronzes are the *Orator* and a 3rd-century B.C. funerary statue of Aulus Metellus, the *Idolino* and *Torso of an athlete*, both original Greek works of the 5th century B.C. On the same floor is the coin collection, jewellery (gems, cameos and silverwork) and above all the *Chimera*, a splendid Etruscan bronze of the 5th century (see Plate 22).

On the SECOND FLOOR Rooms I-VI contain items from northern and southern Italy and from Cyprus and Crete, Greece and the Aegean Islands. Rooms VII-XV contain a rich collection of vases and terracottas, including the famous *François vase*, a masterpiece of archaic Attic work (see Plate 21), from a tomb at Chiusi (p. 152-3). Rooms XVII-XXX have frescoes taken from the tombs, reproductions of Etruscan tomb paintings and the 3rd- to 2nd-century *Sarcophagus of Larthis Salaviti* in polychrome terracotta.

13. **Grosseto** (p. 127). 6 Via Mazzini. Open summer 9-12, 16-19, Sunday 10-13, winter 9-12, Sunday 10-13, closed Wednesday. Contains Etruscan material from excavations in the surrounding region including Rusellae, and Roman items from local villas. Good collection of urns, bronzes, coins and architectural fragments.

14. **Gubbio** (p. 171). Museum in the Palazzo dei Consoli. Open summer 9-13, 15.30-17.30, winter 9-13, 14.30-16, Sunday 9-13. Three rooms contain material from excavations in the neighbourhood, Roman bronzes coins and vases, also the famous *Iguvine Tablets*: seven bronze plates with inscriptions representing religious formulae and texts partly in Umbrian and partly in Latin.

15. **L'Aquila** (p. 184). National Museum of the Abruzzi, housed in the castle. Open summer 9-13, 15-18, winter 9-16, Sunday 9-13. The archaeological section is on the ground floor. There is much material from the Roman cities of Abruzzo, notably from Amiternum.

16. **Naples** (p. 223). The National Archaeological Museum in the Piazza Museo. Open 9.30-16.00, Sunday 9.30-13.20, closed

Wednesday. This is outside the scope of this Guide, but much material fromn Norther Campania is housed there.

17. Orvieto (p. 146). There is a good Etruscan collection in the Palazzo dell'Opera del Duomo (open summer 9–13, 15–18, winter 9–13, 14.30–16.30, always closed Monday) and another in the Civic Museum in the Palazzo Falane (open summer 9–13, 16–18, winter 10–13, 14–16, always closed Monday). The period covered is from the 4th to 2nd centuries.

18. Ostia Antica (p. 96). The museum is in the excavations where several rooms house a fine collection of objects from the city which were found during the work of restoration. Open 9 to one hour before sunset, closed Monday.

19. Palestrina (p. 210). The Archaeological Museum of Praeneste in the Palazzo Barberini on the upper terrace of the monument. Open summer 10–13, 15.30–18.30, winter 10–15.30, Sunday 10–13, closed on Monday. Fine collection of objects from the surrounding area magnificently arranged in fourteen rooms. Room I: statues, etc. from the Sanctuary of Fortune. Room II: funerary stelae and other objects from the 4th- to 3rd-century local necropolis. Rooms IV-VI: funerary altars, fragments of architectural terracottas, heads and portraits of the 1st century A.D. Room VII: architectural terracottas from the 6th and 3rd to 2nd centuries B.C. Rooms VIII and IX: bronze mirrors, toilet boxes and tomb furniture, bone tablets, bronze statuettes and reliefs. Room X: sarcophagus covers and mosaics and a reconstruction of the Sanctuary of Fortuna Primigenia. Rooms XI-XII: antefixes, frescoes and statuettes in terracotta covering the 7th to the 2nd centuries. Room XIV: 4th-century B.C. architectural items in terracotta and in bronze, and a mosaic representing the Nile in flood, a copy of an original 1st-century B.C. Alexandrine painting formerly in the lower apse of the Sanctuary. In the internal courtyard of the Palace are reconstructions with original material of the *Tholos* which crowned the top of the Sanctuary and housed the Statue of the goddess.

20. Perugia (p. 175). The National Archaeological Museum of Umbria, housed in the ancient Convent of San Domenico. Open 9–13, closed Monday. This museum has one of the most important pre-

historic collections in Italy. There are eight rooms of objects representing the evolution of the cultures through the Palaeolithic, Neolithic, Eneolithic, Bronze, and Iron Ages. The Etrusco-Roman
section comprises inscriptions, sarcophaghi, stelae, etc., arranged
under the portico and in the main cloister. Of particular importance
are the series of cinerary urns grouped according to their provenance.
Amongst the most celebrated pieces is the stele with the *Cipus
Perusinus*, or 'Perugian Inscription', an extremely interesting
Etruscan document. One room contains a fine collection of bronze
objects and also Greek and bucchero vases.

21. **Pesaro** (p. 173). The Archaeological Museum is at No. 97 Via
Mazza. Open 9–12.30, 16–18, Sunday 10–12. Contains items from
the prehistoric tombs at Pesaro and from the necropolis at Novillara.
There is a famous bi-lingual Etruscan-Latin inscription, some beautiful bronzework and some orientalized bronzework of the 6th century.

22. **Rome** (p. 84). Barracco Museum in the Piccolo Farnesina
Palace at 168 Corso Vittorio Emanuele. Open 9–14, Wednesday and
Thursday also 17–20, Sunday 9–13, closed Monday. Selection of
antique sculpture and a Babylonian and Egyptian section. Numerous
Greek items such as the *Head of a Priest* which is thought to be a
Romano-Egyptian portrait of Julius Caesar, *Head of a Youth*, *Head
of Minerva*, a group of Cypriote sculptures, copy of a *Head of
Marsyas* by Myron, *Head of Apollo*, possibly by Praxiteles and three
funerary stelae from Palmyra.

23. **Rome** (p. 80). Capitoline Museum in the Piazza del
Campidoglio. Open 9–14 (also Saturday 21–23.30 in summer),
Sunday 9–13, closed Monday. Rich collection of classical sculpture.
   GROUND FLOOR: in the courtyard a fountain by Giacomo della
Porta incorporating a large antique statue of *Fluvius* (the so-called
Marforius—one of the 'Talking Statues' of Rome). Rooms I-III:
monuments of Roman oriental cults. Room V: the 3rd-century B.C.
Amendola Sarcophagus with scenes of a battle between Gauls and
Greeks.
   FIRST FLOOR Room I: *The Dying Gaul*, Roman copy of a 3rd-
century B.C. original from Pergamon, a Hellenistic *Eros and Psyche*.
Room II: *The Laughing Silenus* in red marble, copy of a Hellenistic
bronze of the 3rd century B.C., *Boy with Goose*, copy of a Hellenistic

bronze of the 2nd century B.C.; a bronze tablet with the famous *Lex de imperio Vespasiani* listing the powers of the Roman emperor. Room III: *Child Hercules*, a basalt statue of Imperial date; the *Old Centaur and the Young Centaur* in grey marble, a Hadrianic copy of a Hellenistic original. Room IV: 79 busts of savants, poets and philosophers; amongst them Homer and Cicero, and on the walls Greek votive reliefs. Room V: 64 busts of Roman emperors and empresses, including the famous 2nd-century A.D. statue of *Agrippina seated*. On the walls are high-reliefs of Hellenistic type of Perseus and Andromeda, Selene and Endymion. In the Gallery: the *Minerva of Velletri*, copy of a Greek bronze of the 5th to 6th centuries, *Drunken Old Woman*, Pergamo School, end of the 3rd century B.C. Room of the Doves: on the wall a mosaic from Hadrian's villa of four doves drinking at a vase; other mosaics with masks, etc. and Roman portraits from the late Republican Age. The 1st-century A.D. *Tabula Iliaca* with small reliefs of the siege of Troy. Room of Venus: the *Capitoline Venus*, a famous statue in Parian marble, after an original by Praxiteles.

24. **Rome** (p. 80). Palazzo dei Conservatori, opposite the Capitoline Museum. Same ticket valid for, and same entry times as, the Capitoline Museum. In the courtyard: fragments of a colossal statue of Constantine; reliefs from the temples to Hadrian. The First Floor and Second Floor stairways have grand reliefs in honour of Hadrian and Marcus Aurelius.

The FIRST FLOOR is mainly illustrative of the story of Rome in reliefs and frescoes of the 16th and 17th centuries A.D. On the same floor, Room III: *Boy with a Thorn in his Foot*, bronze of the 1st century. Room IV: the famous Etruscan Bronze *She-Wolf* of the 6th to 5th centuries—the twins were added to the wolf by Pollaiolo in A.D. 1400 (see Plate 5); also *Portrait of L. Junius Brutus* of the 4th to 3rd centuries; fragments of the *Fasti Consulares* and *Fasti Triumphales* formerly on the sides of the arch of Augustus in the Forum. These are lists of the Consuls and of the Triumphs celebrated by victorious generals and are valuable evidence for some dates in Roman history. Room V: *A Dog*, Roman.

On the SECOND FLOOR is the 'museum of the Conservatori', containing Graeco-Roman sculpture. On the right is the *Sala degli Orti Lamiani*, containing items found on the Esquiline Hill, the *Esquiline Venus*, a *Seated Girl*, an *Old Fisherman*, a fine bust of *Commodus as*

Hercules; and in the Room of the Magistrates are two statues of magistrates in the act of starting a race in the circus. They date to the reign of Constantine in the 4th century A.D. Rooms of archaic material: 5th-century B.C. headless statue of a young girl, Greek; 5th-century B.C. sepulchral stele of a girl holding a dove; charioteer mounting his chariot, copy of a 5th-century Greek original. Room of the Litter: terracotta statuettes and ceramics of Etrusco-Italiote origin from a tomb at Palestrina. Castellani Room: amphorae, Corinthian, Cyrenian and Attic vases, a 7th-century B.C. crater by Aristonothos and signed by him. Room of the Bronzes: bronze ornaments of Roman date, also a fine bronze bed of the same date, head of a horse and fragments of a bull, etc. The New Wing holds finds from more recent excavations and in the first three rooms remains of the foundations of the 6th-century B.C. temple of Jupiter Capitolinus can be seen. A further ten rooms in the new museum, in the Palazzo Caffarelli, contain urns, funerary vases and numerous fine statues including a *Minerva* or *Athena* of the 4th century B.C. in Room V.

25. **Rome** (Chapter 2). The Forum Antiquarium. Open 9–13. Occupies the ex-convent of San Francesco Romano. Contains material from the Archaic necropolis and marbles from the Forum.

26. **Rome**. Lateran Museum (Museo Profano), in square of St. John Lateran. Open Monday, Wednesday, Friday 9–14. Room I: *Torso of Hermes* from a Greek original of the 4th century B.C. *Roman Relief with Procession of Magistrates* of the 1st century A.D. Room II: fragments from the Trajan Forum. Room III: the Emperor Hadrian's lover Antinous with the attributes of the deity Vertumnus, 2nd century A.D. Room IV: on the floor and on the walls are mosaics of the 3rd century A.D. from the Thermae of Caracalla, head of Medusa, etc. Room V: 1st-century A.D. *Faun with Dionysus as a Boy* and a large historical relief of the same century. Room VI: fragments from the Roman Theatre at Cerveteri. Room VII: relief of Medea and the daughters of Pelias (perhaps a Greek original of the 4th century B.C.); *Sophocles*, a copy of Greek original; reliefs with Menander and Comoedia, copies of Greek originals; *Marsyas*, also a copy. Room VIII: objects from the tombs of the Haterii, 1st century B.C. Room IX: a fine mosaic on the floor. Room X: statue of Neptune, and Roman busts. Room XI: Roman sarcophagi of the 3rd century

4

A.D. Room XII: a sarcophagus with the myth of Niobe, and an altar dedicated to Piety. Room XIII: 1st-century B.C. funeral furniture from the tomb of the *Gens Furia* with portraits. Rooms XIV, XV and XVI all contain fragments from tombs.

27. Rome. National Museum (p. 91). Open 9.30–15, Sunday 9–13, closed Monday. Entrance at the side of the church of Santa Maria degli Angeli in the Piazza Esedra. Contains a most important collection and occupies several halls of the Baths of Diocletian. Hall I: a mosaic pavement of early Imperial date with animal motifs, and a sarcophagus with the legend of Phaedra. Hall II: reconstruction in plaster of the basement of the Temple of Hadrian (2nd century A.D.) and the *Sarcophagus of the Muses*. Hall III: Christian sarcophagi. Hall IV: a fine mosaic pavement of Nile scenes, from Colle Mancio; a colossal *Statue of Kore* from an original by Alkamenes; 2nd-century A.D. sarcophagus with battle scene between Romans and Barbarians; 2nd-century B.C. sarcophagus with Dionysus and Ariadne. Hall V: 2nd-century B.C. group of *Mars and Venus*; 3rd-century A.D. sarcophagus with Eros and Psyche. Hall VI: mosaic with chariot race motif of the 5th century A.D.; relief of dancing girls from the Via Praenestina. Hall VII: plan of the Baths of Diocletian. Hall IX: fine mosaic of the 3rd century A.D. showing *Neptune driving his Chariot of Seahorses*. Hall X: reconstruction of the 1st-century A.D. tomb of the Platorini with painted walls and ceiling. Hall XI: mosaics. Hall XII: the ancient latrine of the Thermae. From the garden one enters the museum proper.

In the small cloister: the famous Ludovici Collection with the *Hermes*, a copy of a 6th-century original; *Athena Parthenos*, copy of the celebrated statue of Phidias, *Galatian Killing Himself and His Wife*, *Satyr* from an original by Praxiteles, the *Ludovisi Throne*, Greek work of the 5th century B.C. which perhaps represents the birth of Venus, colossal head of Hera, colossal archaic head of a goddess (Sicilian art of the 5th century B.C.), *The Sleeping Erinyes* (Fates) of Hellenistic date, *Orestes and Electra*, altars and a 3rd-century B.C. sarcophagus with battle scene. Room II: *Apollo del Tevere* (copy of work by Phidias), *Nereid*, fragments of a young *Dancing Girl* of the 5th century B.C., *Torso of peplophorus*, a Greek original of the 5th century B.C., *Venus of Cyrene*, an original of the 4th century B.C., *Juno of the Palatine*, possibly a copy of a work by Phidias. Room III: the *Discobolus*, copy of a 4th-century bronze by

Myron, *Niobid* from the gardens of Sallust, a Greek original of the
5th century, 5th-century B.C. torso of a Hero or of an Athlete,
Hellenistic bronze of a *Youth leaning on a stick*, bronze *Boxer* signed
by Apollonius, an original of the 4th century B.C., *Apollo of Actium*
a Roman copy of a 4th-century B.C. original, *Young Girls from Antium*
(a 4th-century original). Room IV: Hellenistic art: *Amazon on
horseback with Galatian*, an original from Pergamon; *Sea Deity*;
statues of the Muses; the *Maiden of Anzio*, a Greek masterpiece of the
end of the 4th century B.C. Room V: Roman decorative art. Room VI:
statue of Augustus as a priest, *head of an old woman, head of Nero,
bust of a vestal virgin*. Room VII: sarcophaghi. On the UPPER FLOOR:
two rooms containing mosaics. And finally rooms containing wall
paintings from the Empress Livia's Villa at Prima Porta (see p. 173)
and the Farnesina villa—a Roman villa found in 1879 on the Tiber
bank in the Farnesina garden, probably the villa 'across the Tiber'
where Caesar kept Cleopatra as his mistress. Most of the inner walls
of Roman houses were plastered and this plaster was richly decorated
with paintings. These two villas provide the most important collection of antique paintings after the great collection from Pompeii
(now in the Naples National Archaeological Museum).

28. **Rome**. The Luigi Pigorini Prehistoric and Ethnographical
Museum, Piazza Marconi, EUR. (The EUR suburb is about five
miles south of Rome and can be reached by bus or metro.) Open
9–14, Sunday 9–13, closed Monday. The Prehistoric Museum, the
Museo del Lazio, illustrates every period of the prehistory of Latium,
the province of Rome, from the Lower Palaeolithic to the Iron Age.
The collection is well organized and splendidly displayed.

29. **Rome**. Museum of Roman Civilization, Piazza G. Angeli,
in the EUR Zone. Open 9–14, Tuesday and Thursday also
17–20, Sunday 9–13, closed Monday. Contains the story of Rome's
expansion over the Mediterranean, with many plans and reconstructions. The collection occupies 60 rooms.

30. **Rome** (p. 91). The Vatican Museum. Open 9–14, closed on
Sunday and religious feasts. Entrance on the Viale Vaticano. The
Museum of Popes Clement and Pius. The Room of the Greek Cross:
4th-century A.D. sarcophagus of Saint Helena in porphyry; sarcophagus of Constantina, daughter of Constantine in porphyry, about

4th century A.D. In the Rotonda or Circular Hall: on the floor, 1st-century A.D. mosaics with centaurs, tritons and nereids; statues along the walls and in niches, statue of a goddess (copy of a Greek original), colossal 1st-century B.C. statue of a goddess (copy of a Greek original), colossal 1st-century B.C. statue of Hercules in bronze, bust of Jove from Otriculi, 4th-century copy of Greek original of 4th century B.C. Room of the Muses: along the walls, alternate statues of the Muses and of Apollo (copies of 3rd-century Greek originals), also many portraits of philosophers. Animal Room: *Meleager and his Dog*, copy of a 4th-century B.C. Greek original by Scopas. Gallery of the Statues: *Eros of Centocelle*, a famous copy of a 4th-century B.C. Greek original, bust of a Triton, copy of a Hellenistic original of the 2nd century; *Penelope*, from a Greek original of the 5th century B.C., *Apollo Sauroctonus* copy of a 4th-century B.C. bronze by Praxiteles, two grand candelabra, Roman 2nd century B.C.; *Sleeping Ariadne* from a Hellenistic original of the 2nd century B.C. The Gallery of Busts comprises four rooms; one is devoted to Roman portraits: *Caracalla* (A.D. 211–17), *Trajan* (A.D. 98–117), *Octavian* as a young man (63 B.C.–A.D. 14), and a 1st-century B.C. *Man and Wife*. Room of the Masks: 2nd-century A.D. pavement in mosaic from Hadrian's villa. Cnidian Venus, a copy of the famous 4th-century B.C. statue by Praxiteles. Octagonal Courtyard: four bays open out from the portico of this with *Laocoon* copy of a late 2nd-century B.C. Hellenistic original, *Apollo Belvedere* from an original of the 4th century B.C., and *Hermes*, a copy of a 4th-century B.C. statue by Praxiteles. Round Vestibule: the *Apoxyomenos*, or athlete with the strigil, copy of a bronze by Lysippus *c.* 330 B.C. Atrium of the Torso: *Torso Belvedere* of Apollonius (1st century B.C.). From here one passes to the next museum.

31. **Rome** (p. 91). The Vatican. The Chiaramonti Museum consists of a long corridor with the statues of secondary importance. The Galleria Lapidaria contains over 5,000 inscriptions. The New Wing houses a number of sculptures, amongst which are *Silenus with Dionysus in his Arms*, the *Augustus of Prima Porta*, *Bust of Julius Caesar*, *The Wounded Amazon*, *The Nile*, *The Giustiniani Athena*. Room of the Chariot: a Roman chariot in the centre. Gallery of the Candelabra: a fine collection of lamps from Otriculi, and numerous statues.

Plate 2. Tomb contents from Tomb 7, Palledrara at Bisenzio from the Iron Age in Lazio: vases, cups, (and in foreground from left to right) a spindle-whorl, a fibula, three rings and a razor. These are typical of tomb contents found throughout Central Italy.

32. **Rome** (p. 91). The Vatican. The Etruscan Museum contains 9 rooms of material from the excavations in Southern Etruria. Room I: items from the 7th to 1st centuries B.C. Room II: Regolini-Galassi tomb at Cerveteri and a marvellous collection of gold jewellery. Room III: bronzes, especially the *Mars* from Todi. Room IV: funerary urns of various dates; vases and bronzes from Vulci. Rooms VI-IX contain a precious collection of Greek vases, also Etruscan and Italiote vases arranged chronologically.

33. **Rome** (p. 91). The Villa Giulia Museum in the Viale delle Belle Arti. Open 9–15, Sunday 9–13, closed Monday. The museum contains southern Etruscan material and other items from Latium and

Umbria. GROUND FLOOR, Rooms I-II (Vulcian territory): sculpture from the necropolis of Vulci. Note the 6th-century B.C. Centaur, and the *Man on a Sea-monster*. In cases, material from the archaic necropoleis of the 9th to 6th centuries, urns, ossuaries, vases, etc. Room III (Vulcian and Volsinian territory): in cases, furniture and objects from the tombs of the 6th century, objects from the necropolis of Castro (7th to 6th century), ceramics of the 3rd to 1st centuries and 6th-century bronzework. Rooms IV-V (Tarquinian territory): in cases, material from the necropolis of Bisenzio of the 8th to 6th centuries (see Plate 2) and other material from this region. Room VI (Territory of Veii): in the centre are three statues, *Apollo*, *Hercules with the Stag*, and *Goddess with Child* which were found at Veii in the Sanctuary of Apollo. They are masterpieces of Etruscan sculpture of the 6th century B.C. by the sculptor Vulca. In cases are terracotta, votive and other religious items from Veii. Rooms VII-IX (Territory of Cerveteri): in the centre of the first room an 'orientalized' sarcophagus from a tomb of the 5th century B.C. In cases are objects from Cerveteri and the archaic cemeteries, terracottas of Etrusco-Roman age, among them a fine male portrait; sepulchral furniture, vases from an Archaic tomb of the 7th to 6th centuries. In the second room, *Sarcophagus of the Married Couple*, a masterpiece of the second half of the 6th century B.C. (see Plate 12). In the third room are many cases of items from the tombs in the necropolis of Banditaccia at Cerveteri arranged in chronological order from the 7th to the 1st century; vases of *impasto* to imitate metal, bucchero with reliefs and incised decoration, native Italian pottery, Greek geometric, Italo-geometric, Proto-Corinthian and Italo-Corinthian pottery, Spartan ware, Attic Black and Red Figured ware, Arretine vases. On the UPPER FLOOR, Rooms X-XIV contain the Antiquarium of bronzes, Etruscan and Italiote *fibulae* (safety pins) from the 8th to 6th centuries, bronze tablets and statuettes of gods, warriors' votives and offerings, arms and various items of bronze and iron; rich series of *cistae* (ossuaries), copper boxes for toilet items, incised mirrors, candelabra and other domestic items. Rooms XV-XVII: antiquarium of wood, glass and terracotta.

34. Siena (p. 148). Archaeological Museum at 3 Via della Sapienza. Open 9.30–16, Sunday 10–13, closed Tuesday. There are eleven rooms of prehistoric, Etruscan and Roman material from the surrounding area.

35. **Tarquinia** (p. 120). National Museum in the Palazzo Vitelleschi. Open 9–16, Sunday and Monday 9–13. Parties to visit the Necropolis are made up at the museum. There is a splendid collection of items from the local cemeteries including the *Twin Horses* (see Plate 14) and many frescoes from the tombs showing *The Chariot Race, The Banquet, The Funeral Bier, etc.*

36. **Todi** (p. 175). Civic Museum in the Piazza Umberto. Open summer 9–12, 16–18, winter 10–12, 15–18. Good little museum of Etruscan and Roman items and coins.

37. **Viterbo** (p. 143). Civic Museum, near the Porta della Verità. Open 9–16, Sunday 9–13, closed Monday. On the ground floor there is a fine collection of Etruscan material from the surrounding area, also Roman items from the city.

38. **Volterra** (p. 134). The Guarnacci Museum at II Via Don Minzoni. Open summer 9–13, 15–18, winter 9–13, 14.30–16.30, Sunday 9–13. There are 20 rooms with over 600 urns and other items from the 6th to 4th centuries. Besides the prehistoric material there are sculptures, ivories, vases and bronzework, all from the local cemeteries.

PART I

Prehistory

Students of prehistory tend to be a specialized group visiting sites which would have little to interest the general visitor. It seems right, therefore, to have a special chapter on the prehistoric sites, so that they can easily be traced by their addicts, and the material from them inspected in the relevant museums.

1 . SOME PREHISTORIC SITES IN CENTRAL ITALY
(by Graeme Barker)

The study of Italian prehistory is still somewhat in its infancy, although much good work has been done, especially since the last war. Central Italy is fortunate in having several important concentrations of sites (see Map 3). They have been arranged here in chronological rather than geographical groups, to try to give a broad picture of prehistoric remains within the story of prehistoric development. It is hoped that visits to the sites can be tied in with the archaeological itineraries of the main chapters of the Guide: Luni could be seen, by the energetic at least, at the same time as Tarquinia; the Avezzano caves and Alba Fucens; the Villa of Tiberius at Sperlonga and the Middle Palaeolithic caves between Sperlonga and Gaeta; and so on. There is a strong bias towards caves in the selection of sites, but it often happens that all traces of the simple huts found in the excavation of Neolithic and Bronze Age settlements have long since vanished once more and there is usually nothing to be seen but the fields of the modern farmer. Inevitably it is more rewarding to visit sites that are more than just a map reference: the caves and rock-shelters that provide warmth and shelter particularly to the hunters of the Palaeolithic or Old Stone Age; later farmers and herdsmen were wont to use other caves for shelters (Grotta del Orso, Grotta dei Piccioni, Grotta a Male, Grotta Lattaia, le Tane del Diavolo, la Romita di Asciano); for religious sancturies (Belverde, Grotta del Leone); or as burial places for their dead (Grotta Patrizi and some of the Avezzano caves). The few sites where something more remains have all been included: Conelle, Mirabella Eclano and Luni for example. The museums of central Italy hold rich collections of material from all periods of the prehistory of the area arranged on a regional basis. The best summary of the prehistory of central Italy is the recent book by Dr Trump, included in the selected bibliography of some background reading at the end of this chapter. His series of distribution maps can be compared with Map 3 in the Guide showing the sites selected for discussion. Also his map of sites in the Gola del

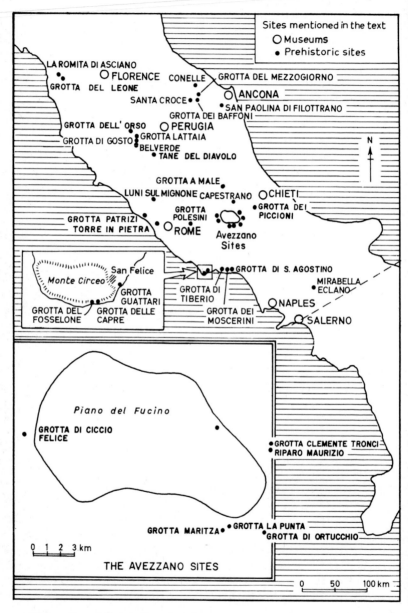

Map 3. Central Italy: selected prehistoric sites discussed in the text, from the Lower Palaeolithic to the Villanovan Iron Age.

Sentino (Fig. 45, p. 145), may be useful in conjunction with the notes given below on caves in the gorge.

LOWER PALAEOLITHIC

We are especially fortunate in having traces of the earliest inhabitants of central Italy preserved in one of the finest Lower Palaeolithic sites known in Europe. 26 km west of Rome on the Via Aurelia is the village of **Torre in Pietra** or **Torrimpietra**; excavations by the University of Rome in 1955-8 discovered a stratified deposit reaching back to almost half a million years ago. Gravels and volcanic deposits near the base of the sequence were dated by the potassium/argon method to 431,000–438,000 years ago. At the base of the overlying sediments traces of light windbreaks and hearths of a Lower Palaeolithic camp occupied by hunters using *Acheulean* hand axes were found, some of the earliest tools in Europe. Their hand axes and flakes were in the occupation debris of their camp together with the traces of their meals: the bones of red deer, horse, cattle and even the occasional elephant and rhinoceros. Today one can see the gigantic section of the deposit that overlaid the camp and even the living floor where the men (or women?) dismembered the kills, which has been preserved under a hut built at the termination of the excavations. Ask for the custodian of the site in the village, who is delighted to take the visitor out to the excavations (*scavi archeologici*) which lie some two kilometres from the village and are fenced off. A living floor has also been removed to the Museo del Lazio in EUR (see p. 51).

MIDDLE PALAEOLITHIC, from perhaps 60,000 or more years ago

Near the top of the section at Torre in Pietra the flake tools were found that formed the major part of the flint tool kit of the groups using a Middle Palaeolithic (Mousterian) industry. The best material available for a hunting band on the coastal plains of central Italy was the shingle left on beaches by the sea as it retreated during the periods of glaciation, when a vast amount of sea-water became transformed into mighty ice-caps. This coastal Mousterian industry has been named the Pontinian Mousterian because it was originally

found on the fossil beaches north and east of Anzio, the area of the
Pontine Marshes; naturally it consists mostly of very small tools
manufactured from beach pebbles. It has also been found in caves
along the rocky coast; and another deposit, found during the cutting
of a ditch during drainage operations in the Pontine Marshes, has
been dated by the 'Carbon 14' method to over 55,000 years ago
(expressed as years B.P., or before the present). Between Gaeta and
Sperlonga three caves have produced evidence of Mousterian occupation: the **Grotta di Tiberio,** 1 km south of Sperlonga, is much
better known for the excavations and recovery of Roman statuary
from both inside the cave and from the villa immediately beside it
(now displayed in the new museum above the cave), but the excavations also found traces of a Middle Palaeolithic occupation during the
Last Glaciation. 3 km nearer Gaeta, a small signpost marks the path
which runs down from the main road to the **Grotta dei Moscerini.**
This cave is much smaller than the Grotta di Tiberio and lies a few
metres above the modern sea level. The Pontinian band camped here
on a fossil beach, still visible at the front of the cave. During the
coldest period the sea level was as much as 100 m below today's level,
and the hunters could look out over the plain for the game they
sought. In the same period a band camped in the **Grotta di
Sant'Agostino,** on the left about 3 km towards Gaeta; this cave can
be seen from the road at the southern end of the bay of Sant'Agostino,
about 30 m above sea level in the crags above the plain. It is signposted from the road at this point as the Grotta delle Marmotte and
is reached by taking the road to Formia that bypasses Gaeta, then the
farm track that leaves on the left 10 m after the junction; this track
curves back round the cliffs and passes directly below the cave.

Three other Mousterian caves can be visited at Monte Circeo,
which can easily be reached from the Via Appia. The **Grotta
Guattari** is the celebrated cave where Professor Blanc found a
Neanderthal skull; the base of the skull had been widened, probably
to extract the brain in a cannibalistic rite. This skull can be seen
today in the Museo del Lazio in Rome. The cave is in the grounds
of the Hotel Neanderthal and the Villa Guattari, on the sea-shore
outside the village of San Felice, and the management will show the
visitor around the cave and point out the corner of the cave where the
skull was found. The second cave is as impressive but in a very
different way. The Grotta Guattari is dank, cold and illuminated
today by artificial lighting; the **Grotta del Fossellone** booms and

reverberates as the sea crashes in. The fossil beach can be seen in this cave as in the Grotta dei Moscerini, upon which the Pontinian hunters made their camp, although most of the deposit has been carried away by the waves curling round within the rocky walls. The **Grotta delle Capre** is a huge dry cavern that took its name from its use years ago as stalls for a herd of goats. Pontinian flints were found in excavations in this cave too, and food refuse even included the bones of hippopotamus, which must have roamed the swamps around Monte Circeo. Take the Via del Faro from San Felice along the southern coast of Monte Circeo (the only road). A kilometre west of Torre Fico a road leads down towards the sea (signposted to the Grotta della Capre) to a parking place, from which a foot-path drops straight down to the cave. The Grotta del Fossellone is in a tiny cove 150 m to the west of the Grotta delle Capre. With some care it is possible to climb into the cave through a natural tunnel, but some dexterity is needed to negotiate the rock face at the base of this, over the waves, in order to reach the archaeological deposit! But the more timorous can contemplate the stratigraphy from a distance without attempting this. Surface scatters of Mousterian tools are frequently found on eroded hills and terraces in central Italy and several inland cave sites have been excavated. From Belverde (see below) it is possible to visit the nearby Mousterian cave called the **Grotta di Gosto**, where stalagmite containing animal bones and Mousterian tools has recently been dated by the Th^{230}/U^{283} method to $48,000 \pm 4,000$ years B.P. The site was used by a band to hunt red deer, roe deer, pig, cattle and even an occasional rhinoceros. The services of a guide ought to be obtained at Belverde because the cave is hidden in crags in the woods and could easily be missed.

UPPER PALAEOLITHIC, from c. 35,000 B.P.
MESOLITHIC, from c. 12,000 B.P.

Surface scatters of Upper Palaeolithic tools are extremely rare in central Italy, and most of our knowledge of life in the coldest period of the Last Glaciation comes from caves and rock-shelters. The tool kit of Upper Palaeolithic hunters in Italy, for the most part, is very similar to the Gravettian industries of the 'classical' sites in France. In Italy these industries of backed blades and points, scrapers and burins have often been named Romanellian, after the site in the heel of Italy called the Grotta Romanelli. Backed blades were battered on one surface to blunt the edge of the 'back', and were probably hafted as delicate cutting instruments; scrapers were presumably for working wood or cleaning hides; burins are specialized tools for engraving bone and wood. The **Grotta Polesini** was one of the richest Upper Palaeolithic sites in Italy. To reach it, take the rough unmade road which climbs up from the left-hand side of the main road from Rome to Tivoli, immediately before the bridge over the Aniene at Ponte Lucano. Take the first road on the right (after 500 m), and continue along this for another 500 m to the fields beyond the last houses. At this point leave the road and walk off to the right towards the river. The path winds down in front of a cliff face onto a river terrace; the cave is immediately on the right when the path reaches this terrace. It is a large rock shelter, probably the winter base camp of a Romanellian band of hunters, when the lower snowlines in the Last Glaciation forced game and hunters alike down to the coastal plains in the winter months. The cave was ideally placed at the exit of the Aniene valley from the Apennines, on the edge of the plains. The main trench of the excavations can still be seen. The faunal sample from the cave was huge and consisted largely of red deer and the steppe horse, *Equus hydruntinus*. The most notable discovery at the site was the fine collection of Upper Palaeolithic engraved art on stones and fragments of bone. This important manifestation of cave art can be seen in the Museo del Lazio at EUR near Rome (28). Occupation at the site has been dated by Carbon 14 to 28,000–12,000 years ago.

In Umbria there is a dramatic Upper Palaeolithic cave near Parrano that is best reached from the Fabro exit of the Autostrada del Sole to the north of Orvieto. Just before the road from Fabro begins to climb up to Parrano it crosses a tributary of the river Chiana called the Fosso del Bagno, for this spring is thought by the locals to have healing properties. Less than 500 m from the bridge (upstream) this tributary stream tumbles through a rocky gorge. High up in the crags to the left of the waterfall two caves were found, **le Tane del Diavolo** ('the Devil's caves'), with Romanellian material similar to the industry at the Grotta Polesini in one, and Bronze Age material in the other very like that from Belverde, which is quite near on the other side of the Chiana valley. From this site the Palaeolithic hunting band killed cattle, red and roe deer, pig, horse and occasionally goat. In the Bronze Age the caves were occupied by a group of herdsmen who probably stockaded their animals in the narrow valley below the cliffs.

One further group of Upper Palaeolithic caves can easily be visited around the ancient lake basin of the Fucine Lake near Avezzano in the Abruzzo (see inset, Map 3). Seven caves have now been excavated, principally by the members of the Istituto di Paletnologia at Pisa, directed by Professor Radmilli. The material can be seen in the museum at Chieti. On the eastern shore of the lake two caves were occupied during the last millennia of the Last Glaciation by Upper Palaeolithic hunters: the two caves are next to each other and can be seen in a small quarry less than a kilometre north of the village of Venere: the **Grotta Clemente Tronci** and the **Riparo Maurizio.** The latter unfortunately is almost quarried away. The hunters probably occupied these sites during the summer months when the snow had receded from the hills above and herds of red deer and steppe horse moved up to graze around the lake. The wild goat, still seen occasionally in Abruzzo, is frequently found in the refuse of these inland sites. Three other caves of this period can be seen round the lake. Between Trasacco and Ortucchio on the southern shore, on the north-western flank of Monte Praticelle, the **Grotta la Punta** is hidden among crags some 50 m above the level of the lake basin; the stratigraphy included Mesolithic, Neolithic and Bronze Age levels above Upper Palaeolithic hearths, which were dated by Carbon 14 to 14,448 $\pm$800 B.P. (the basal hearth) and 10,581 $\pm$100 B.P. (an upper hearth). The cave can just be discerned amongst the boulders from the junction of the Trasacco-Ortucchio road with the Fucine farmroad (No. 30); it lies *above* the line of the telegraph poles and wires. 200 m to the west (to the right as seen from the road) the **Grotta Maritza** is similarly hidden, at about the same height above the basin. The stratigraphy of this site, which is a cleft in the rock face rather than a cave, contained Upper Palaeolithic, Neolithic, Eneolithic and Bronze Age layers. It is still possible (1971) to see the stratigraphy left by the excavations, together with the layer numbers painted on the rock face. From top to bottom these are: 1–5 Bronze Age; 6–7 Eneolithic; 8–12 Neolithic; 20–35 Mesolithic and Upper Palaeolithic. On the western shore the **Grotta di Ciccio Felice** was used especially for hunting goat and deer. This cave lies about 4 km to the south of Avezzano near the hamlet of Casale Incile on the road to Trasacco. (The official Avezzano camping site is here.) It can be seen as a wide and obvious cave at the foot of the

hills about 300 m from the road, just north of Roman arches that
survive from the Emperor Claudius' attempts to drain the lake into
the upper waters of the Liri river. Perhaps this cave was occupied
in order to trap game seeking to move out to the western lowlands
at the end of the summer.

At the end of the last glaciation, some 12,000 years ago, the lake
began to dry up. Both caves and open sites were occupied during

Plate 3. Grotta di Ortucchio, also known as the Grotta dei Porci, on the edge
of the Fucine Lake basin near Avezzano. A cave used by prehistoric hunters
and fishers over 10,000 years ago.

the Mesolithic: traces of a camp have been found out on the plain a
kilometre from the modern village of Ortucchio, which before the
drainage work of the last century was a fishing village at the water's
edge; and I have already described the stratigraphy at the Grotta la
Punta, where the upper hearths are clearly post-glacial. 1 km south
of Ortucchio is a large cave immediately to the west of a prominent
gravel quarry visible from the village (see Plate 3). The occupation
layers from the excavation (the trench of which can still be seen)
were dated by Carbon 14 from 12,619 ±410 B.P., which was from
a sample from one of the lower hearths—in other words from
about the end of the last glaciation, when the cave was occupied by

hunters and fishers. In the excavation reports the cave is called the **Grotta di Ortucchio,** but the local name is the Grotta dei Porci.

NEOLITHIC, from c. 4500 B.C.

By the term Neolithic, archaeologists mean something that is both economic and cultural: cereal and stock husbandry, the use of pottery and polished stone, life in settled villages. Pottery and polished stone tools appear at a fairly early date in central Italy, compared with developments in the rest of Italy and the Mediterranean in general; but the most remarkable aspect of the Neolithic in central Italy is the strength of earlier traditions. The new economy made little headway in some areas, perhaps for millennia, and in any case had to adapt to the climate, the terrain, the seasonal pastures and so on, much as game and hunters had always adapted for thousands, indeed tens of thousands of years. The shepherds on the high summer pastures above L'Aquila, Avezzano, or Norcia, close and taciturn men in flowing black cloaks who still remain with the flocks at night to protect them from wolves, are the survival of a tradition that is probably of immense antiquity.

Five caves have been selected with Neolithic deposits, all excavated since the last war. Two are just outside Pisa at the foot of the Colli Pisani between the villages of Agnano and Asciano. The **Grotta del Leone** lies directly by the road just west of Agnano; it was probably an Upper Palaeolithic home base, but after the collapse of the entrance the site was used as a burial cave in the Late Neolithic. The **Romita di Asciano** is a shelter 1 km to the west, about 100 m from the road behind the *Ristorante il Montecelio* and about 60 m above the level of the road. This very important site has given us a stratified sequence from the Neolithic to the Middle Ages. The *Grotta Patrizi* is a burial cave near Sasso Furbara, a village in Latium off the Via Aurelia 25 km before Civitavecchia, travelling from Rome. The Neolithic material from this cave is especially interesting because it was identical to the pottery and flint work of the Fiorano culture situated in the Po Valley. The cave is some way from the village in private land, but well known to all the villagers, and quite accessible. In recent years a second cave has been found with this Sasso-Fiorano assemblage, the **Grotta dell'Orso** at Sarteano in the province of Siena in Tuscany. The site is 1 km north of Sarteano, a few hundred

metres east of the Chancano road. Take the farm track on the right
when the main road suddenly curves to the left. The cave commands
a wonderful view over the Val di Chiana, situated right on the edge
of a wooded ridge, and has been dated to 1430 ± 200 B.C.

Chieti museum has a rich collection from excavations at the type
site of the Neolithic of the Abruzzo—Ripoli, near the village of
Corropoli in the Vibrata valley. This valley has produced a great
deal of evidence of settlement by Mesolithic, Neolithic and Bronze
Age populations, but there is nothing to be seen today of a score of
sites. It is more worthwhile to visit an important site at Bolognano,
a few kilometres off the road from Popoli and Sulmona to Chieti.
The **Grotta dei Piccioni** is set high on the side of the gorge of the
Olta river a few hundred metres from the village and commands a
magnificent view of the gorge. Anyone in the village will direct you
to the cave, which is approached by an impressive but safe path along
the wall of the gorge. The basal layers were Middle Neolithic, dated
by Carbon 14 to 4297 ± 130 B.C., and Late Neolithic layers to 2820
± 110 B.C. Ripoli pottery was widely traded across Italy and sherds
were found at the **Grotta Lattaia** near Belverde (see below), at the
Grotta dell'Orso and the Grotta Patrizi.

COPPER AGE, from c. 2500 B.C.

The Eneolithic or Copper Age in Italy is characterized by a few
burials rich in exquisite flint work and occasional simple copper
objects, especially daggers. The grave goods from the type site of
the Copper Age in Tuscany and Latium, Rinaldone near
Montefiascone, can be seen in the Museo del Lazio in EUR near
Rome. There is also a fine reconstruction of a burial in a rock-cut
tomb at this museum from a Copper Age cemetery at Ponte San
Pietro in the Fiora Valley. However, two Eneolithic sites are also
well worth seeing in themselves: the first is the type site of the period
in Marche at **Conelle**, about 4 km north-east of Arcevia. Take the
road from Arcevia to Senigallia; after about 5 km turn left on to the
gravel road to San Mariano, turn left again at the T junction and
the site is on the left after the road crosses a stream bed. Conelle
was a large ditched settlement and it is still possible to see the deep
open ditch, which has been protected by a metal shelter. The second
is the site of **Mirabella Eclano** in Campania. This was a rich

cemetery of several rock-cut tombs, which can still be seen today because they also have been covered by a shelter after their discovery and excavation. The village of Mirabella Eclano is on the main road from Avellino to Foggia, 35 km from Avellino; the archaeological site is by the church of Madonna delle Grazie 2 km from the village on the road to Taurasi. The grave goods, fabulously rich for the period, are beautifully displayed in the museum at Avellino.

One element often found in small quantities in Neolithic and Eneolithic sites in central Italy is obsidian, a black volcanic glass. Work on linking these blades and flakes with known sources of obsidian has been conducted especially in Malta, Greece and further east. (A. C. Renfrew, J. E. Dixon and J. R. Cann, *Papers of the Prehistoric Society* 1966, 1968.) A programme of analysis of Italian obsidian samples on the same lines as this is currently under way at Rome University but results of this work have not yet been published. The few known sources of obsidian are off the west coast, particularly Lipari, Palmarola in the Pontine Islands and in southern Sardinia. So far it seems that obsidian began to be traded across peninsular Italy in the Neolithic and Eneolithic; most sites just have one or two tiny bladelets, the odd core and so on, but in a few cases it is present in such quantities that presumably it was used instead of flint tools. Sometimes the blades are so tiny and fragile that they may have been purely ornamental or even of a magical significance. The obsidian trade is interesting, not for its own sake, but because it is the one solid hint about the extent of trade in prehistoric Italy—trade in material, foodstuffs and so on, presumably in the manner of primitive exchange patterns known from ethnographic evidence; it also implies, necessarily, sea travel from the islands to the mainland at a very early date, beginning more than 6,000 years ago.

BRONZE AGE, from c. 1800 B.C.

There is an overall similarity in the pottery of much of the Bronze Age in central Italy which is therefore thought by archaeologists to imply an overall culture—the 'Apennine Bronze Age'. Some sites are so high in the mountains that they can only have been occupied in the summer, probably by shepherds. Today you can still see huge flocks on the summer pastures, which are taken down to the coastal lowlands in the winter. There is one cave, for example, at the foot of the southern wall of the Gran Sasso, the highest mountain of the Apennines. This is the **Grotta a Male,** a cave 3 km north-west of the village of Assergi, not far from L'Aquila, near the foot of the chair-lift up to the ski slopes on Gran Sasso, and a site has even been found on Campo Pericoli at over 2000 m above sea level, just below the topmost peak of Gran Sasso, the Corno Grande. The occupation debris of the farmers and herdsmen of the Apennine Bronze Age has been found in several of the caves already mentioned: the Grotta Polesini, the Grotta Maritza, le Tane del Diavolo, the Grotta dell'Orso, the Grotta del Leone, la Romita di Asciano and the Grotta dei Piccioni. However, the richest site is undoubtedly **Belverde** on the eastern slopes of Monte Cetona, a few kilometres south of Sarteano. The cave is sign-posted from the villages of Cetona and Sarteano, although the track is fairly testing for a motor car! However, there is an excellent *ristorante* operating at the site in summer, which is a favourite Sunday outing for local Italians. Most of the extraordinarily rich material is displayed in the museum at Perugia, but there is a small museum in Cetona too. The cave of Belverde produced a quantity of fine pottery, miniature pots and metal work, together with several jars of carbonized grain, thought to be votive offerings. The material from the site was not divided stratigraphically in the excavations, although Belverde was clearly used throughout the Bronze Age. A guide will take you from here through the woods to the **Grotta di Gosto** (Middle Palaeolithic—see above) and the **Grotta Lattaia** (Neolithic).

In contrast to this little understood cave is the habitation site of the acropolis at **Luni** on the river Mignone, recently excavated by Professor Östenberg, Director of the Swedish Institute in Rome. The acropolis rises above the deserted railway station of Monte Romano. It is best reached by taking the Viterbo-Tarquinia road, and turning off south at Monte Romano on the road to Blera. Leave the road just west of Civitella Cesi station where a farm track heads south, then take the track that strikes south-west after 1 km. Luni is directly south-west at about an hour's distance away from this junction, but the acropolis can be seen below in the distance after a quarter of an hour. The country is wild and desolate around the site, which has a strong claim to be one of the most beautiful in Italy. The walk is well worth it! To the south forested hills climb into the distance towards Tolfa and Allumiere; the rest is an expanse of pasture with perhaps an occasional shepherd and his flock in the distance. On the top of the acropolis are traces of the Villanovan and Etruscan occupation, when the site guarded the southern boundary of the territory of Tarquinia. The ruins of a medieval chapel, Etruscan city walls and the foundations of an Iron Age house can still be seen on the acropolis. Most interesting of all was the discovery in the centre of the plateau of several rectangular trenches which proved to be the rock-cut foundations of houses inhabited by Bronze Age families. Presumably these were covered by a wooden ridged framework and thatch, like rather similar buildings still used by local farmers. These families kept cattle, sheep and pigs and culti-vated wheat, barley, millet, beans and lentils. There were even a few sherds of pottery from Mycenae in Greece, a tantalizing hint of prehistoric trade into central Italy towards the end of the second millennium B.C. The Bronze Age occupation at Luni is dated from *c.* 1300 to 800 B.C. 40 km to the east there was a contemporary occupation at the foot of the acropolis at **Narce** between Mazzano and Calcata on the banks of the Treia River, which like Luni was also occupied later in the Villanovan and Etruscan Iron Ages; this site has been excavated in recent years by the British School at Rome, with the collaboration of Italian archaeologists.

The later period of the Apennine culture is frequently called the Subapennine phase, although pottery developments show strong regional divergence. On the east coast, the richest Bronze Age site was the type site of the culture in Marche, at **San Paolina di Filottrano.** The farm nearby can point out the small hill where excavations took place, although there is nothing to be seen on the ground to compare with the rich finds from the site now in Ancona Museum. The Gola (gorge) of the Sentino river, east of Sassoferrato, also in Marche, has a series of Bronze Age sites set in superb scenery. On the road from Sassoferrato to the gorge (the road to Iesi and Ancona) a quarry can be seen on the opposite bank to the left of a church, now a farm, **Santa Croce.** 300 m west of the farm and 70 m above it there is a cave which was broken into by the quarry work and where a rich Apennine deposit was found, now in Ancona Museum. Farm and quarry both lie less than a kilometre east of Sassoferrato. On the left bank of the entrance to the Sentino gorge is the modern village of Pianello; below the village was a huge Late Bronze Age *urnfield* cemetery. Then going downstream through the gorge: the **Caverna di Frasassi** is reached first by a path (sign-posted) on the left of the road about a kilometre into the gorge. This

Plate 4. The 'Warrior of Capestrano', a life-sized terracotta statue found during drainage work near Capestrano in the province of L'Aquila, Abruzzo in the 1930s. Nearby were 33 inhumation graves, 21 of which could be dated to the end of the seventh and the sixth centuries B.C. The statue is probably sixth century, an exceptional example of an ancient form of Italic statuary. Archaeological Museum, Chieti.

huge cave, which contained Apennine and Subappenine deposits, is only a few minutes' walk up the path from the road and now contains a Christian shrine. The other Bronze Age sites are at the end of the gorge and the **Grotta dei Baffoni** can easily be reached from the village of San Vittore; it in fact is still within the gorge, 70 or 80 m above the river, but the path curves round from the village. The **Grotta del Mezzogiorno** can be reached by Herculean efforts from the village, straight up through the wooded slopes to the cave, which is at the top of the crags above. However, it is possible to escape this obstacle course by driving up to Pierosara village, from where an easy path winds round to the cave. The scenery in any case is breathtaking. For the faint hearted, guided tours can be arranged at San Vittore to these and other caves. Similar material has also been found in the excavations at **San Omobono** in Rome on the site of the Roman Forum, sporadic and tantalizing finds of the early peasant bands that settled the hills of Rome at the turn of the first millennium B.C.

IRON AGE, from 900/800 B.C.

The prehistory of central Italy merges into protohistory during the Iron Age, when the tribal groupings known in the Roman period can gradually be distinguished across the peninsula. Over much of the area life seems to have continued little affected by Etruscan and early Roman expansion, and the dearth of Roman remains in the archaeology of Marche and Abruzzo is remarkable. Perhaps the strangest relic of these 'silent peoples' of much of central Italy is the extraordinary *Warrior of Capestrano* now in the Chieti museum, a monumental clay figure buried near a score of 7th- and 6th-century Picene graves in the Capestrano basin near the source of the Tirino river in Abruzzo (see Plate 4).

PRINCIPAL MUSEUMS CONTAINING MATERIAL FROM THE PREHISTORIC PERIOD

Material from the prehistoric sites has been collected and preserved in the following museums in central Italy:

Province	*Town*	*Museum*
Toscana	Florence:	The National Archaeological Museum, Piazza S. Annunciata, and the Museo Fiorentino di Preistoria in the Istituto di Paletnologia, Via S. Egidio 21.
Umbria	Perugia:	The National Archaeological Museum of Umbria.

Province	*Town*	*Museum*
Marche	Ancona:	National Archaeological Museum of the Marche.
Abruzzo	Chieti:	National Archaeological Museum of Abruzzo and Molise.
Lazio	Rome:	Museo Preistorico del Lazio L. Pigorini, Piazza Marconi, EUR.
Campania	Naples:	National Archaeological Museum.
	Avellino:	Museo del Sannio (housed with the town library).
	Salerno:	National Archaeological Museum.

BIBLIOGRAPHY

Bloch, Raymond, *The Etruscans*, Thames and Hudson, London, 1958.

Hencken, H., *Tarquinia and the Etruscan Origins*, Thames and Hudson, London, 1968.

Radmilli, A. M., *Piccola Guida della Preistoria d'Italia*, Sansoni, Florence, 1962.

Radmilli, A. M., *La Preistoria d'Italia alla luce delle ultime scoperte*, Istituto Geografico Militare, Florence, 1963.

Trump, D. H., *Central and Southern Italy before Rome*, Thames and Hudson, London, 1966.

PART II

Rome and Ostia

2 . ROME AND OSTIA

ROME

To do justice to the archaeological treasures of Rome is far beyond the scope of this Guide. Nevertheless the Eternal City is the main attraction and the key to all visits to Italy. There are so many things to see that a considerable amount of time will inevitably be spent in looking round the city on plain sightseeing. I have therefore felt it wiser to leave detailed descriptions to specialized works (a selected list of which will be found on pp. 248–9) and to concentrate on indicating the main items of archaeological interest, and above all the museums. This I have done by suggesting some itineraries by which the archaeological sites can be visited with the minimum of travel and on foot if necessary. The time required for each itinerary for a general appreciation of the sights is roughly one day.

To the visitor and to the archaeological student, professional or amateur on his first visit to Italy, I would give a caution constantly to bear in mind that side by side or superimposed, he will find items of very different dates. Sometimes these differences amount to several centuries. It is essential to think in terms of these differing dates and their effect on one's picture of the architecture, the way of life, or whatever aspect of the ancient civilization appeals to the visitor. It is very easy to overlook this aspect and to be led badly astray in dating a particular item. Great changes can occur in the life and customs of a nation in the course of one, two, or three centuries. One has only to recall the England of Queen Anne, when America was still an English colony.

Rome was traditionally founded by Romulus in 753 B.C. and resulted from the union of the settlements founded by the Latin tribes on the tops of the seven hills. Livy tells the story well, and the modern reader can follow his account in the excellent translation by Anthony de Sélincourt in the Penguin Classics series. The original city was on three hills, the Palatine, Capitoline and Quirinal.

Excavations recently carried out in the Forum have brought to light a necropolis containing a mixture of cremation and inhumation graves, suggesting perhaps a fusion of different tribes. One is reminded of the Rape of the Sabine Women in this connection.

The Gauls sacked Rome in 390 B.C., but immediately withdrew, having taught the Romans that defence walls are a discouragement to aggressors. The 'Servian wall', whose name suggests that it should date from the period of the Kings, is believed by many scholars to have been begun by the Romans in 390 B.C. and when completed had a circuit of nearly seven miles.

It was not until after the defeat of King Antiochus the Great in 188 B.C. and the final destruction of Macedon in 168, that fabulous wealth began to flow into Rome and the city was adorned with fine public buildings and many beautiful private houses. In the days of Augustus even more was done to 'turn Rome from a town of brick to a city of marble'. A great fire in Nero's reign destroyed most of the poorer quarter of the city with its wooden houses. During the rebuilding Nero instituted a town-planning scheme, and Rome became a worthy capital for the Empire. The population continued to increase, and Aurelian in A.D. 271 began a greatly increased circuit for the defence walls which was completed during the reign of his successor, Probus.

Of the bridges over the Tiber, the oldest was the *Pons Sublicius*, the scene of the famous legendary battle with Lars Porsena, King of Clusium, when Horatius Cocles and two others held the bridge until it could be demolished by the Romans. It was traditionally built by King Ancus Marcius and was destroyed by floods several times, but was always rebuilt on the same site and always of wood. Naturally, nothing of it now survives. The central arches of the Ponte Sant' Angelo originally formed part of the *Pons Aelius* built by Hadrian. The *Pons Fabricius* (62 B.C.) now called the Ponte dei Quattro Capi, and the later *Pons Cestius*, both linking with the *Isola Tiberina*, now the Ponte San Bartolomeo, are also ancient bridges still in use.

There were over four hundred temples, of some of which there are sufficient traces for their former magnificence to be recognized. Circuses, theatres and amphitheatres for the amusement of the people were all a part of state policy.

In Imperial Rome, the *Thermae*, or Baths, were the most magnificent buildings and served as meeting places for the daily gossip, as well as for bathing and massage. They usually comprised hot and cold water baths, steam 'Turkish' baths and small private baths. There was also a large open space for sun-bathing and great halls for those who preferred shade. The National Museum is housed in the Thermae of Diocletian, and part of the Thermae of Caracalla is now used as a theatre. They have also inspired architects of all times with the spacious beauty of the Great Hall. Pennsylvania Station in New York is one example. The water brought into the city by the network of aqueducts from the surrounding hills was intended primarily for the Thermae and public drinking fountains. Only what was surplus to these requirements was available for private houses.

The most conspicuous monuments are listed in the itineraries, but remember, there are many thousands of fragments incorporated in the walls of modern shops and houses, and much of ancient Rome is still buried. Reference to the list of museums on pp. 47–54 will remind visitors of the fabulous collections they contain. Only the architect can appreciate and picture the complete building from a couple of columns that remain in the field, but in the museums are the little human items that made up the life of the people. One can see reconstructions of palaces and of cities, or of a villa that will give an overall setting for the chairs, tables and beds, the toilet boxes and jewel cases, the cooking pots in the museums, even the false teeth that some Etruscan wore four hundred years before Christ was born, the silver and gold plates of the wealthy, the chariots and horse trappings of the knights and the litters of the ladies and the senators. Truly the museum is the place to reconstruct the daily life of the inhabitants of Rome under the Caesars, their religious beliefs and their burial customs.

Later on when tramping over a rocky hillside amongst the scented thyme and marjoram, the thistles and brambles, the find of a pottery fragment like that seen in the museum will immediately create a living picture, and the crumbling wall will once again become the patrician's country villa. This is the real joy of archaeology, the realization that the ruins once housed living folk. Take away the television aerials, and the motor cars and I say there is precious little difference between the old Roman and you and me.

NOTE. In the Itineraries that follow, in order not to distract attention from the object of this Guide, only items of archaeological interest are mentioned. But Italy is a treasure-house of the past, and all along the routes taken by the Itineraries, and even alongside the ancient buildings there are many beautiful examples of churches and palaces from ancient to modern times.

ITINERARY I: Piazza del Popolo—Via del Corso—Piazza Colonna—Piazza Montecitorio—Piazza del Campidoglio
(Plan 1a)

The Piazza del Popolo is one of the finest squares in the city. Standing in the centre is the obelisk of Flaminius, the hieroglyphs on which celebrate the triumphs of the Pharaohs Rameses II and Merenptah. It was brought by Augustus to Rome (originally to the Circus Maximus) in a large ship specially built for the purpose, which carried, in addition to the obelisk, over 800 tons of grain. The column was erected in the square in 1589 by Pope Sextus V. From here, take the Via del Corso, which is still the principal street of Rome. The Piazza Colonna was for centuries the political centre of Rome. On one side is the Palazzo Chigi, the Italian Foreign Office. In the centre is the Column of Marcus Aurelius, erected between A.D. 176 and 193; the shaft is 28 m high, in 28 blocks of white marble, with a spiral pictorial account of Aurelius's victories over the Marcomanni and the Sarmatae. In 1589 Pope Sextus V placed the statue of St Paul on the top. Just to the west of the Piazza Colonna is the Piazza del Parlamento, by which stands the Palazzo di Montecitorio, one of the main Italian Parliament buildings. In the centre of the square is another Egyptian column, that of the Pharaoh Psammeticus II, also brought to Rome by Augustus. From here proceed by the Corso to the Piazza Venezia, on the right of which is the Piazza del Campidoglio. This was the *Capitol*, the political and religious centre of Roma Antica, founded by Tarquinius Priscus, who built the first temple dedicated to Jupiter Optimus Maximus Capitolinus. Tradition says that when the foundations of the temple were being dug, a head was found, hence the name *Capitolinus* for the temple. In 78 B.C. the *Tabularium* was built to house the state archives. In the centre of the square is the superb equestrian statue of Marcus Aurelius. Around the square are numerous statues and fragments from the ancient Via Appia. Note especially those on the stairway, called La Cordonata. Two superb museums are housed in the palaces on either side of the square—the Capitoline museum (23) and the Palazzo dei Conservatori (24). Outstanding pieces are the statue of the *Dying Gaul*, the

Plate 5. The She-Wolf, symbol of their past to the Romans. It is one of the largest and finest Etruscan bronzes and stands about 850 mm high. Probably of the school of Veii, the wolf is dated to about 500 B.C. Palazzo dei Conservatori, Rome.

Etruscan bronze *She-Wolf* (see Plate 5) and the busts of the emperors.

ITINERARY II: Piazza del Popolo—Via della Scrofa—Pantheon—Piazza Navona—Corso Vittorio Emmanuele—Largo Argentina (Plan 1a)

From the Piazza del Popolo, take the Via di Ripetta to the *Mausoleum of Augustus* erected in 28 B.C.; the original appearance of the Mausoleum has been restored as much as possible after excavations in 1926–30. In the central chamber were three niches in which cinerary urns of the imperial family were found. Opposite the Mausoleum between it and the Tiber is the *Ara Pacis*. This famous altar was dedicated by Augustus in 9 B.C. to celebrate the return of peace to the Roman world following the troubled times after the death of Julius Caesar. Its original site was in the Campus Martius, but the stones were widely scattered in the following centuries; the

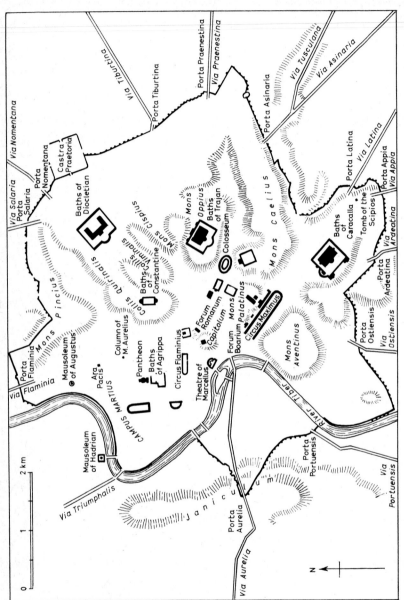

Plan Ia. Ancient Rome.

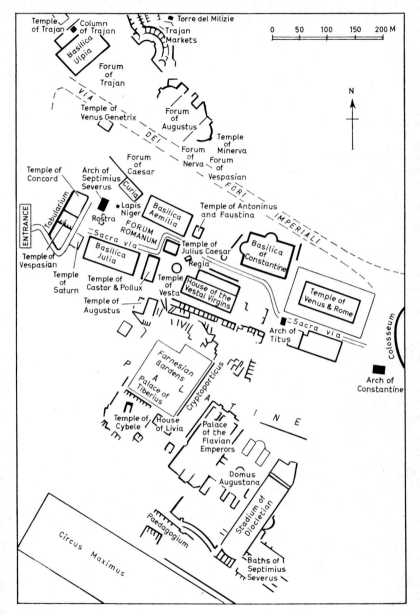

Plan 1b. Ancient Rome.

removal and re-erection of the altar on its present site is a triumph
for the archaeologists. Before this was carried out in 1937–8, some
of the altar stones had been taken from Rome: some were in Florence,
one was in the Vatican Museum, another in the Villa Medici and
some were even in the Louvre in Paris. One was found acting as a
cover for a tomb in Rome, and more still were in the National
Museum. In spite of the removal of all this material, the foundations
and podium had remained intact, and it was possible to reconstruct
the altar to the original design at its present site. The side panels are
decorated with reliefs telling the story of the birth of Rome and
showing Augustus and his family in procession to make a sacrifice.
From here take the Via della Scrofa as far as the Palazzo Madama
(the Italian Senate House), and there turn left to the *Pantheon*. The
original building was erected by Agrippa in 27 B.C. The building
you now see, with its great dome in a perfect state of preservation,
was built by Hadrian and further adorned by Septimus Severus. The
dome is 43 m in diameter and is semicircular. The only lighting is
by a circular hole in the centre of the dome. The Pantheon has been
used as a mausoleum for famous men and also as the tomb for Italy's
kings.

Return to Piazza Navona, which was a sports arena in Roman times,
used mainly for horse and chariot racing at the *Feast of the Lupercalia*;
this feast is still observed by the Christian church as the Feast of
the Epiphany (La Befana) on January 5 and 6 when a fair and toy
market is held in the square. The Egyptian obelisk in the centre
was erected by Domitian. At the south end of the Piazza Navona
is the Museo di Roma. From here take the Corso Emmanuele past
the Barracco Museum (22) to the Largo Argentina where there are
remains of temples of the Republican Age.

ITINERARY III: Piazza del Campidoglio—Forum Romanum —Via Sacra (Plan 1b)

Proceed to the Piazza del Campidoglio. Descend to the *Roman
Forum* by the Via di Monte Tarpeio; beside it, and behind the
Tabularium, runs the ancient *Clivus Capitolinus*, once the scene of
Julius Caesar's Gallic triumph when he lined the road with forty
torch-bearing elephants. In the valley between the Palatine,
Capitoline and Esquiline hills was the public centre of Rome (see
Plate 6). On the left as one descends, is the *Porticus of the Temple
of the Dei Consentes* restored in 1858. Then follow three columns of

Plate 6. The Roman Forum as seen from the Temple of Antoninus and Faustina.

the *Temple of Vespasian*, erected after his death by Titus and Domitian in A.D. 79. Below the Tabularium was the *Temple of Concord*, a reconstruction by Tiberius of a sanctuary erected by Camillus in 367 B.C. to mark the end of the controversy between the patricians and the plebeians. Here also is the *Mamertine* prison, also called the *Tullianum*. Tradition says that St Peter was imprisoned here.

One now enters the *Roman Forum*, the largest of the great public squares that adorned the ancient city (see Plan 1b and Plate 6). Here at public meetings the orators harangued the crowd from the *Rostra*, a raised platform adorned with the bronze beaks of galleys captured in battle. The Forum has been fully excavated and is undoubtedly one of the most impressive and historic localities of the world. The following is a brief description of the layout of the various buildings, beginning at the entrance in the Via dei Fori Imperiali. It is open from 9 a.m. to one hour before sunset. A general panoramic view can be obtained from the terrace alongside the Senatorial Palace as one descends from the Piazza del Campidoglio. In the foreground is the main central plain, on the right is the Palatine hill and in the background the Colosseum. In the foreground are the eight columns of the temple of Saturn; a little to the left are the Arch of *Septimius Severus* and the *Curia*, the Senate House. In the middle distance on the plain is the *column of Phocas*, set up in A.D. 608, and further on the three columns of the *Temple of the Dioscuri*, on the left the colonnade of the *Temple of Antoninus and Faustina*, and in front the Campanile of the church of San Francesco Romano; behind the latter is the *Basilica of Constantine* and on the right the *Arch of Titus*. From the entrance proceed to the *Basilica Aemilia*, first built in the 2nd century B.C. and restored several times; the last restoration was carried out by Honorius in the 5th century A.D. Opposite this is the *Temple of Antoninus and Faustina*, now the church of San Lorenzo in Miranda: six columns of the front porch are still standing. Then follows the *Curia*. The present building is a restoration of the Curia Julia, begun by Julius Caesar. A second hall for secret meetings, the *Secretarium Senatus*, occupied the site of the church of SS. Luca and Martina. Nearby, the six rows of black stones are said to mark the *Tomb of Romulus* and are named the *Lapis Niger*; recent excavations, however, found no trace of any burial here. Here also was the site of the *Comitium* for public meetings, mentioned above. Modern archaeologists date the Lapis Niger to the 6th century

B.C. Next comes the *Arch of Septimius Severus* erected in A.D. 203. This Emperor was born at Leptis Magna in North Africa, and his wife was Julia Domna, a Syrian Princess. Severus himself at the end of his life campaigned in Britain and died at York. Near the arch the remains of the *Rostra* can still be seen. Here also was the *Umbilicus Urbis Romae*, the spot marking the centre of the city upon which stood the *Miliarium Aureum*, the 'Golden Milestone' from which all distances were measured along the Imperial roads.

Further along the *Via Sacra*, which was the street leading to the *Templum Sacrae Urbis*, are the remains of part of the foundations of the *Basilica Julia*, erected by Julius Caesar in 40 B.C. to mark the protection given to Rome by the gods during the wars with the Etruscans and the Latins in 496 B.C. Next is the *Temple of Augustus* and the *Temple of Julius Caesar* built in 29 B.C. over the place where his corpse was burned. Then follow the *Temple of Vesta* and the *House of the Vestal Virgins*. The Temple of Vesta is a circular building of twenty Corinthian columns and was partially reconstructed in 1930. The temple was burned down in Nero's fire of A.D. 64 and again in A.D. 191. The holy Palladium, or statue of Pallas Athena, was kept inside the temple. The House of the Vestal Virgins is a large rectangular building nearby dating to Republican times. Both in Greek and in Roman times, Vesta was a most important deity as she protected not only the state but also the hearths and homes of the people. The first of the daily sacrifices was always made to her, and the greatest care was made to maintain the Sacred Fire, which, in its way, represented the life of the nation and of its people. The six Vestal Virgins were chosen from the daughters of prominent families: for their office was much sought after. Once elected the priestess had to serve for thirty years, under very strict regulations and taboos. She served ten years as a neophyte, ten years as a full priestess, and ten years teaching the neophytes their duties. Any breach of the regulations was very severely punished, and unchastity was followed by being buried alive. Their main duty was to guard the Sacred Fire, which was rekindled on 1st March each year by rubbing two sticks together. The Festival of the goddess was held on 7th–15th June, and involved a great deal of food-ritual—prayers in the Storehouse of Vesta for the prosperity of households, and on 15th June the ritual cleansing and sweeping of the Storehouse when the Vestal Virgins ceremonially swept all the dirt and rubbish out of the Temple and threw it into the river

Tiber. The day was marked in the Roman Calendar at Q.ST.D.F. (*Quando stercus delatum fas*): as soon as the cleansing operation was completed the Festival was over. Nearby was the *Regia*, the official residence of the Pontifex Maximus, the Priest of Jupiter Optimus Maximus. Now comes the biggest *Basilica* of all, erected by Maxentius and Constantine, followed by the *Arch of Titus* (A.D. 81) recording his victories over the Jews in Palestine. On the interior panels are some very fine reliefs depicting his triumph.

ITINERARY IV: The Palatine hill (Plan 1b)

It was upon this hill that Romulus founded the original city with a small band of adventurers from Alba; the traditional date is 753 B.C. The hill was also the scene of the Feast of the Lupercalia (see above). Cross over the Farnese Gardens to the *Temple of Cybele* (the Great Mother, or *Magna Mater*); a silver statue of Cybele was brought to Rome from Phrygia in 204 B.C. following a prophecy of the Cumaean Sibyl, that, if this were done, the Carthaginians would leave Italy. The prophecy was duly fulfilled, as in the very next year Hannibal was back in Africa to meet his final defeat at Zama. The identification of the temple was confirmed by the finding of a statue of the goddess within its precincts. The Temple, built in 191 B.C., was twice burned before its restoration by Augustus. Close by is the *House of Livia*, which was the residence of Augustus; the palace is very well preserved, although the roof is modern, and is particularly famous for the mural paintings preserved in the rooms. At the northern side of this is the *Palace of Tiberius*, skirted by the *Cryptoporticus* or vaulted passage which Nero built to his *Golden House* and the Imperial Forum; there is some fine stucco lining in the vault of the passage. Then follows the *Palace of the Flavian Emperors*, which was built by the architect Rabirius, and adorned with such splendid statuary and other embellishments that even contemporary Romans considered it a marvel. Adjacent to this was the *Domus Augustana*, the official residence of the emperors, containing a vast number of rooms in which official business was conducted. Across the *Stadium of Diocletian* are the *Baths of Septimius Severus*, the arches of which still form an excellent viewpoint, and from which the Emperor and his family could look out over the Forum or watch the races in the *Circus Maximus*. The aqueduct to the north of the Baths supplied water to the Palace of Domitian. Nearby to the south was a seven storeyed building also built by

Septimius Severus, named the *Septizonium*, which survived until
nearly A.D. 1600, when it was destroyed by order of Pope Sextus V,
and used as a stone quarry to build churches. Return by the Stadium
to the ruins of the *Paedagogium*, in which the court pages had their
College. Nearby is the *Altar to the Unknown God* erected in 129 B.C.
and connected with the Feast of the Lupercalia. It was used for
sacrifices to any unknown gods that might exist and who might
take umbrage at being left out of the general worship and feasting
to the unknown deities.

ITINERARY V: Piazza Venezia—Forum of Trajan—Via dei Fori Imperiali—Colosseum—Colle Oppio (Plan 1b)

From the Piazza Venezia, facing the Monument to Vittorio
Emmanuele, turn left to the *Forum of Trajan*, now the home of
Rome's stray cats, built by the architect Apollodorus of Damascus,
who also built Hadrian's *Temple of Venus and Rome*, and the *Trajan
Arch* at Ancona on the Adriatic coast (see Plate 26). He eventually
came under the Emperor's displeasure for his outspoken criticism of
the Emperor's technical incompetence and was banished. The Forum
of Trajan comprises a large Square, the *Basilica Ulpia*, a Greek and
Latin Library and the *Temple of Trajan*, at present hidden in the
structure of the modern Prefettura. *The Column of Trajan* dedicated
to him in A.D. 113, was also his tomb, and consists of 18 marble
drums, around which winds a spiral frieze; this shows about 2,500
figures enacting scenes from the emperor's wars against the Dacians,
who lived in modern Rumania. *The Trajan Markets* backing on to
the slopes of the Quirinal Hill, are in two storeys with many shops
and mosaic floors. From this great commercial area the visitor can
obtain a vivid idea of the commerce of 1st- and 2nd-century Rome.
Through the *Forum of Trajan* runs the modern Via dei Fori
Imperiali, which was built without any respect for the valuable
monuments that stood there. Tradition says that Nero watched the
burning of Rome from the *Torre delle Milizie*, the tower behind the
Forum of Trajan. The monuments on either side and the *Colosseum*
at the end, remain isolated without the logical connection that must
have existed in the past. In quick succession are the subsidiary
public spaces, the *Forum of Augustus*, the *Forum of Caesar* and the
nearby *Forum of Nerva*, or *Forum Transitorium*, so called because
it connected the other fora with the *Forum of Vespasian*. Next are
the ruins of the *Temple of Venus Genetrix*, from whom the Julian

family claimed descent; three fine Corinthian columns with their architraves remain. The temple was demolished by Paul V, who used the stones to build the Fontana dell'Acqua Paola on the Janiculum Hill. Close to the Temple was the *Basilica Argentaria*, presumably an international banking exchange; there were similar facilities in other major cities, such as Alexandria in Egypt or Antioch in Syria, whereby transfers of credit could be effected to oil the wheels of trade. The *Forum of Augustus* is dedicated to Mars and was built to commemorate the battle of Philippi and the completion of the vengeance taken upon the assassins of Julius Caesar. The *Temple of Mars Ultor* stood in the centre of the Forum, where the Standards of the Legions were kept; only the podium remains. The *Forum of Nerva* was demolished by Paul V to use as a stone quarry although the basement of the *Temple of Minerva* can still be seen.

The *Colosseum* is the largest monument extant from ancient times, and in spite of having been a stone quarry throughout the centuries it is still a most impressive sight. It was begun in A.D. 72 by Vespasian and completed by Titus in A.D. 80. It takes its name from a nearby colossal statue of Nero (now no longer there), which stood near the *Arch of Constantine*. The amphitheatre is 187 m long, 155 m wide; the maximum height is 57 m above the ground. It could accommodate 50,000 spectators and was used for gladiatorial combats, fights between man and beast, and hunting scenes. The enormous cost of these shows was borne, not by the state but by the Emperor, or even private persons. In recent years the floor has been removed and the understructure where the beasts and prisoners were kept is now revealed.

The *Arch of Constantine* is decorated with motifs of previous monuments of the reigns of Hadrian, Marcus Aurelius and Trajan, but was erected in A.D. 315 to commemorate Constantine's victory over Maxentius. On the nearby hill of the Colle Oppio, stood the *Domus Aurea* of Nero. This must have been a fabulous place, but unfortunately it was demolished by Trajan to build his Thermae, and all that can be seen today are the foundations and some of the basement rooms, which escaped destruction at that time. At one time the space between the Palatine and the Caelian Hills was an artificial lake fed by a special aqueduct which had to be destroyed by Vespasian before work could begin on the Colosseum. After the death of Nero the extravagant Golden House was soon destroyed or covered up by the building works of his successors.

ITINERARY VI: The Vatican City

Recent excavations under St Peter's Cathedral have found traces of the original church built by Constantine approximately between A.D. 322 and 337. Underneath the church there are also extensive remains of the Roman cemetery which stood beside the road from the Tiber. Archaeological opinion is divided, but the Church authorities believe that their excavations discovered the bones of St Peter in a tomb below the present altar and dome. It is possible to visit the excavations, for a small tour is taken round each afternoon on weekdays. Application should be made well in advance to the Monsignore Economo. This is more likely to be successful if you are prepared to join tours given in other languages as well as in English. Hard by was Nero's *Circus*, traces of which were found in the excavations under St Peter's. The magnificent museums of the Vatican contain the very best examples of Greek and Roman art, also much Etruscan and Italic material (30, 31, 32). The Castel Sant'Angelo was begun in A.D. 135 by Hadrian who intended it to be used as his mausoleum, and was completed in 139, a year after his death, by his successor Antoninus Pius. Under Aurelian it became a fortress, then a prison, which capacity it retained until modern times; see, for example, Verdi's *Tosca*.

ITINERARY VII: The Villa Borghese and the Viale delle Belle Arti

Within the gardens of the Villa Borghese is the *Fountain of Aesculapius* with an antique statue. On the northern edge of the Park, in the Viale delle Belle Arti, is the splendid museum of the Villa Giulia (33), which houses a superb collection of Etruscan material.

ITINERARY VIII: Porta Pia—Piazza della Republica

Near the Central Station is the Porta Pia; on the right of the square is the ancient *Porta Nomentana* from which it is a short step to the Piazza della Republica and the *Thermae of Diocletian* which now house the National Museum (27). The Thermae, built in A.D. 305–6 by Diocletian and Maximian, cover no less than 11 hectares and could accommodate more than 3,000 bathers at one time. Part of it has been built into the church of Santa Maria degli Angeli.

ITINERARY IX: Piazza Venezia—Teatro di Marcello— Circus Maximus—Porta San Paolo (Plan 1a)

Take the Via del Teatro di Marcello from the Piazza Venezia to the *Theatre of Marcellus* which was begun by Julius Caesar, and completed by Augustus in 13 B.C. who dedicated it to Marcellus, the son of his sister Octavia. Some fine examples of superimposed arches remain out of the original structure of three tiers of arches with fifty-two columns in each. The Piazza della Bocca della Verità nearby occupies part of the site of the antique *Forum Boarium* or cattle market. On the right are two temples: the so-called *Temple of Vesta* is the small round *cella* surrounded by twenty fluted columns, probably dating to the 1st century A.D. and perhaps dedicated to Portunus, god of harbours; the second temple, usually called the *Temple of Fortuna Virilis*, was probably dedicated to the Mater Matuta. It was built at the end of the 3rd century B.C. and because it escaped alterations during the Empire is an invaluable example of Graeco-Italian temples of the Republic. Between the Palatine and the Aventine Hills was the site of the *Circus Maximus*. According to Livy, it was first used in the time of Tarquinius Priscus, *c.* 600 B.C. The Circus was repeatedly destroyed and rebuilt by different emperors (Augustus, Nero, Vespasian, Titus, Domitian, Trajan), but today imagination alone can serve to reconstruct the past glories of the Circus for the visitor.

Follow the Viale Aventino down to the *Porta San Paolo*, the ancient Porta Ostiensis in the Aurelian Wall. The outer side of the Aurelian Gate was rebuilt by Honorius in A.D. 402 and has since been restored. Just outside the gate is the *Pyramid of Gaius Cestius*, (37 m high), the tomb of a Praetor and Tribune of the plebs who died in 43 B.C. This is the start of the road to Ostia. Take the Via della Marmorata from the inside of the gate north-west to the Tiber. The Ponte Sublicio here is on the site of the original Pons Sublicius (mentioned earlier). Nearby is the outlet of the *Cloaca Maxima*, the great drain built to carry off the rainwater and drain the space around the Forum area in the valley between the three hills.

ITINERARY X: Colosseum—Via San Gregorio—Via Terme di Caracalla—Via Porta San Sebastiano—Porta Latina (Plan 1a)

From the Colosseum take the Via San Gregorio to the *Thermae of Caracalla* which were perhaps the grandest and most luxurious of all the ancient Roman Baths. The immense complexity and grand aspect of the halls has inspired architects of all ages. The construction was begun in A.D. 212 and on completion in A.D. 217 remained functioning until the 6th century. A surrounding wall limits the project, which in addition to the baths also contained gymnasia, libraries, assembly halls and gardens. The Baths are open from 9 a.m. until one hour before sunset. In the ruins of the *Caldarium* a theatre has been built in which ancient plays and modern operas are performed. Recent excavations have provided considerable new areas accessible to the visitor, including a sanctuary covered by the Baths which may have been a Mithraeum. The Via di Porta San Sebastiano proceeds from the Baths to the Aurelian Wall and the Appia Antica. On the left, near the Gate, is the *Tomb of the Scipios*, a mausoleum built in the 3rd century B.C. for L. Cornelius Scipio Barbatus, the great-grandfather of Scipio Africanus. Just in front of the Gate is the *Arch of Drusus*, probably an arch of the aqueduct that brought water to the Baths of Caracalla. The Porta San Sebastiano, the ancient Porta Appia, was rebuilt by Honorius in the 5th century and restored in the 6th by Belisarius. On the exterior are two medieval semicircular towers. One can return to the city by the Porta Latina if one turns to the left at the gate and follows the Aurelian wall round to this Gate, built by Belisarius.

ITINERARY XI: The Via Appia Antica (Plan Ia)

The Via Appia Antica begins at the Porta San Sebastiano; its construction was begun in 312 B.C. by the Censor Appius Claudius to connect the capital to the towns of southern Italy (see Chapter 9). The section just outside the city is sufficiently well preserved to give the visitor a realistic impression of the 'glory that was Rome'. The *Catacombs* are of great interest and those of San Callisto (St Calixtus) contain many frescoes of the 3rd century A.D. It should be remembered that, though we think of these burial places in connection with Christian martyrdoms, they were often originally pagan. One of the more fascinating finds which may come from St Callisto was made in the tomb of a lady called Caecilia Secundina. This was a thin gold plate some $7\frac{1}{2}$ cm long by 5 cm wide upon which are scratched the following lines

She comes from the pure, o pure Queen of the underworld
And Eukles and Eubuleus. O child of Zeus, receive here the armour
Of Memory, a gift celebrated in song among men.
O Caecilia Secundina, come, by law grown to be divine.

A small number of similar gold plates have been found in tombs in southern Italy, Greece and Crete. They are all couched in approximately the same terms, but with minor differences that may perhaps indicate a Degree in Initiation of the possessor. They belong to what is known as the Orphic religion, and seem to be a sort of passport for the soul of the dead person, with instructions to the gods of the Underworld as to how he should be treated. This attitude towards the gods was a feature of ancient religions. One made one's 'sacrifice' according to the proper ritual, and one could then demand the assistance of the god in the project one had in mind. The principle applied not only to day-to-day affairs; if proper observance of the religious dogmas and practices was carried out and especially if the person had been initiated in the cult of the god, entry into the Elysian Fields was assured.

In a field on the east side of the Via Appia Antica is the *Circus of Maxentius* with a seating capacity of 20,000. It was built in A.D. 309 by the Emperor Maxentius in honour of his son Romulus;

Fig. 3. The tomb of Cecilia Metella on the Via Appia Antica. She was the wife of Crassus, son of the famous and extremely wealthy banker who died at the battle of Carrhae in 53 B.C.

traces of the *Tomb of Romulus*, a circular structure, can be seen to the left of the Circus. A little further on is the *Tomb of Cecilia Metella* (see Fig. 3). She was the daughter-in-law of Marcus Crassus (115–53 B.C.) the millionaire who had made his fortune under the dictator Sulla by buying up confiscated estates. For example, the villa of Gaius Marius on Cape Misenum was acquired for the sum of 75,000 sesterces and was bought shortly afterwards by Lucullus for 2,500,000. Crassus also owned a small army of slaves which he hired out as labour in factories.

The whole length of the Via Appia Antica until it joins the modern road (S.S.7) some 12 km from the Porta Sebastiano is littered with statues and fragments of statues, marble facings and wall-footings of tombs. The *Tomb of Seneca*, Nero's Minister of State (on the left after the fourth milestone) has a relief depicting a boar hunt. The *Tomb of the Sons of Sextus Pompeius Justus* has inscriptions in verse. There are ruins of the apse of a *Temple of Jupiter*, the pyramidal *Tomb of the Licinii*, and the *Tomb of the Freedmen of Claudius*. Some of the tombs were demolished when the Emperor Aurelian built the new wall in 274 B.C.

Return to the city by the Circumvallazione Nomentana, and pass through the wall at the *Porta Maggiore*, where, at No. 7 Via Prenestina, about 150 m from the gate, there is a splendid underground basilica of the 1st century which was discovered in 1916 when part of the railway was built. The basilica comprises a large vaulted chamber with the roof supported on six massive columns. The vault of the roof is decorated with a series of allegorical paintings which, although badly damaged, are still sufficiently clear for the motif to be interpreted. The central panel is Ganymede being taken up to Olympus to be Cup-bearer to Zeus. In the surrounding panels are Hercules rescuing Hesione, Helen with the Palladium at Troy, Orpheus escorting Eurydice back to Earth from Hades, Medea obtaining the Golden Fleece. In the apse is another great picture, representing a woman entering the sea and being urged on by a small winged figure behind her. In the water stands a man with his cloak spread out and a naked man with a bow in one hand and the other stretched out in welcome. There is a Triton in the sea, and a seated figure with his head in his hand. It appears to be a painting of Sappho being invited to join her lover in eternity. The general interpretation of the basilica is that it might have been the meeting place of the Neo-Pythagoreans, a sect which had revived the beliefs of the Greek sage who lived at Croton in Magna Graecia in the 6th century B.C. (Applications to visit the Basilica should be made at the Soprintendenza di Monumenti behind the Baths of Diocletian.)

The author would appreciate any suggestions for improving these itineraries for incorporation in any future editions of the Guide. There are so many things to see and one's personal interests are so varied that the choice of material should be made from specialist sources. The Bibliography contains a selected list of books to do just this.

OSTIA

To appreciate Ostia it is necessary to know a little about commerce in the Mediterranean at the beginning of our era, the ships that carried the goods and the routes that they followed. This in turn calls for a general picture of the conditions ruling when Ostia was built.

Many centuries before the Romans became a naval power, Cretans and Egyptians, Greeks and Phoenicians had been trading along the shores of the eastern Mediterranean, Sicily, North Africa and as far west as Spain. In all probability the ships that these early trader/pirates used were the fifty-oared galleys that had fought at Troy and were the standard seagoing vessels until the 5th century B.C. The fifty-oared galley was an open vessel with twenty-five oarsmen aside. The oarsmen were also the fighting men of the ship. Slaves were not used as oarsmen at that time. The ship was a trader or a pirate as occasion offered. There was a mast amidships on which was set a square sail, or a lateen. The latter type has survived until today in the Red Sea as the Arab dhow and in the Mediterranean in the small coasting vessels of the Levant and the Italian coastal trade. They had an overall length of about 21 m, a beam of 6 m and a draught of only about a metre. There was a small deck fore and aft. The trade goods included slaves (at the top of the list), wine, grain, bronzework (including weapons), salted fish and hams, also probably linen and wool fabrics and maybe silk. These goods were exchanged for iron, copper, gold, silver and amber that had come overland from the Baltic.

By the 5th century B.C. the wine trade, with the heavy amphorae that contained it, had increased to such an extent that special merchant ships capable of carrying a greater pay-load had to be built. The typical coaster was then a sturdily-built wooden vessel, fully decked with a hold. She was felucca-rigged or had two masts with square sails. The length was about 30 m, beam 8 m, with a draught of about 4 m. The 'tonnage' was calculated by the number of amphorae that the vessel could carry. The weight of an amphora can be taken at about one hundredweight, therefore a vessel of 3,000 amphorae would be a ship of about 150 tons today.

By the beginning of the 1st century Rome was a large city and the grain required to feed the population had mainly to be imported, either from Sicily, or from Sardinia and Corsica. To complicate matters still further, the river Tiber was silting up all the time and shallowing rapidly. Strabo tells us 'Ostia is without a harbour, on account of the silting up of the river Tiber which is fed by numerous streams. Although it is dangerous for the merchant ships to anchor off shore, the lure of profit prevails and the cargoes are unloaded into lighters which bring back fresh goods to enable the ships to depart without entering the river, or alternatively, they partly discharge their cargo, then sail up the Tiber to Rome which is distant 190 stadia' (5.3.5). Dionysius of Halicarnassus says that an oared ship of any size or merchant ship of up to 3,000 amphorae could still pass up to Rome, whilst a larger merchant ship was forced to anchor at the river mouth to discharge her cargo into barges for the journey up to Rome (3.4.4).

Down to the early empire Puteoli (Pozzuoli) was the 'greatest port in the whole world' according to Strabo, and was the principal link with Egypt and the Levant. But obviously a port in the Bay of Naples 200 km distant from the capital was an unsatisfactory state of affairs. The Emperor Claudius created an artificial harbour at Ostia. But he made no provision for combating the silting, and his harbour rapidly became unusable except for the smallest ships. The rate of silting is such that today Ostia beach lies no less than 5 km beyond the walls of Roman Ostia.

In A.D. 104 the Emperor Trajan built a new inner harbour basin with a hexagonal plan, protected against silting by a narrow, right-angled entrance from the Claudian harbour. The traffic of the trade to and from the most luxurious city in the world soon made Ostia immensely prosperous, with a population of some 25,000–30,000,

7

mainly the merchants and their staffs and labour. Later the Emperor and a number of patricians had seaside villas in the town.

The excavations were carried out with great skill and care by Guido Calza, who even restored the ancient drainage system. Following a study of the brick-stamps by H. Bloch, dating of the various structures and the subsequent repairs can be followed with considerable accuracy. The brick-stamps are 'trade-marks' impressed upon the bricks before firing; they usually give the factory's name and the consul's name, thus fixing the year in which they are made. The history of the town is one of developing prosperity followed by a decline. In the reign of Trajan, some 15 per cent of the 69 hectares that make up the ground covered by the town had been built up. Hadrian added another 45 per cent during what seems to have been the period of its greatest prosperity, as in the period A.D. 138–92 only some 18–20 per cent more was taken in, leaving the remaining 10 per cent to be completed under Septimius Severus.

The plan is much on the lines of all Roman towns, based upon the Etruscan town-planning scheme of *cardines* and *decumani*: north-south and east-west streets with the *Decumanus Maximus* running through the Forum, and originally flanked by a colonnade throughout its whole length, from the *Porta Romana* to the *Porta Marina* (see Plan 2). The ancient-looking street names are of course modern. The site is open to visitors from 9 a.m. to one hour before sunset every day. Cars can drive in and park near the entrance to the museum.

At the entrance is a large very well-preserved medieval castle that was built in 1483–6 by Baccio Pontelli for Julius II. The actual entrance to the excavations is at the end of the avenue which begins at the castle.

The first street entered is the Via Ostiense; parallel to this is the Via delle Tombe, flanked by sepulchres of various epochs, as far as the remains of the *Porta Romana*, one of the original gates to the town. Immediately to the left is the Piazza della Vittoria, with a colossal statue of *Minerva Victoria*, dating to the reign of Domitian: the buildings on the right are the *Horrea*, a great complex of shops and warehouses dealing with all kinds of foodstuffs. Here also were flour mills for grinding grain which was the staple food in antiquity. At this point the Decumanus Maximus begins, the main street of Ostia, which is over one mile long. Further down the street on the right are the *Baths of Neptune* on a platform; the large entrance hall has a very fine mosaic floor, representing Neptune driving his four

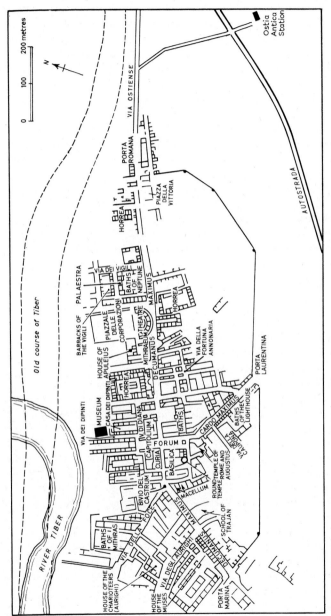

Plan 2. Ostia.

Plate 7. A mosaic at Ostia showing the loading or unloading of ships which are moored two deep at the quay. Piazzale delle Corporazioni.

Plate 8. Detail from a mosaic at Ostia illustrating the trade network around the ancient port of Rome. Piazzale delle Corporazioni.

horses, surrounded by tritons, nereids and cupids riding dolphins, sea-monsters of all kinds and two youths swimming. Adjoining the Baths is the *Palaestra* surrounded by columns. At the side of the Thermae is the *Via dei Vigili* (Street of the Watch) and behind the Thermae, the *Barracks of the Vigiles*. The *Vigiles* were a night watch, whose main, but not only duty, was fighting fires; they were a detachment of the Roman night watch, maintained at Ostia to protect the valuable stores of grain, furs, silks, and other inflammable merchandise in the warehouses and offices of the merchants. The *Theatre* on the right, originally built by Agrippa, has been restored so that performances of ancient plays can be given. Beyond the stage of the Theatre is the grandoise *Piazzale delle Corporazioni* (Square of the Guilds), with the remains of the double colonnaded cloister that surrounded it. The trade-marks of the Guilds can be seen in the mosaic floors of this arcade. In the centre of the Square is the *podium* of the *Temple of Ceres*, the goddess of the grain crops. In these cloisters were the offices of the shipping companies, merchants and artisans, and each office had a mosaic floor symbolizing the business carried on there (see Plates 7 and 8). This gives an insight into the high degree of Roman civilization and the luxurious way of

Plate 9. Ostia, an oil store. One of the vast warehouses that can still be seen in the excavations.

life. Inscriptions and the mosaics tell the story of the far-flung shipping lines to Gaul, Spain, Sardinia, North Africa and the eastern Mediterranean. Roman trade goods included olive oil, salted fish, fish sauce (the famous *garum,* the prototype of Worcester Sauce) without which no Roman feast was complete; wines from the Greek islands; furs and skins from the Black Sea, silks from China; spices from India and Arabia; grain from Egypt; hams from Gaul; toilet requisites like henna from North Africa; gold and silver from Spain, tin from Britain and amber from the Baltic. In addition to their offices these corporations had their warehouses where the goods were stored (see Plate 9). The architectural styles had a lasting effect on the design of buildings right through the Middle Ages.

The contrast between the offices of these well-to-do merchants and the squalid backstreets with their wine bars or little snackbars, which also catered for more dubious activities suited to a seafaring population, makes a vivid picture for all to see of the proximity of wealth and penury always present in great ports.

West of the *Piazzale delle Corporazioni* is the *House of Apuleius* with an *atrium* and a general plan similar to the Pompeian houses in the Bay of Naples. At the side is the *Mithraeum of the Seven Heavens* with the Meeting Hall decorated with the symbols of the Cult of Mithras. There were seven degrees of initiation in the cult, each with its appropriate symbol, the Crow, the Bridegroom, the Soldier, the Lion, the Persian, the Sun, the Father. It was a purely masculine religion. The birth of Mithras (see Fig. 4) was celebrated on

Fig. 4. Mithraism: the birth of Mithras from an egg. A relief found in the Mithraic temple at Housesteads (Vercovicium) in England.

25th December, a date that caused a lot of embarrassment to the Early Christian Fathers, as the dawn was greeted by the Mithraeans with cries of 'The Virgin has given birth to the light'. It is suggested that in order to suppress this the original date of the birth of Christ was changed from 6th January (Epiphany) to 25th December. In about A.D. 150 Christianity was established at Ostia in the little Basilica near the Porta Marina. Perhaps this is the place recorded by Saint Augustine in his *Confessions*. The altar of the Mithraeum next door was found by the excavators to have been destroyed in antiquity, probably by the Christians. This was in the 4th century A.D. and by this time the glory that was Ostia was gone, and the Claudian harbour was useless. Trade had gone to Trajan's new harbour 3 km away, where a new town, Portus, had grown up.

Returning to the Decumanus Maximus, alongside the *Horrea* runs the *Via di Diana*, flanked on both sides by houses with several floors, provided with balconies and gardens. These were all apartment houses or lodging houses. At the end of the street is a typical *Thermopolium* or snack-bar, with marble counter, large bowls for the food, and a fine painting of various foods and fruits. On the right along the Via dei Dipinti, are large two-storeyed houses with mosaic floors and wall paintings in the post-Pompeian style.

The Forum is dominated by the great *Capitolium* (see Plate 10), the grandiose *Temple to Jupiter, Juno and Minerva* that adorned all the central squares of Roman municipia. The walls, six marble columns and the beautiful steps remain of the temple, which dates to the first half of the 2nd century B.C. On the south side of the Forum is the *Temple of Rome and Augustus* dating from the 1st century A.D. with a fine statue of *Roma Victrix*; at the side there is a portion of the façade with a reconstructed *Winged Victory*.

On the long eastern side of the Forum are the *Baths of the Forum*, a luxurious complex of the 2nd century A.D. On the western side is the *Basilica*, a long rectangular hall surrounded by a portico. Beyond the Basilica is the *Round Temple*; this temple, dating from the 3rd century B.C., was probably erected to the worship of the emperors. On the opposite side of the Decumanus is the *Curia*, the Hall in which the Council of the Municipium met. There is also the *Casa del Larario*, a kind of supermarket or bazaar. In the Via della Horrea Epagathiana is a great commercial house with a fine entrance to an inner courtyard.

At the top of the street on the Decumanus, is the so-called Bivio

Plate 10. The great Capitolium at Ostia, the Temple of Jupiter, Minerva and Juno, dated to the first half of the second century B.C. Their temple adorned the principal square in all Roman 'municipia'.

del Castrum, an important cross roads where the Decumanus forks to the left, with the Via della Foce (Street of the River Mouth) on the right. This was the sacred area of the town, and three Republican temples are situated here. Behind one of them on the right is the 3rd-century A.D. *House of Amor and Psyche*, in the Pompeian style with porch, atrium and surrounding rooms. A little further up the street are the *Thermae of Mithras* with an underground *Mithraeum*, dating to Trajan's reign. Next come the *Apartment Houses of Serapis* with several floors (2nd century A.D.). Opposite are the *Thermae of the Seven Wise Men*, so named from an amusing painting, where the seven are discussing the effects of constipation on learning. Finally there is the *Apartment House of the Charioteers*, with a shrine to some oriental cult. In the Via degli Aurighi, there are also the *House of the Muses* and the *House with the Painted Ceilings*, both of them rich in paintings and mosaic floors. Continuing along the street leads back to the Decumanus.

From the Bivio del Castrum, follow the Decumanus Maximus on

the left to its termination at the *Porta Marina*. On the return, immediately on the right is a large building of the 2nd century A.D. called the *School of Trajan*, perhaps the seat of some large corporation. Opposite this is the *Temple of Shipwrights*, in which there is a deposit of columns. Next comes the small Christian basilica mentioned above, with two naves and Christian symbols and inscriptions on the architraves. And next to this is the Mithraeum, the 'Mitreo delle Sette Poste' that was almost wholly destroyed in antiquity. The seven grades of the Mithraic cult are displayed in the seven arches. Finally there is a market (*Macellum*) with stalls and counters for the sale of fish.

The *Cardo Maximus* is a wide street that begins at the Forum and runs obliquely to the *Porta Laurentina*. Along it are Republican

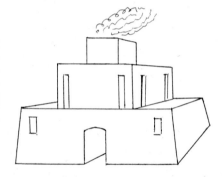

Fig. 5. Ostia lighthouse, a sketch from a mosaic. This was a standard pattern duplicated at Cumae and elsewhere. Note the through passage to break the force of the heavy seas.

houses; on the right is the *Domus of Jupiter Fulminator*, then the *Domus della Nicchia a Mosaico*, with a colourful mosaic in a statue niche. Next is the neat little *Nymphaeum Eroticum* with marble-covered walls and lastly the 4th-century A.D. *House of the Columns*. In the Via della Caupona del Pavone are two interesting buildings: *The Peacock Inn* (Caupona del Pavone), a hotel-restaurant with several paintings, and the Christian *House of the Fish*. In the *Terme del Faro* (Baths of the Lighthouse) is a mosaic representing *Ostia Lighthouse* (see Fig. 5). Then follows the triangular *Ager Matris Magnae* with three temples.

Another street that should be visited is the *Via della Fortuna Annonaria* in which the house is given the same name, of Pompeian style with marble pavements, mosaics, paintings and statues. To return to the Decumanus Maximus take the *Via degli Augustali*, flanked by houses of Hadrianic date. From here the entrance to the excavations lies on the right.

One of the features of the town were the numerous apartment houses. These were arranged with a common garden, a common store for oil, foodstuffs and goods, and a common latrine. The gardens were shady resorts with flower beds and a pergola, shrubs and trees. The *Casa dei Dipinti* is a typical example with mosaic floors depicting scenes of the chase, mythology, dancers or portraits. But in spite of the enthusiasm of the visitor, these apartment houses are very like those of any large suburban main street in England, or the Bronx in New York, inhabited by the lower middle class, minor civil servants, clerks and other small fry.

So Ostia tells its story. Four hundred years of development and prosperity, then decline into sixteen hundred years of oblivion. Now the archaeologist has created a new interest and a new life for this fascinating relic of antiquity.

The *Villa of Pliny* is best visited from Ostia; these ruins lie on the Viale di Plinio which is a turning to the right off the road to Rome from the Lido di Castel Fusano. About 2 km further on is the site of **Laurentum,** on the Via Severiana from Ostia to Antium (Anzio).

ENVIRONS OF ROME

Many of the sites described in the following chapters are within a day-trip's distance of Rome if the visitor prefers to stay in the city (see Maps 5 and 6). If he is not a car owner, many of the places can still be visited by train or the local bus services. When planning such trips be sure and check that the sites are open to view and not closed on account of some special event.

PART III

Etruria

3 . VIA AURELIA (S.S.1)

The founding of the Roman colonies generally preceded the construction of the paved roads linking them with the capital (see Fig. 6). Cosa, for example, was founded in 273 B.C., some twenty years

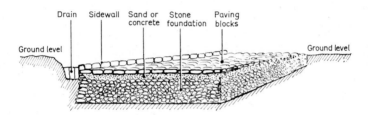

Fig. 6. A diagrammatic section of a Roman road showing the method of construction.

before the suggested date of the Via Aurelia. The actual date is uncertain, but was probably about 241 B.C. It originally ran northwards from the Aurelian Gate of Rome to Alsium possibly via Fregenae, and thence along the coast to Cosa. Later on in about 109 B.C. it was extended to Populonia, Genua and Dertona. For the major part of its course in central Italy (now as S.S.1) there are long flat stretches over the Maremma coastal plain, and gentle rolling hills. The whole length of the route is covered with farms, as doubtless most of it was in antiquity too, and in Roman times emperors and patricians had their villas at least as far north as Civitavecchia (Centum Cellae).

VIA AURELIA, S.S.1 (see Map 5)

Leave Rome by the Porta Aurelia.

Torre in Pietra or **Torrimpietra.** The finest Lower Palaeolithic

26

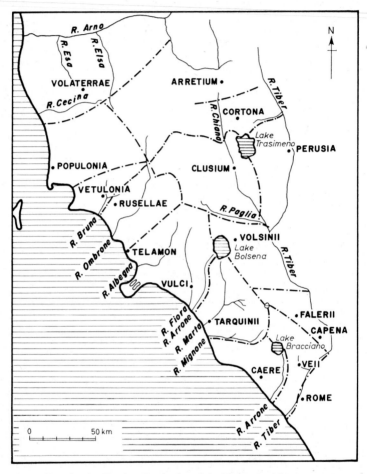

Map 4. Etruria: the Twelve Territories of the Etruscan cities.

site in Italy (see Map 3 and Chapter 1). Ask for the custodian (*il custode degli scavi archaeologici*) in the village—he is normally to be found on the Bowling Green on the right as you enter the village from Rome! You can see the surface of the camp used hundreds of thousands of years ago by prehistoric hunters. It is now preserved under a modern hut. Their axes and flakes are strewn on the ground amongst the food debris of the hunters—bones of deer, horse, cattle, rhinoceros and elephant.

Palo (Alsium). Of Etruscan foundation, the town belonged to the territory of Caere. It was colonized by Rome in 245 B.C. and there are extensive remains of villas, including those of Pompeius Magnus and the Antonine emperors.

DIVERSION TO CERVETERI

Turn right for 4 km to **Cerveteri** (Roman Caere, Greek Agylla, Etruscan Cisra or Chaire but usually known by its Roman name). The city belonged to the Etruscan League (see below) and its territory extended from the river Mignone in the north to the river Arrone in the south, and eastwards to Lake Bracciano (see Map 4). Pyrgi, Alsium, Punicum and Fregenum were all busy ports serving the city which flourished from the 7th to the 6th centuries. Within the city walls there were at least eight temples, with that dedicated to Uni (Hera) having the place of honour. Many terracotta decorations and antefixes, also votive offerings, indicate the luxury of the temple furnishings. At the height of its power Caere would have had about 25,000 inhabitants, judging from the extent of its remains. This prosperity was based on the mines of the Tolfa region which gave rise to an important bronze working industry. In addition there were gold and silver workers of surpassing skill producing magnificent jewellery like that of the funerary furnishings found in the late 6th century B.C. Regolini-Galassi tomb, now in the Vatican Museum (32), and the beautiful cups and plates in the Villa Giulia Museum (33). Pottery was manufactured and exported all over the Mediterranean, to the Levant, the Aegean region and North Africa, in exchange for Corinthian and Attic vases, gold and silver jewellery, and wines from Athens and the Aegean islands. Caere even maintained a Treasury at Delphi, showing how close a relationship there was with the east. The ships of Etruria held command of the seas and there was a trading alliance with Carthage. Punicum may have been a colony of Carthaginian merchants founded in about 600 B.C. After a naval defeat by Cumae in 474 B.C. which followed the revolt of the Latin tribes with the expulsion of the Etruscan kings from Rome, Etruria lost her command of the seas. Pyrgi was sacked by the Syracusans in 384 B.C. and thereafter Caere declined into an

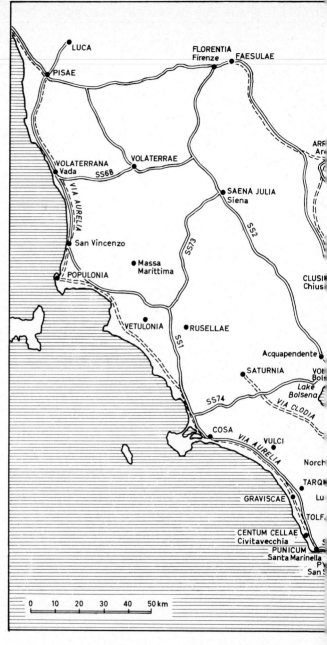

Map 5. Main modern roads and ancient sites north of
ing and where there is no Roman name the Italian nam

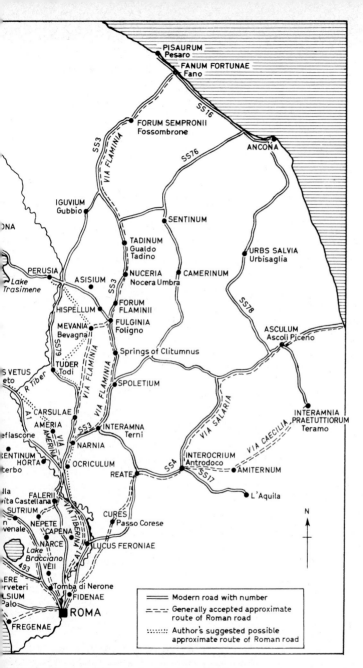

odern Italian name of the site is given in smaller letter-

agricultural state. In 390 B.C. she had made a treaty with Rome and
during the Gallic invasion the Vestal Virgins found refuge at Caere.
But later she sided with Tarquinia against Rome and was incorporated into the Roman confederacy.

The main necropolis is on the Banditaccia hill about 2 km from
the modern town of Cerveteri, and covers a vast area—over 270
hectares (see Plate 11). Part has been excavated and is open to view.
It is open from 9 a.m. to an hour before sunset every day. An official
guide-book is obtainable at the booking office. There are tombs
dating from the 7th to the 1st century B.C. The oldest types are

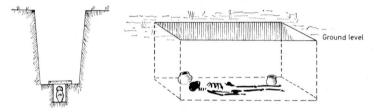

Fig. 7. A diagrammatic   *Fig.* 8. A diagrammatic section of a 'fossa'
section of a 'pozzo' or   grave.
'pozzetto' grave.

pozzetto and *fossa* graves (see Figs. 7 and 8), and the more recent
are round *tumuli* built upon a circular base excavated in the tufa
rock, and containing chambers modelled in the form of Etruscan
houses. Furnishings from the tombs are to be found in museums all
over the world. The principal collection in Italy is in the Vatican
(32). Some of the largest tombs have a diameter of 30 m. About
two hundred have been excavated and restored. The plan of these
tombs is an approach passage leading to a chamber in the form of a
house, or in some cases a room, with roof beams and tiles. The
sarcophagi are either resting upon shelves cut in the tufa, or are
excavated in the rock (see Plate 12). The walls are decorated with
magnificent frescoes representing various aspects of the way of life
of the deceased, or religious motifs. In the absence of the possibility
of reading the Etruscan language it is from these frescoes that we
have been able to learn what we know of the Etruscans. Besides the
Banditaccia necropolis there are others along the gorge of the river
Manganella, where the Regolini-Galassi tomb is situated, south of
Cerveteri. After its incorporation into the Roman confederacy

Plate 11. Cerveteri, the vast necropolis of the Etruscan city.

Plate 12. The terracotta sarcophagus of a married couple, from Cerveteri, illustrating the excellent status enjoyed by women in the Etruscan states. Villa Giulia Museum, Rome.

Caere rapidly declined. This was possibly due to malaria, as a mass migration of the population to another site at Caere Novum, Ceri, took place at some unknown date.

RETURN TO THE VIA AURELIA

San Severa (Pyrgi). This town was the main seaport of Caere. *Km* Excavations begun in 1957 uncovered the foundations of two temples, which were adjacent to one another. The larger one was built about 480–470 B.C. and the other about 500 B.C. Inscriptions indicate that one of these temples was dedicated to Uni (Juno), and in 1964 three thin gold plates were found in the space between the temples; their date is agreed to be about 500 B.C. The text on one of the plates was inscribed in Phoenician, and the others in the Etruscan language. It was hoped that there might be a bilingual inscription but it turned out that though the three plates were couched in similar terms they were not identical. They record the dedication of the shrine, or of a statue by Thefarie Velianas, King of Caere to Uni-Astarte. The importance of this discovery, apart from the linguistic aspect, is its confirmation that a close relationship existed between the Etruscans and the Carthaginians at this date. It also tends to support Polybius' claim that Rome had a commercial treaty with Carthage about the same time.

2   **Santa Marinella** (Punicum). A pretty little seaside resort today, but formerly probably a colony of Carthaginian merchants trading with Caere. Some of the ancient port works still remain. There was also a temple to Minerva in use from the 6th to about the 3rd century.

DIVERSION TO THE TOLFA REGION

2   **Civitavecchia.** After the harbour at Ostia began to silt up, a new harbour, the Portus Romae, was built nearby by Trajan. At the same time he instructed his architect Apollodorus in about A.D. 106 to build a new port here at Civitavecchia, called Centum Cellae. The central basin of this harbour can still be seen at the port. From the port take the road signposted to the Autostrada station 'Civitavecchia Nord'. Continue past this for another kilometre, to the *Thermae Taurianae* or Bagni di Traiano, built at approximately the same time as the harbour. At the Thermae there are extensive remains of an open swimming pool and the men's baths. If possible, leave the Aurelia and take the second-class road from Civitavecchia across the hills to *Tolfa* and *Allumiere*. The scenery is magnificent as the road winds upwards through chestnut woods with plunging views down into the valley on the left. This was the centre of the mining region which was the main source of Caere's wealth. Both Tolfa and Allumiere are hilltop villages built of the local stone which has weathered until they are almost invisible against the lichen-covered rocks. The whole area has scarcely been explored archaeologically, and there is a wide-open field for the ambitious student. The road descends to lower levels as it proceeds towards Lake Bracciano. There are many Etruscan tombs along the side of the road. The topography is one of high narrow plateaux dissected by the stream ravines cut into the soft volcanic rock. On the plateaux are many Villanovan settlements, and rock-cut tombs in the cliffs of the river gorges.

Turn right on Road 1 *bis* (secondary road) for the sites of the
Etruscan settlements at **Luni sui Mignone** and **San Giovenale** *Kn*
(see Plate 13), where the Swedish Institute in Rome with the active
co-operation of King Gustav has carried out a valuable series of
excavations. (For specific details as to how to reach Luni from
Civitella Cesi station see page 70.) Take Road 1 *bis* to Monte
Romano, then take the country road signposted right to Barbarano,

Plate 13. San Giovenale. The photograph shows the impressive Etruscan
walls around the acropolis.

as far as the deserted railway station at Civitella Cesi. *San Giovenale* is 5 km east of Luni: the best way to reach the site, however, is to continue on the track taken for Luni south from the station, over the level crossing and on for another 3 km, where the track arrives at the Vesca river to the immediate east of the acropolis of San Giovenale. The country is magnificent and the visitor may well prefer to walk, leaving his car by Civitella Cesi station; the best maps are those of the Istituto Geografico Militare—No. 142 for Luni and 143 for San Giovenale in the 1:100,000 series (one kilometre to the centimetre). On the other hand, from personal experience, it is not asking too much of the average car to struggle about halfway along the track in dry weather! From the Via Clodia (see Chapter 4), turn off to the left 3 km north of Veiano, past Barbarano (2 km) to the T-junction, left down the hill and straight on (ignoring the road left to Civitella Cesi village) to the station— about 8 km from the Via Clodia.

At **Luni** the Villanovan and Etruscan settlement was preceded by a Bronze Age village of houses cut into the *tufo* or volcanic tuff of the acropolis. The life of the village began in the second half of the second millennium B.C., about 1400 or 1500 B.C., at about the same time as the first village at *Narce* (see p. 70). Six Mycenaean potsherds were a surprising find in the Bronze Age levels at Luni, dating to the 14th to 13th centuries B.C.—a tantalizing glimpse of far-flung trade networks in the Bronze Age. This prehistoric settlement is described in Chapter 1. The first village at **San Giovenale** was also Late Bronze Age, dated about 1000 B.C., followed by a Villanovan and Etruscan occupation on the western end of the acropolis. Etruscan burials contained imported Greek Proto-Corinthian and Attic pottery. Oval huts were replaced by rectangular houses of *tufo* blocks *c.* 600 B.C., in which pottery was found inscribed with Etruscan letters. Today the visitor can see traces of these Etruscan houses, together with roads, wells and a defensive ditch. The settlement lasted until the end of the 3rd century B.C. At Luni there are ruins of defence walls probably constructed after the fall of Veii in the 4th century B.C., when the threat of Rome loomed dangerously large. A ditch was cut across the acropolis at this time. Also at Luni there is a very interesting cult grotto at the western end of the acropolis, with shafts cut from the roof to the cliff above, perhaps to play some part in a religious ritual.

The most striking feature of these sites is the continuity of

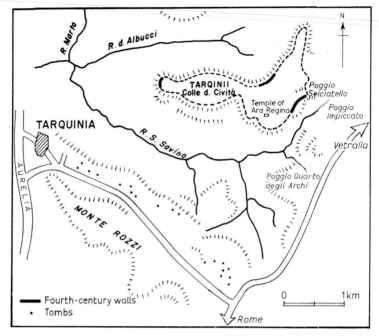

Plan 3. Tarquinia.

settlement: the Bronze Age villages at Narce, Luni and San Giovenale all developed into Villanovan and Etruscan settlements. A basic continuity also exists in the domestic pottery, whose gradual evolution seems to rule out any significant or dramatic population changes during the occupation of these sites. Most archaeologists believe that older theories over-emphasized the importance of changes in burial rites seen in the cemeteries; in many ways the recent excavations of Villanovan and Etruscan settlements discussed above are telling us far more about the sort of life led by the *mass* of the population than decades of 'cemetery archaeology'.

RETURN TO THE VIA AURELIA

Tarquinia (Roman Tarquinii, Etruscan Tarcauna or Tarchna). Plan *Km*

3. Formerly known as Corneto, the town lies on a hill about 1 km to the east of the Via Aurelia overlooking the coastal plan and about 5 km from the sea. There is a magnificent National Museum housed in the Palazzo Vitelleschi (35). The territory of Tarquinia was bounded on the north by the river Arrone, and on the south by the frontier with Caere along the river Mignone, thence to Nepet and the headwaters of the Mignone (see Map 4). Tarquinia was the principal city of the Etruscan League until about 650 B.C. when Caere began to take the lead. After 600 B.C. even Vulci became its commercial rival in the production of the beautiful black bucchero vases.

The old city stood on a hill some 4 km to the east of the modern town, where there survives the *Temple of Ara Regina*, the 4th-century B.C. temple whose ruins are the most impressive monument of the ancient city. The famous terracotta *Winged Horses* (see Plate 14) were found here. The intervening area is covered by the vast underground cemeteries containing tombs dating from the 9th to the 4th centuries B.C. Four periods are recognized by M. Pallottino, demonstrating an unbroken sequence from the Villanovan village to the great city: I to before 700 B.C., II to 675 B.C., III to before 600 B.C., IV to 550 B.C. *Tomba a pozzo* cremation burials in urns (see Plates 1 and 15) were supplemented and superseded (*c*. 750–700 B.C.) by *tombe a cassa* (stone coffin burials) and *tombe a fossa* (trench inhumations); burial furnishings grew ever richer in time, culminating in those of the Tomb of the Warrior. Then inhumation became the rule in the 'orientalizing' period, and correspondingly rock-cut tombs and inscriptions in the Etruscan language appear. Painted chamber tombs (see Plate 16) date from about 550 B.C. at the same time as a renewal of cremation, which, however, only lasted until about 500 B.C. Legend has it that Tarquinia supplied Rome with several of the Etruscan kings. The city finally became part of the Roman Confederacy in 353 B.C.

Numerous fragments of inscriptions found in 1948 at Tarquinia and known as the *Elogia Tarquiniensia* give tantalizing glimpses of the city's history: they are of early Imperial date and were placed at the base of statues or monuments of famous men; they draw on the city's Etruscan history and often give family genealogies as well as the rank and honours of the individual.

The exact site of the port for Tarquinia has been the subject of some discussion. It was more likely to have been Martanum at the mouth of the river Marta rather than the malarial Graviscae (Porto

Clementino), where a Roman colony was founded in 181 B.C.
(Incidentally malaria is supposed to have reached Italy as early as
the 2nd century B.C., for Cato wrote in 180 that Graviscae was
already dangerously unhealthy. Others say it was brought by
Hannibal's army.) In the eastern part of the Tarquinian territory
the hills were covered with dense forest which greatly restricted
communications and led to the construction of a network of cross-
country roads, running generally east and west. The principle
Etruscan highway was probably the route of the modern Road 1 *bis*,
which connects Tarquinia with Vetralla-Viterbo-Orte and thence to
Narni (Narnia), giving access to Chiusi (Clusium) and Perugia
(Perusia), and the upper Tiber valley. Livy records a list of gifts sent
by the Etruscan cities to aid Scipio Africanus in his expedition to
North Africa which led to the battle of Zama (28.45). Tarquinia sent
'linen for the sails of the warships and transports'. The wines of
Graviscae and Statonia were famous and were being exported to
Greece from about 350 B.C. Pliny (N.H.14.24) tells us that the most
popular was a perfumed muscatel, a sweet wine with the name
Apianae. Pliny thought it had this name because it was sweetened
with honey, but it seems more likely that Appius was the name of the
grower. Many of the peasants' tools are depicted in the tomb
paintings at Tarquinia, while most of the actual artifacts have also
been found in excavations, especially at Telamon and Luna: these
can be seen in the Archaeological Museum in Florence (12). They
include mattocks, hoes, billhooks, sickles, ox yokes and a plough
remarkably similar to the simple iron plough still used in Tuscany.
In the Villa Giulia Museum in Rome (33), too, is a charming model
in bronze of a ploughman and his team of oxen (see Fig. 13). Emmer
wheat, (*far* in Latin, *Triticum dicoccum*), which was the staple food
in Roman times in Italy, was also widely cultivated by the Etruscans.
In ancient Italy, not much meat except pork was eaten even by the
troops. Tacitus (*Annals* XIV, 24) recalls an occasion on which a
legion in Armenia was forced to live on mutton owing to the shortage
of corn supplies. Sheep breeding for milk and especially wool was,
however, one of the principal sources of wealth; the coastland of
Etruria, the Maremma, has always been one of the traditional winter
pastures for transhumant flocks which spend the summer on the
high Apennine plateaux; undoubtedly the Etruscan cities in western
Etruria controlled these lands and the drove roads to them. The
aristocracy were great huntsmen, and the tomb frescoes provide

Plate 14. The terracotta
Winged Horses from
the temple of Ara della
Regina at Tarquinia,
dated to the fourth
and third centuries B.C.
Museo Nazionale,
Tarquinia.

Plate 15. A Villanovan cinerary hut urn.
Villa Giulia Museum, Rome.

Plate 16. The Lady Velcha from an Etruscan
tomb painting in the tomb of the Velcha
family (Tomba dell'Orco) at Tarquinia.
About 500 B.C.

many vivid hunting scenes. Perhaps the most famous is the fresco in the *Tomba della Caccia e Pesca* at Tarquinia, in which one man is seen shooting at a flying duck with a sling, whilst in a boat another is fishing with a line over the side and dolphins are playing round the boat.

Forest timber, notably the *pinus etruscus*, a close-grained variety of fir specially suitable for ship building, was mentioned by Pliny the Elder as being used in the Roman Navy. Much hydraulic engineering work in connection with irrigation was carried out in all Etruscan territories. Some of the tunnels (*cuniculi*) to divert the streams are several miles long, and some are still in use today.

RETURN TO THE VIA AURELIA

Montalto di Castro. Here is an AGIP hotel and a camping site.   *Km 1*

DIVERSION TO VULCI

Turn right on to Road 312 and in 8 km reach the site of **Vulci** (Etruscan Velch) which lies on a hill in bleak countryside on the right bank of the river Fiora (see Plan 4). An ancient bridge with possibly Etruscan foundations, the *Ponte dell'Abbadia* (see Fig. 9) and also the Ponte Rotto over the river, give access to the site. In 1927 D. Randall-MacIver wrote that the site 'is extremely difficult of access and desolate beyond description'. The visitor today, however, can reach the site on a new tarmac road built in recent years. This branches off to the left on the road from Montalto di Castro to Canino, just before Musignano; there is a prominent sign by the road that reads *Ruderi di Vulci* (Ruins of Vulci). The town stood on a low hill and was continuously occupied from the 9th century B.C. until the fall of the Roman Empire. Vulci was one of the leading cities of the Etruscan League (she supplied a king, Servius Tullius, to Rome) and her immense wealth can be judged by the five thousand Greek vases so far recovered from the tombs. The first tomb was discovered in 1828, which was followed by large-scale grave robbing and 'excavation' by local land-owners. In 1857 a tomb with wall paintings was found by G. François and is now named after him (see

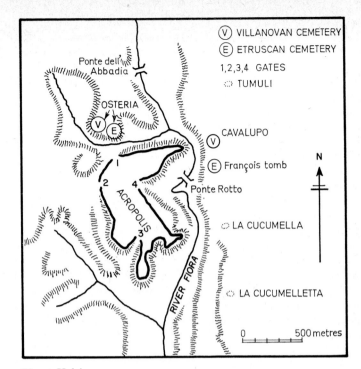

Ponte dell'
Abbadia

OSTERIA
Ⓥ Ⓔ

Ⓥ CAVALUPO
Ⓔ François tomb

Ponte Rotto

ACROPOLIS
1
2
4
3

N

RIVER FIORA

⋯ LA CUCUMELLA

⋯ LA CUCUMELLETTA

0   500 metres

Plan 4. Vulci.

Fig. 9. The Ponte dell'Abbadia at Vulci; the bridge may rest on Etruscan foundations. The river Fiora here cuts a deep ravine through desolate countryside.

Plan 4). The territory of Vulci was one of the largest. It extended from Telamone on the coast to the north, to the headwaters of the river Paglia in the east, thence to Lake Bolsena and the river Arrone in the south (see Map 4). The general line of the city walls can still be traced and the 4th-century portion can be seen near the East Gate. Excavations are now in progress. A milestone was found within the walls with an inscription AUR(elia) C(otta) CO(s) M(ilia) A RVMA LXX, indicating that the city was seventy miles from Rome. The inscription probably dates to the 2nd century B.C. and is also interesting in that it shows that after the loss of Vulci's independence the Etruscan spelling of Rome had survived.

There are extensive Villanovan cemeteries at Osteria, Cavalupo and also near the Ponte Rotto. A votive deposit found near the north gate included statuettes which may be of the divinities Liber and Libera or Fufluns and Turan, also of Jupiter (Etruscan Tinia); a great many places have him as their eponymous founder. There were also many little models of babies in swaddling clothes, reminiscent of similar votive offerings at Paestum far away to the south in Magna Graecia. Many tombs probably had tumuli, but only three mounds survive (see Plan 4): la Cucumella, la Cucumelletta and la Rotonda. (The last of the three is just off Plan 4, to the north.) Two painted tombs have been found. The François tomb shows the sacrifice of the Trojan prisoners by Achilles to the shade of Patroclus. The paintings in the Campanari tomb disintegrated soon after their discovery but there is a copy in the British Museum showing Charon and the Underworld. Vulci was at its peak in the 6th or first half of the 5th century B.C. It was not greatly affected by the naval defeats off Cumae, nor by the Latin tribal revolt, as it transferred its trade with Greece to a route via Spina at the mouth of the river Po. During the 6th century, Vulci was perhaps the producer of the black-figure *Pontic* vases, and her bronzework was exported to all parts of Italy, Greece and even Central Europe. The territory included a number of subsidiary towns. Suana (Sovana), Aurinia (Saturnia) Statonia, Heba (Magliano) and Cosa at the mouth of the river Fiora. The identification of the port of Vulci's territory is not yet settled, as Cosa seems to have been a Roman construction, but there may have been something at Orbetello, where there are Etruscan tombs and walls.

RETURN TO THE VIA AUREI IA

125 **Ansedonia** and **Cosa.** Cosa may have been an Etruscan port, but more probably it was founded as a Roman colony in 273 B.C. as part of a general policy of establishing naval colonies along the coasts of Italy about this date. The site has been excavated in recent years by F. E. Brown, the Director of the American Academy at Rome at the time, and much of the old town and port works has been recovered. Remains of the *Capitolium*, a Roman temple dedicated to Jupiter, Juno and Minerva, can still be seen at the top of the hill. The interesting feature of the harbour construction is the *Tagliata Etrusca*, a channel built for the prevention of silting of the harbour and its entrance. The problem was common to all ports on sand dune coasts in ancient times, and it was first solved by the Phoenicians in the construction of their port of Sidon in Palestine. The essential feature was to have a supply of sand-free water. This was obtained by collecting clean seawater on a rocky coast, and bringing it by canal to the head of the harbour. The clean water was collected by constructing a tunnel at right-angles to the direction of the prevailing winds and waves, and provided with a ramp some one and a half metres higher than the highwater mark. The breaking waves would run up this ramp and spill over into the tunnel, thus filling a reservoir and providing a good head of water (some two metres) above low water level. The reservoir was at the head of the harbour, and after a storm or other occasions when silting had occurred, sluice gates were opened, and the clean water then flushed out the sand from the harbour (see Plates 17 and 18). The method was used in many ancient ports. Another example is that of Cumae where the canal is still in use to feed fresh seawater into Lake Fusaro, to provide brackish water for mussel cultivation. (See R. F. Paget, 'The Ancient Ports of Cumae' in *Journal of Roman Studies*, Vol. 58, 1968.)

180 **Grosseto.** Here there is an AGIP hotel and a camping site. In the town near the Duomo is a fine museum (13); this contains Etruscan and Roman antiquities, including a black bowl on which the Etruscan alphabet is scratched.

Plate 17. Cosa: Part of the system for the provision of sand-free water to flush out the harbour and prevent silting.

Plate 18. Cosa: another part of the scheme for prevention of silting in the harbour.

DIVERSION TO RUSELLAE (Plan 5)

Take Road 223 (signposted to Batignano) for about 10 km to **Terme di Roselle.** Here on a wild and desolate hill covered with brambles stood the Etruscan city of Rusellae, one of the twelve towns of the Etruscan League (see Map 4). Excavations begun in 1959 have already given very promising results. The territory of Rusellae followed the banks of the river Bruna to the north as far as the head-waters of the river Ombrone, and thence followed roughly the route of the Via Cassia to the frontier with the territory of Vulci. The hill site comprises two plateaux with a small saddle between them, upon which stood later the Roman forum. The site was occupied from the later Villanovan period in the early 7th century. Parts of a 7th-century B.C. wall of sun-dried bricks were found on the northern hill. By the 6th century B.C. there was a complete ring defence wall of great limestone blocks with a circuit of nearly 3 km. These walls are earlier than those of most Etruscan cities, and possibly they can be attributed to the city's rivalry with Vetulonia, only 10 km away to the north-west. The town on the northern hill antedates that on the southern by about a century; Etruscan buildings, streets and drains can be seen on the southern hill. The peak of prosperity was at the end of the 6th century. From the similarity of their terracottas Rusellae seems to have had a close connection with Orvieto. It was finally captured by the Romans and incorporated into the Confederation in 294 B.C. The site remained inhabited until 1138, when the whole population was removed to Grosseto. Lizards and thorn bushes then took possession of the site which was soon to disappear and be forgotten.

RETURN TO THE VIA AURELIA

202   Turn left along a short signposted approach road to **Vetulonia** (Etruscan Vetluna or Vatluna). This was one of the earliest of the Etruscan towns. It is situated at 221 m on a hill 345 m high protected by cliffs on three sides, and is some 15 km from the sea. Ancient writers speak of a Lake Prilius here, which may indicate that a lagoon or bay offered port facilities to the town, but more likely that the plain between the rival cities of Vetulonia and Rusellae was already marshy. These marshes were very extensive in the

9

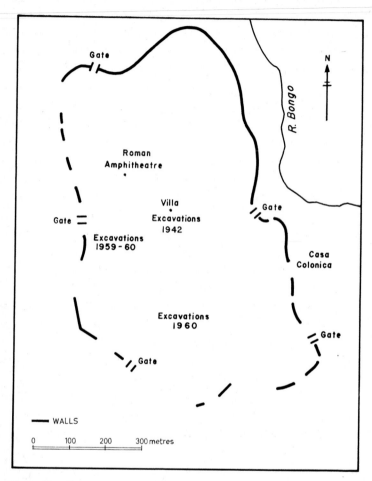

Plan 5. Rusellae.

Middle Ages and were only drained in recent years. Excavations were begun in 1942, and have given rich rewards. The more important finds have been removed to the Archaeological Museum in Florence (12), and there is also a small museum at the site. Whilst some of the earlier material may be assigned to the wrong tombs, owing to lack of care in recording when excavating, the dating is not at fault. The later Etruscan items from the 7th century are from a special type of grave, known as the 'circle grave'. These tombs consist of a circular wall of slabs, within which are one or more rectangular trenches. They continued to be used until the 6th century when the city was depopulated, perhaps destroyed by Rusellae. Among the tombs whose fabulous contents are a silent witness to the enormous wealth of the city, is the *Tomba del Duce*, the contents of which have survived intact and are now also in the Archaeological Museum in Florence. The occupant of the grave was probably a wealthy noble, one of many similar with tombs of equal luxury. The furnishings included a large bronze ossuary containing the deceased's ashes wrapped up in purple linen; the remains of a chariot and harness for the horses; a bronze helmet and shield; many bronze and pottery vases, a chalice with an Etruscan inscription

Fig. 10. The original 'fasces' of Vetulonia, adopted by the Romans as the insignia of consular power. An iron model dating to *c*. 600 B.C.

and bronze candelabra. The *Tomb of the Lictor* in addition to the usual luxurious furnishings, contained a set of iron *fasces* (see Fig. 10). In fact Rome believed that she had received these insignia of the Magistrates, together with their curule chair, purple toga and the trumpets from Vetulonia. The tradition is mentioned by several Latin writers, amongst them Silius Italicus who lived in the 1st century A.D. The Etruscan title for their Magistrate was *Zilath*. Socially there was no middle class: their place was occupied by the upper servants and freedmen of the aristocracy. The serfs and slaves of the lower classes must have led a life of misery and hard labour, half starved and badly housed.

RETURN TO THE VIA AURELIA

n 228 **Fullonica** was an Etruscan settlement dependent on Vetulonia, but there is little to be seen there now.

DIVERSION TO THE COLLINE METALLIFERE

Turn right along Road 439 for 17 km to **Massa Marittima,** with its
extensive traces of Etruscan mining activities—caves, workings and
galleries. It was the exploitation of these metalliferous deposits and
veins that converted the primitive Villanovan communities into
wealthy cities. Mine galleries, slag heaps, and remains of furnaces
are not only still visible—for example, in the Val di Fucinaia near
Campiglia—but the slag heaps are being worked over again to
extract some of the rare metals essential to the production of nuclear
power.

RETURN TO THE VIA AURELIA

Venturina.   *Km 2*

DIVERSION TO POPULONIA

Turn left for 12 km to **Populonia** (Etruscan Fufluna or Pupluna).
The ancient city is built on a high promontory overlooking the sea.
At the foot of the hill is a little bay, surrounded with pine-clad
slopes covering the necropolis. The territory of Populonia was
considerable. On the north the frontier was along a line just south
and parallel to the river Cecina as far as modern Siena, and thence
southwards to the river Ombrone, and to Fullonica on the coast.
It was visited by Strabo in the 1st century B.C., and he describes it
as 'now entirely deserted except for the temples and a few houses.
There are more inhabitants in the harbour-town, which has a small
port and two docks at the foot of the promontory; in my opinion
this was the only one of the Etruscan cities that was established on
the coast itself.' Excavation has shown that the port settlement is
built on the necropolis of an older settlement, and it can be dated
to the beginning of the large-scale exploitation of the iron industry:
the early tombs in the San Cerbone cemetery are covered by the
iron slag of the industries of the later town. Servius, the commentator
on Virgil, has suggested that Populonia was founded by pirates from
Corsica, others that it was a colony of Volterra, but the excavations
demonstrate no connection with either of these places. On the

contrary, Etruscan Populonia developed from an autonomous Villanovan settlement. The material from the tombs is now all in the Archaeological Museum in Florence (12). The principal cemeteries are at San Cerbone and Poggio delle Granate, a little to the north-east. They contain tombs from the 6th to the 3rd centuries, when the town was incorporated into the Roman Republic. Early Villanovan cremation and inhumation *a fosso* burials were superseded by small chamber tombs *a pozzo* covered with mounds. The largest circle graves are more than 30 m in diameter. The actual tomb chamber is built of large rectangular blocks of stone, surrounded by a wall of uncemented slabs laid horizontally. This forms a base for an earth-covered tumulus laid upon a 'roof' of overlapping slabs. The outside of the circle is further surrounded by a paved path. Entry is along a passage with side chambers. The usual rich

Fig. 11. A coin of Populonia showing ironworkers' tools.

furnishings in gold and silver, and vases and bronzework, especially Attic vases, have been recovered in large numbers. There are not many Proto-Corinthian vases; later Corinthian and Attic vases, both black- and red-figure, form the main treasure. Populonia was first and foremost an industrial city: her wealth was in metalwork, first in copper and bronze from the mines around Massa Maritima in the Colle Metallifere, then, by the middle of the 7th century, in iron from the island of Elba. The quantity of iron extracted during the next four hundred years was of the order of ten thousand tons annually. Considering the population of the known world at that time, this was a prodigious quantity. During the general decline of Etruria, Populonia continued to flourish, and in the 4th century B.C. was issuing her own coinage, with the heads of gods on the obverse and a hammer and tongs as the sign of their trade on the reverse (see Fig. 11). Of the city nothing remains but the walls, but the propaganda message of the coins of Populonia testifies to its prosperity.

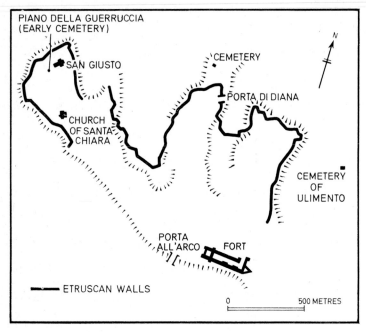

Plan 6. Volterra.

RETURN TO THE VIA AURELIA

San Vincenzo. There was small Etruscan settlement here dependent *Km 2*
on Populonia.
Cecina.   *Km 2*

DIVERSION TO VOLTERRA

Turn right on Road 68 up to the very scenic valley of the river
Cecina for 30 km to **Volterra** (Etruscan Velathri, Roman Volaterrae).
The town is built upon a precipitous hill, which is flat on the crest
where the walls of the city still stand (see Plan 6). Strabo saw it and
said 'their settlement is in a deep ravine. In the ravine there is a high
hill, which is precipitous on all sides and flat on the top, and it is on
this top that the walls of the city are situated. The ascent to the city

from the base is fifteen stadia long, an ascent that is steep all the
way and difficult to make.' The territory of Volterra is difficult to
assess; it probably extended from the river Macra (between Pisa
and Spezia, and outside the limits of this Guide) southwards along
the Val D'Arno south of Florence to the vicinity of the modern
town of Figline Val D'Arno, to the frontier with Populonia south of
the river Cecina.

Of the city walls long sections survive, especially near the church
of Santa Chiara on the west side; altogether they are some 6 km
in circumference. The acropolis was in the south-east of the city

Plate 19. Volterra: the Porta all'Arco. The lower part of the gate is Etruscan
in date; the three heads in the arch are also Etruscan.

(now under the medieval fortress) and was further surrounded by an additional wall for secondary defence. The walls date from the 5th and 4th centuries. Two gates have survived, the Porta di Diana and the Porta all'Arco; of the latter, only the lower part and the three heads of the arch are of Etruscan construction (see Plate 19). The city is still famous for its alabaster industry which, with the production of funerary urns and other items, was the principal source of wealth in antiquity. There seems to have been only one temple, which stood on the acropolis, and was built on the remains of an earlier one (perhaps of the 7th century). The cemeteries are rock-hewn tombs, cut into the cliffs of the gorge of the river Cecina and in the course of time, many of them have fallen away. The tombs cover a long period from late Villanovan times in the 7th century with relatively primitive furnishings, in *pozzo* and *fossa* graves. Then follow the chamber tombs of the 6th and 5th centuries, some of which were large family mausolea covering several generations. One of these, in the cemetery of Ulimento to the north-east of the town, comprises a huge circular compartment deep in the rock. There is a central pillar for additional roof support and the funerary urns were placed around the base of this, and on a bench around the periphery. This tomb, which belonged to the Alia family, was excavated by the Inghirami brothers who found no fewer than 53 urns. It was removed and re-erected in the garden of the Archaeological Museum in Florence (12). The urns are in the Guarnacci Museum in Volterra (38). There are many other tombs of the same type belonging to whole families and dating from the 4th to the 1st centuries. The evidence of the tombs suggests that the peak of Volterra's prosperity was in the 4th century, when the population began mining copper in the neighbouring hills on a large scale. Her trade was largely with the east, with Arretium and Clusium. The staple industry was the manufacture of alabaster urns, in the form of miniature sarcophagi with the portrait of the owner on the lid, and mythological scenes round the sides. It has been noted, however, that there are many duplicates and it would therefore seem that the 'portraits' were somewhat stylized and more in the nature of an indication of the sex of the deceased. A similar device was used at Caere using conventional symbols to differentiate the male and female tombs or urns. The port of Volterra was at **Vada.** There were numerous other Villanovan settlements in the vicinity of Volterra such as Cerrate, Casaglia, Montescudaio and Pomerance.

RETURN TO THE VIA AURELIA

295   **Castiglioncello,** has a small local museum with items from local
sources of the 3rd to the 2nd centuries.

336   **Pisa.** The city was an Etruscan foundation and later, in 180 B.C., a
Roman naval station. Strabo says that in his day it exported timber
and building stone. In view of its obvious importance it is strange
that there is so little to be seen. The sites have probably not yet
been located. There is an important collection of Roman, Greek and
Etruscan sculptures and of Roman sarcophagi in the Camposanto,
the building at the northern end of the Piazza del Duomo. In the
Moute Pisano, the hill nearby, a cave has been found near Agnano with
interesting Upper Palaeolithic and Neolithic deposits, and a rock
shelter at Asciano with a stratigraphy from the Neolithic to the
Middle Ages. A description of these is given in Chapter 1.

DIVERSION TO LUCCA

Turn right along Road 12 to **Lucca** (Roman Luca), a town of
Ligurian origin, later Etruscan and still later, in 180 B.C., a Roman
colony. From Lucca the Autostrada can be taken to Florence (see
Chapter 4). Alternatively one can return to Pisa and take Road 67
through Empoli to reach Florence in about 85 km.

4. VIA CLAUDIA (S.S.493), VIA CASSIA (S.S.2), VIA AMERINA (See Map 5)

The Via Cassia (S.S.2) was, and still is, the main highway between Rome and Florence. The Via Claudia forks left from it soon after leaving Rome, to skirt the south and west sides of Lake Bracciano. The Via Amerina was constructed earlier to connect the capital with Falerii Novi. North of Veii the Via Cassia forks to the left, whilst the Via Amerina went on to Nepi. The region to the north of Veii and east of Lake Bracciano was inhabited by Faliscan tribes who were not Etruscans, but Etruscanized Italians who spoke a dialect akin to Latin. The Via Amerina no longer exists as a road but its route has been plotted by J. B. Ward-Perkins (see particularly the Papers of the British School at Rome, Vol. 36, 1968). Indeed the British School at Rome has done a lot of work in this area and their published records of the ancient roads are of great value. Livy mentions the Falerians and says they tried to assist Veii against Rome, then later fought alongside Tarquinia, and so were then incorporated into the Roman state with the loss of all their wealth and movable property. The inhabitants of their principal town Falerii Veteres (now Civita Castellana) were removed in 241 B.C. to a new site at Falerii Novi, about 5 km to the west.

The Via Cassia leaves Rome by the Ponte Milvio. It was probably paved in 154 B.C. by the censor C. Cassius Longinus, some time after the Via Amerina, which ran through Nepet to Falerii Novi. The construction was dictated by the need for controlling the narrow saddle between the Monti Cimini and the Monti Sabatini. The striking difference between the ancient Etruscan network of country roads and the Roman strategic highways, is that the former follow the contours of the hills, whereas the latter go direct to their objective, overcoming obstacles with viaducts, bridges and tunnels. Some of the Etruscan roads have very spectacular stretches, cut along the sides of precipitous ravines, with rock-hewn tombs in the nearly vertical cliffs. Consult the *Papers of the British School at Rome* for full details of the region immediately to the north of the city.

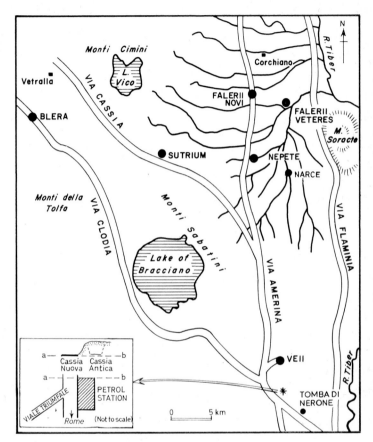

Plan 7. Faliscan road network.

18   The **Tomba di Nerone,** a prominent landmark on the roadside
which is in fact the tomb of P. Vibius Maranus (2nd century A.D.).
Via Claudia/Braccianese. Just here the old Via Clodia known
today as the Via Claudia and Via Braccianese forks to the left, and
follows the line of the Etruscan roads round the southern end of
Lake Bracciano. It passes first through the territory of Caere, and
then that of Tarquinia. The geology of the area consists mostly of
volcanic *tufo* (or tuff) plateaux, cut by dramatic stream ravines. The

medieval villages and towns such as Civita Castellana, Calcata and
Nepi are built on isolated tuff pillars which have resisted erosion.
Tuff is a comparatively soft rock to cut: at Norchia (see below),
Breda and Castel d'Asso, Etruscan tombs can be seen cut into the
walls of the river ravines and Etruscan drainage canals (*cuniculi*) can
often be found in the countryside of Etruria. Numbers of Etruscan
rock-cut tombs are broken into each year; the area has been ravaged
for decades by systematic grave robbing and the *clandestini* or tomb
robbers are still a terrible menace in Etruscan studies.

Modern research is beginning to offset decades of clandestine
excavation and destruction. The British School at Rome has excavated a settlement at the foot of the acropolis of *Narce* between the
Viae Cassia and Flaminia, more specifically between the villages of
Calcata and Mazzano—instructions to visit the site from both roads
are given on pages 142–3 and 159. The excavations, on the right bank
of the Treia river, have found traces of Bronze Age, Villanovan,
Etruscan and Roman occupation. They have thrown important light
on the kind of life led by ordinary people in a small rural village or
farmstead in Etruscan times, to compare with our mass of evidence
from the famous cemeteries round the chief cities.

Return to the Via Clodia, which can be followed to Manziana
where the fork on the left goes to Tolfa and Civitavecchia (see
Chapter 3). From Manziana the Via Clodia continued northwards,
probably to Blera, Norchia and Tuscania, but the modern road
returns to the Cassia at Quercie d'Orlando between Sutri and Vetralla.

RETURN TO THE TOMBI DI NERONE ON THE VIA CASSIA

The ancient Cassia can be seen at the junction of S.S.2 with the Viale *Km*
Trionfale. On the right at this point there is an AGIP petrol station;
the ancient road can be seen as a cutting in the *tufo* wall at the
northern end of the service station, behind a kiosk (see inset to Plan
7).

Via Cassia. Just after the Via Clodia forks left, turn right off the
Cassia to Isola Farnese and **Veii.** (See Plan 8.)

The ancient city stood at the twelfth Roman milestone from the *Km*
capital. Her territory was bounded on the north by the river Arrone
and Lake Bracciano, thence to the source of the river Mignone; on

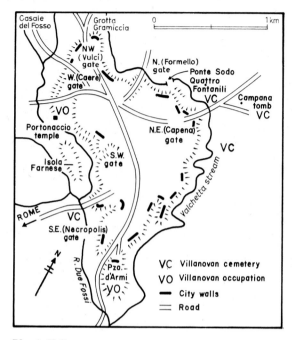

Plan 8. Veii.

the east from Nepi to the river Tiber near Capena, and so along the Tiber to Rome (see Map 4). With Roman expansion, a clash was inevitable and the city was captured and sacked by Rome in 396 B.C. A detailed account of the field-work and excavation at the site has also been published by J. B. Ward-Perkins: 'Veii, the Historical Topography of the Ancient City', *Papers of the British School at Rome*, Vol. 29, 1961.

The town was built on a *tufo* plateau with precipitous sides, formed by the confluence of a river, the Cremera or Valchetta, with a tributary stream, the Fossa dei due Fossi (see Plan 8). Traces of the walls remain round the edge of the plateau, but little of the Etruscan city is left. There were six gates opening on to roads leading to Vulci, Capena and Rome. The occupation of the site and its subsequent evolution from Villanovan to Etruscan settlement, follows much the same pattern as at Caere or Tarquinia. The early Villanovan villages were scattered settlements, each with its own necropolis. The main Villanovan cemeteries were around the acropolis, especially to the north of the city at Grotta Gramiccia, Quattro Fontanili and Casale del Fosso. Pottery in Villanovan huts to the north-west has revealed that the domestic items were local in style rather than typically Villanovan, suggesting that a close relationship existed between the local Latin tribes and Villanovan elements. From the centre of the Etruscan city roads passed out through the gates to all the neighbouring towns. Just outside the western walls are the foundations of the Temple of Apollo (or the Portonaccio temple); a cult of Minerva was established here in Republican times. In earlier years there must have been several other temples, to judge from the number of votive offerings that have been found. The cult of Minerva practised in the temple was probably connected with an unknown ritual using the elaborate system of water cisterns. The famous terracotta statue of the *Apollo of Veii* was found here in 1916 and dates from about 500 B.C.

The prosperity of Veii depended largely upon agriculture. The city carried out extensive irrigation works to the north, to bring the water from the rivers to the fields: channels, *cuniculi*, were cut to drain the fields, and a 550 m-long tunnel diverted one stream to another so that water would always flow round much of the city. Legend says the Romans captured the city by driving a tunnel which came up into the Temple of Uni. In gratitude, she was taken to Rome, where a new temple was built for her. It is possible that this lady was the same as Juno Curritis at Falerii Novi.

Veii's prosperity also depended upon her terracotta industry, which was not only commercial, but artistic as well. Masterpieces like the *Apollo* were the work of great artists like Vulca who made a terracotta statue of Jupiter for the Temple of Jupiter Capitolinus, in Rome itself. Bucchero pottery was also made in quantity. This is a fine black-glazed ware made from a black clay, thus distinguishing it from another type mainly from northern Campania, which is also black-glazed but upon a red clay body. Veii was not a great importer of Greek vases, possibly on account of her distance from the sea. The town was also the central market for a very considerable agricultural area. After its capture by the Romans it remained a small market town until the 2nd century when it was by-passed by the construction of the new Via Cassia.

Turn right on the road signposted to Mazzano Romano (8 km) to *Kn* visit the acropolis of *Narce* (see p. 140). Go straight past Mazzano towards Calcata and Rignano; the road descends sharply down to the river Treia. The acropolis is both on the left and right of the road on the far side of the river (the right bank). The British School excavations of the prehistoric settlement were at the foot of the acropolis on this bank of the Treia, immediately north of the bridge.

50   **Sutri** (Sutrium). In Etruscan times Sutrium was a small settlement. There is one 8th-century burial and some 7th- to 4th-century Etruscan graves. Early in the 4th century, the Romans established a colony here and also at Nepete to control the narrow pass between the Monti Cimini and Monti Sabatini, a region then covered with thick forest. At Sutri one Etruscan tomb was converted into the church of the Madonna del Parto. There are also remains of Etruscan *cunicili* and walls, and a Roman amphitheatre. Continue on the Via Cassia over the saddle, to come out onto the volcanic tuff region to the south of Lake Vico which was one of the Etruscan mining areas.

68   **Vetralla.** Just before reaching the town the Via Clodia rejoins on the left; also in the town is the crossroads with Road 1 *bis*. This was probably one of the Etruscan east/west cross country highways, connecting the western coastal territories with Clusium and the settlements along the Tiber valley.

DIVERSION TO NORCHIA (see above, p. 140)

Take the small road that forks left from Vetralla at the northern end of the town, to the end of the road at the ravine of the Torrente Biedano (9 km); the Etruscan town lies to the south of the road-end and the tombs are cut into the ravine wall on the right bank of the stream below the town.

81   **Viterbo** (Etruscan Surrina?). An important city of the Volsinians situated at the foot of Monte Cimino. Viterbo has a fine archaeological museum (37). There are very few remains of the ancient occupation. The Porta Romana was restored in the 17th century in the Baroque style. 7 km north of Viterbo, along the road leading to Bagnoregio are the ruins of **Ferentinum.** A track leads right, by the school building, to the ruins (20 minutes' walk). This was an Etruscan city which later flourished under Roman rule. There are many interesting remains, including the Theatre, sections of the walls, and parts of the Thermae. Ferentium was the birthplace of the Emperor Otho.

Montefiascone at the south-eastern corner of Lake Bolsena and a *Km* candidate for the site of the **Fanum Voltumnae,** which was the great religious and cultural centre of the Etruscans. Every year a religious festival was held at which games were staged to which merchants and athletes from all the Etruscan states came to demonstrate their products and their prowess. The meeting must have been somewhat on the lines of the international fairs of today, but there must also have been much religious pageantry. The Zilaths, or Magistrates, were elected at these meetings. These were the equivalent of the Roman Consuls. The actual site of the Fanum Voltumnae is still under discussion. The only thing certain is that it was near Lake Bolsena, where the Games were still being celebrated in the 4th century A.D.

Bolsena (Etruscan Velzna, Roman Volsinii), lies on the shores of *Km* Lake Bolsena surrounded by pine-clad hills. The territory of Volsinii extended to the river Paglia in the north-east to the river Tiber, south to Magliano Sabino and Viterbo, west to Lake Bolsena (see Map 4). Pliny (NH.2.139) and many more of the Latin writers describe Volsinii as one of the richest of the Etruscan cities, as well as one of the most ancient. After a revolt of slaves in 265 B.C. Volsinii appealed to Rome for assistance. The old Etruscan city was destroyed and an enormous booty in slaves, vases and statuary was removed to Rome. A new city was founded at Bolsena on the north-eastern shore of the lake in 264 B.C., and from that moment the ancient site disappeared into oblivion. The search for the lost site began about a hundred years ago when Orvieto, a corruption of Urbs Vetus, was thought to be the site. Excavations begun at Bolsena by R. Bloch in 1946 convinced him that he had solved the problem. But the question cannot yet be regarded as finally settled for the Etruscan graves at Orvieto are older and richer. His excavations revealed continuous occupation throughout the Late Bronze Age, Villanovan and Etruscan periods. Divers in 1969 discovered a Villanovan settlement under the waters of the lake, which today seem to be at least 10 m higher than they were in antiquity. There are also extensive Late Bronze Age and Villanovan remains on a hill (La Capriola), some 3 km south of the Roman site, and Etruscan walls and a temple on a second hill a few hundred yards to the south-west. All of this complicates the solution of the problem of siting the Fanum Voltumnae, but indicates the concentration of population round the lake shores. On the Mozzetta hill north-east of Bolsena much of the defence wall still remains with a circuit of 4 km (see Plan 9). That the walls are Etruscan is well authenticated as many of the blocks are marked with 'masons' marks' in Etruscan letters. Traces of at least three temples have been found.

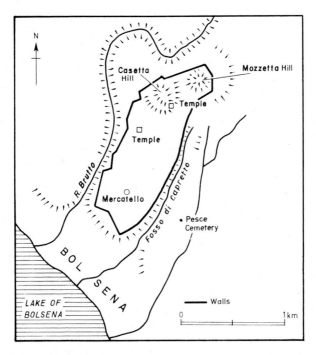

Plan 9. Bolsena.

One of them had been destroyed by fire, a disaster which perhaps occurred in the revolt of 265 B.C. A second temple stands at the northern end of the site on the Casetta hill. These shrines are of a very simple type, with a single *cella* for the statue of the god, with a plain, severe peripheral wall of squared blocks. There is nothing to indicate the name of the deity concerned. But some distance to the north of Bolsena at Pozzarello a large temple, two troughs and a well for votive offerings (now in the museum at Florence) were discovered, dating to the 3rd century B.C. The deity worshipped here was perhaps Nortia, a goddess mentioned by Tertullian and Juvenal; Cincius wrote in the 3rd century B.C. that a nail was driven into the wall of the temple each year to record the passage of time. Summing up the evidence, it is clear that less is known about this, the heart and centre of Etruria, than of any of its component parts. The shores of Lake Bolsena were thickly populated, as the considerable cemeteries prove; the region is very fertile, and the lake also provided an ample supply of fish and marsh birds. The shores also provided reeds and canes for thatching houses and making screens for wind-breaks in the fields. In the summertime the farmers live in reed huts even today. The surrounding hills were covered with good timber.

DIVERSION TO ORVIETO

From Bolsena a short by-road opens on to Road 71 which leads to **Orvieto** in about 17 km. Orvieto was the Urbs Vetus of the Romans and possibly the city of Sappinum of the Etruscans, which fought against Rome in 391 B.C. The city stands on a hill with precipitous sides; it occupied an important position in the communication network between the Etruscan cities. To the north one route led up the valley to Clusium (Chiusi)—the route of the modern Autostrada; and to the east up the Tiber valley to Todi and Perugia (Perusia). The oldest tombs can be dated to the end of the 7th century. The cemeteries at Cannicella, Crocifisso del Tufo, and Poggio Settecamini contain many Greek vases from *c.* 575 B.C. and local copies were soon produced on the site. At Crocifisso del Tufo the necropolis is laid out in streets, with the names of the families owning the tomb inscribed on the lintel over the doors (see Plate 20). There were a number of temples, but only that of Tinia (Jupiter), near the church of San Giovenale where an altar inscribed with this name was found, can be identified with any degree of certainty. The painted scenes of banquets in the tombs at Poggio Settecamini are most interesting and date to the 4th century B.C.

Plate 20. Orvieto: the necropolis with the tombs laid out in streets. Etruscan inscriptions are to be seen on both the outer and the inner walls. Compare Plate 11.

RETURN TO THE VIA CASSIA

123 **San Lorenzo Nuovo** stands on the crossroads with highway 74 at a height of 500 m above sea level. The scenery is magnificent, looking back over the great crater lake of Bolsena, 14 km long by 12 km wide. San Lorenzo stands right on the northern rim of the crater.

131 **Acquapendente** was an important Etruscan town on the northern slope of the Bolsena crater wall. Its ancient name, however, is not known. The town stands where the territories of Vulci, Clusium and Volsinii all meet (see Map 4). Acquapendente doubtless formed a common market for the region. There is some evidence of similarity between the pottery of Rusellae and that of Orvieto, suggesting close contact and even interchange of craftsmen. The valley of the river

Paglia offers an easy means of east/west communication, and fertile
pastures for cereal cultivation. On the north side of the river valley
the road climbs steeply to a height of over 700 m to

Radicofani with splendid views of Monte Amiata to the west,   *Km 1*
Monte Cetona to the east, and the Val d'Orcia to the north. From
Acquapendente to Buonconvento the Via Cassia traverses the ancient
territory of Clusium. Those who are interested in prehistory should
refer to Chapter 1 and pay a visit to the caves and rock shelters on
Monte Cetona, in the valley of the river Chiana near Parrano and at
Sarteano above Chiusi.

San Quirico d'Orcia is on the ridge separating the valleys of the   *Km 1*
rivers Orcia and Asso. It was, and still is, a large agricultural
market. There is little remaining of the Thermae that the Romans
established at Bagni di Vignone, on the banks of the river Orcia.
Road 146 on the right goes to Pienza, Montepulciano and Chiusi
(Clusium).

Siena. The city is the chief town of the province and stands on   *Km 2*
three hills in a rich agricultural region. There is a fine museum (34)
but in the city itself little survives from antiquity for it was not an
important place in antiquity. A Roman colony, Saena Julia, was
founded here by Augustus. The glory of Siena is medieval and it
has preserved its medieval character almost complete. The principal
square of the city, the Piazza del Campo, stands on the site of the
Roman forum, and is the scene of the *Palio*, the famous horse race
on 2nd July and 16th August each year.

   Siena is an important crossroads: the Cassia runs north and south
and is cut by a coast-to-coast route that runs through the town. The
road to the Tyrrhenian sea is to the west, from Monteriggioni to
Volterra and then down the Cecina valley. To the east, a second
route crosses the Sienese hills to Arezzo and Sansepolcro, then
follows the Metauro river to the sea at Pesaro. After the loss of
command of the Tyrrhenian sea, one route for Etruscan trade with
Macedonia and Greece was along this road to the Adriatic, then
north to Spina at the mouth of the Po.

Just before entering **Monteriggioni,** Road 68 forks left to Volterra,   *Km 2*
and the Via Cassia enters the narrow valley of the river Staggia.
Monteriggioni stands on an isolated hill with splendid defence
walls.

Poggibonsi. The town is the main centre for the wines of Chianti.   *Km 1*
Florence, Roman Florentia. The medieval riches of the city are   *Km 3*

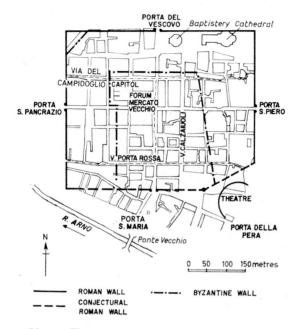

Plan 10. Florence.

well known; again temptation has to be resisted and only the archaeological aspects of the city recorded. It is somewhat surprising to note that Florence was not an Etruscan foundation. There was a Villanovan occupation of the site and from that time until the 2nd or even 1st century, when the Romans founded their colony of Florentia, archaeology shows only the existence of many small agricultural settlements along the valley of the Arno, looking to Fiesole as their market town. The Etruscan expansion into the region and the construction of Fiesole may have been from Volterra to secure the trade routes to the Adriatic. In spite of the attractions of the Pitti and the Uffizi Art Galleries, it is the National Archaeological Museum in the Piazza S. Annunciata that must be the Mecca of all readers of this Guide (12). (Plates 21 and 22.)

It was under the Romans that Florence began her glorious history, that has lasted to the present day. At some unknown date, a colony was founded here, and C. Hardie in *Journal of Roman Studies*

(1965, pp. 122ff) suggests that the city was founded in 41 B.C. and that much land reclamation was carried out by Julius Caesar and completed by Augustus. The plan of the city (see Plan 10) shows the inner Byzantine wall, within the Roman oblong, connected with the campaigns of Belisarius and Narses. Within the Roman wall much of the original Roman grid of streets still survives. Aerial photographs show Roman centuriation (the system of division of the land into holdings) extending towards the north-west along the valley of the Arno for at least 10 km, indicating the importance of the new colony. Other regions which still show Roman centuriation in Italy are the Po Valley, the Tavoliere in Apulia and northern Campania (the Ager Falernus and the Ager Caecubus) (see Chapter 9).

Faesulae (modern **Fiesole**) lies a few kilometres to the north-east of Florence, with wonderful views over the city. It was an Etruscan town. There was a considerable stone quarrying and stone carving industry devoted to the manufacture of funerary urns and stelae during the 6th and 5th centuries. In the 4th century the town and the region generally was under constant threat from the Gauls in the Po Valley and trade was restricted. The Romans founded a strong colony there in the 3rd century. The remains include long stretches of the walls, and some wallfootings on the acropolis. There are also remains of a theatre built in the time of Sulla, and of an earlier temple constructed *c.* 300 B.C.; the last is of particular interest as it has only one *cella* in place of the usual three for the forum temple, to house the statues of Jupiter, Juno and Minerva. Near this Roman temple traces of Etruscan walls and drains of early date, together with Etruscan pottery were found. Two altars can be seen in front of the temple. One of them, protected by a stone cover and Roman walls, may have been the sacred centre of the city.

VIA AMERINA

After the fall of Veii came the establishment of Roman colonies at Nepet and Falerii Novi. The road system became disorganized and called for a new road to connect with the new colonies. This was the Via Amerina which branched off the Via Cassia to the right, eventually to reach Clusium. The volcanic country to the north of

Veii has been cut by erosion into a chaotic pattern of ravines and plateaux over which in places the old Etruscan tracks follow a spectacular course along ledges and through tunnels, with tiers of rock-cut tombs in the cliffs. Further to the north the course of the Via Amerina is uncertain, but the following itinerary follows along the possible route and the towns listed are all of archaeological importance.

37   on the Via Cassia. Here at **Sette Vene** the Via Amerina forked right.

47   **Nepi** (Etruscan Nepet, Roman Nepete). The town was founded in or before the 7th century B.C. A Roman colony was established here early in the 4th century. The medieval walls rest in part on Etruscan foundations.

53   **Falerii Novi.** When Falerii Veteres, the modern town of Civita Castellana on the Via Flaminia, intervened on the side of Veii against Rome, and later allied with Tarquinia, her fate was sealed. In 394 B.C. the city was captured by the Romans; in 241 B.C. it was destroyed and its inhabitants removed to the new site at Falerii Novi some five miles to the west of the old town. The walls are very well preserved and afford an excellent example of Roman military engineering. 50 out of 80 towers and 2 of the 9 gates are preserved. Within the walls it is possible to recognize the areas of the forum and the theatre; the site is best approached from Civita Castellana, on the Via Flaminia (see Chapter 5). At the original site there was a cult of the goddess Juno Curitis (or Curritis), and the new foundation was named after her as the protectress of the town, for a colony there in the 3rd century A.D. was called Colonia Junonia.

The Via Amerina continued northwards through the Faliscan territory and passed through four other Roman colonies within a short distance, but these have not yet been identified with any certainty, though perhaps Corchiano may have been the site of Fescennium. Even the course of the road about here is not yet agreed. It must have reached Orte in due course and the following appears to have been a probable route:

75   **Orte** (Roman Horta) stands on Road 204, the east/west Etruscan highway leading from Tarquinia to Narni. Orte was a town in the territory of the Volsinii.

87   **Amelia** on Road 205. Situated on the ridge between the rivers Nera and Tiber, it was said by Pliny to have been founded three centuries before Rome. Sections of the old Etruscan wall dating from the 6th to the 5th centuries remain with Roman and medieval work in the

upper courses. One Roman gate also survives. A Roman *piscina* is preserved below the *municipo*. The probable route of the Via Amerina from Amelia was to Guardea and the Tiber valley near Orvieto, then north up the Chiana valley to Ficulle, Monteleone d'Orvieto and Chiusi. A few kilometres beyond Ficulle (by the Fabro exit of the Autostrada) the road crosses the river Chiana. Here on the right is a road leading to Parrano, where there are two caves with prehistoric material. For their full description see Chapter I (pp. 64–5).

Here the modern road forks. The right fork goes to Lake Trasimene, *Km 1* the towns around which are described below. On the left the road leads to **Chiusi** (Etruscan Cevsin, Umbrian Camars, Roman Clusium). It is only a few hundred metres from the fork. There is an archaeological museum (the Museo Etrusco) (9). Chiusi was a Villanovan settlement overlooking the long fertile valley of the river Chiana, or Clanis, which runs northwards from near Orvieto towards Arezzo. Before drainage work, the river was slow running and long stretches were navigable to small craft. This led to the valley of the river Clanis becoming one of the principal north/south highways of Italy. By this route the Etruscans reached Rome and spread into Latium. Later Hannibal followed the same route into Samnium and Apulia where he received the hoped-for support from the implacable enemies of Rome in these parts. The development of the prosperity of Clusium began as a series of small agricultural settlements strung out along the banks of the river and of these first Sarteano then Chiusi became the principal market town. By 700 B.C. Clusium was firmly established as the leading city; by the end of the 7th century the original Villanovan cemetery at Poggio Renzo was supplemented by others. Other settlements developed in the region, for example at Sarteano, Castelluccio di Pienza, Dolciano and Cancelli. The Etruscan city was clearly rich and powerful. There were Attic black- and red-figure vases in the graves, including the famous François Vase (see Plate 21), dated to 580–550 B.C. Imports arrived from many other Etruscan cities, including Vetulonia, Caere, Tarquinia and Vulci.

The military power of Clusium made itself felt as far as Rome. The defence of the Pons Sublicius by Horatius Cocles and his two friends, is celebrated in Macaulay's *Lays of Ancient Rome*, when Lars Porsena almost succeeded in taking the city. Pliny and other Roman historians all speak of the great tomb of Lars Porsena, and

Plate 21. The François Vase. The celebrated Greek 'Krater' from Vulci, signed by the potter Ergotimos and the painter Klitias; it is 0.66m. high; a series of ceremonial scenes from Greek mythology is shown in six bands round the body and on the handles. The date of manufacture is between 580 and 550 B.C. so the vase probably arrived in about 550 B.C. or not long after. It is now in the Museo Archeologico, Florence.

the hill of Poggio Gajella, some 4 km north of the town may have been responsible for the tradition as it is honeycombed with a labyrinth of tunnels and burial chambers. Owing to the custom of incising the names of the owners on the lintels of the entrances to the tombs, we know the names of many of the principal families. The sculptured portraits on the lids of the sarcophagi, and painted portraits similar to that of the *Lady Velcha* at Tarquinia (see Plate 16), tell us how they looked and how they dressed. The Romans said they were uxorious, fat and lazy, but this can be dismissed as war propaganda. Their women seem to have enjoyed a good status as many examples of conjugal funerary portraits depict the pair in attitudes of decorous affection. In Villanovan times there was a local custom of making a head or bust portrait on the lid of the funerary urn. But again the discovery of several identical 'portraits' suggests that the sole object was to designate the sex of the deceased. A somewhat similar device was in use at Caere where there were conventional symbols to distinguish the tombs of the two sexes. The hut urns also tell us a great deal about the type of houses used by the Etruscans (see Figs. 12a and 12b). Later a fine arts industry

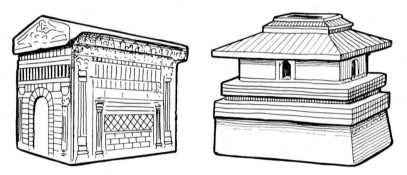

Figs. 12*a* and *b.* Hut urns from Clusium, perhaps models of common types of Etruscan villas.

developed in statuary and decorations for temples which was a great source of wealth to Clusium. At Castelluccio di Pienza, Sarteano and at Chiusi itself, there was a commercial production of hollow seated figures with removable heads to serve as funerary urns from the 5th century. Reliefs on stone stelae, sarcophagi, urns and cineraria of the 5th and possibly 4th centuries depict the chase, banqueting and funerals. There was a pottery industry in heavy bucchero ware, with a decoration rolled on with a cylindrical stamp.

From 600 B.C. the tombs were painted like those of Tarquinia, but unfortunately the climate is not the same, and the paint has become so powdery that it is now impossible to distinguish the motifs. Clusium was little affected by the decline of the west coastal territories after the defeat by Cumae, and continued to flourish long afterwards. Strabo repeatedly calls attention to the trade carried down the rivers in small boats. Lake Trasimene provided a considerable source of fish and fowl, not to mention papyrus and reeds for thatching and luscious pastures for the cattle, with easy intercommunication for the villages round the shores. The plains are good corn land, and the district is still one of the more prosperous agricultural areas of Italy. The scene of Hannibal's victory over the Romans in 217 B.C. is by the northern shore.

195 **Castiglione Del Lago** stands on the lake shore, on a promontory 305 m high, with a splendid panorama.

207 Here Road 71 merges into Road 75 *bis* joining on the right from Perugia.

217 **Cortona** (Etruscan Curtun) stands on a bluff on the eastern side of the Chiana valley with a magnificent view over a wide area. Parts of the walls survive which originally had a circumference of about 3 km, probably of 6th- to 5th-century date. The site has been continuously occupied, with consequent loss of all but a few remains of its importance in antiquity. Its prosperity was linked with that of the other towns in the Clanis valley. When Hannibal invaded Italy, he prudently bypassed Cortona as too strong to attack. Legend would have us believe that Cortona was an Umbrian foundation, later captured by immigrant Pelasgians from the Aegean, and that Dardanus, the founder of Troy was born here (Virgil, *Aeneid* VII, 209). The famous Cortona bronze lamp together with statuettes and a candelabrum dedicated to various deities, suggest a flourishing bronze industry all round the northern shores of Lake Trasimene. Chamber tombs have also been found at Sodo, 2 km west of Cortona, and there are also many other isolated tombs in the vicinity of Cortona.

241 **Arezzo** (Roman Arretium, the Etruscan name is not known). The town lies on a slope dominating the entrance to the valley of the river Chiana, and that of the river Arno leading to Florence. It occupies the site of the original Etruscan settlement, and was the centre of a very large and flourishing bronze industry. The most famous of all Etruscan bronzes, the *Chimera*, was found here in 1552, now in the Museum at Florence (see Plate 22) as well as the delightful little model of a ploughing team shown in Fig. 13. The production was not only artistic but also commercial. As part of the support given to Rome for the expedition of Scipio Africanus to North

Fig. 13. Bronze model of a ploughing scene, Etruscan, from the Villa Giulia Museum, Rome.

Plate 22. The Chimera: one of the most famous of Etruscan bronzes. It was discovered at Arezzo in 1552 and is in the Museo Archeologico, Florence. It is generally dated to the middle or late 5th century B.C.

Africa in 205 B.C., Arretium supplied thousands of spears, lances, helmets, together with the bronze fittings for no fewer than forty warships, and a large supply of grain.

The city was also famous for its pottery with relief decoration of the type known as *Vasa Arretina*, a speciality that was exported all over the Roman West, and even to the east coast of India. This red-glazed ware was one of their main sources of wealth. An earlier craft produced ceramic tiles and antefixes for the roofs of temples in the 5th century. There are some very fine reconstructions of this kind of work in the Villa Giulia Museum in Rome. Little remains of the glory of Arretium on the ground: there are traces of the Roman amphitheatre in the garden of the Convent of San Bernardo, where the fine archaeological museum is housed (5).

From Arezzo, there is access to the Adriatic via Road 73, which passes through Sansepolcro and Urbino to Pesaro. All this area has been little explored from an archaeological point of view. Hannibal must have passed over the mountains from the Po valley somewhere near Sansepolcro. Both Pliny and Vitruvius affirm that the Etruscan walls of Arretium were of brick. A length of such walling has been found in the north-east of the town, but modern scholars still dispute their dating. Arretium seems to have been a dependency of Clusium until about 300 B.C. when it became independent. Apparently it was about this time also that it developed from an agricultural to an industrial city.

In the Second Punic War Arretium was a Roman base and contributed to the defeat of Hasdrubal. Later the city sided with Marius against Sulla, who seized the town in about 80 B.C. and razed the fortifications to the ground and eventually established a strong colony here. The city was also involved in the Catiline plot (see p. 36).

5 . VIA FLAMINIA (S.S.3) AND VIA TIBERINA (S.S.313)

VIA FLAMINIA S.S.3

In antiquity the route from northern Italy into the central and southern provinces was by the passes through the mountains towards the Adriatic coast. At various dates the frontier between Italy and Cisalpine Gaul changed its position from as far south as Senigallia up to Rimini. The Romans planted strong colonies along this line to secure the narrow coastal plain from invasion from the north. Hannibal followed this route and so did Julius Caesar when he 'crossed the Rubicon'.

The Via Flaminia was the principal highway northwards from Rome. It had existed from very early times from the west coast as far as Spoleto. In 220 B.C. the Censor, C. Flaminius extended it to Ariminum on the Adriatic coast. It follows the foothills of the Apennines along the right banks of the river Tiber. It was clearly one of those ethnic migration routes like the Belfort Gap in Alsace, the Po Valley and the Meuse Valley. This was the way by which Lars Porsena reached Rome from Clusium, and the Etruscans expanded into Latium and Campania. Later, in Roman times the importance of this route was seen during the struggle for power that followed the murder of Julius Caesar, when Octavian laid siege to, and captured, Perugia and Mark Antony's wife and brother. A little later Octavian was engaged in a war with Sextus Pompeius who had seized control of Sicily and had command of the seas with a powerful fleet and good sailors. Octavian established the Adriatic naval base for his ships at Ravenna, also reached from Rome by the Via Flaminia.

Even today, travel along the Via Flaminia to the north of Narni emphasizes the contrast between the fertile plains and valleys to the west and the line of forbidding mountains on the east, the foothills of which are covered with olive groves. The plains are good farming country. In July at harvest time, one sees the splendid

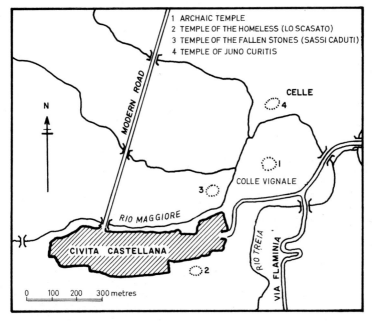

1 ARCHAIC TEMPLE
2 TEMPLE OF THE HOMELESS (LO SCASATO)
3 TEMPLE OF THE FALLEN STONES (SASSI CADUTI)
4 TEMPLE OF JUNO CURITIS

Plan 11. Civita Castellana.

teams of great white oxen hauling wagons with tremendous wheels
that seem to have stepped right out of a Roman picture. In the fields
the long lines of stooks of grain drying in the sun have a 'corn dolly'
at each end to ward off the earth spirits. Survival of such folk-lore
beliefs is eloquent testimony to the antiquity of peasant farming
in the region. In the mountain villages many relics of the old gods
still persist in the Saint's Procession round the villages. In one village
in Abruzzo a large model of a serpent is carried before Saint Biagio,
which seems to suggest his rites have replaced those of Dionysius
at the harvest festival.

Rignano. Turn left here to visit the acropolis at Narce. The road
passes through Faleria, where it turns *sharp* left out of the Piazza to
Calcata (an extraordinary and very beautiful village on an isolated
tuff pillar) then winds round the acropolis to the river Treia. The
recent excavations were on the right, immediately before the bridge.

Civita Castellana (Roman Falerii Veteres) lies just to the west of the Via Flaminia (see Plan 11). It was the chief town of the Faliscans, in the northern part of their territory. The choice of the site was imposed by the topography; the city was built on a plateau carved out by the action of the rivers Treia and Maggiore, tributaries of the river Tiber. Access to this plateau is only possible from the west; on the other three sides the sheer drop into the valley is as much as 90 m in places. The original Villanovan settlement was probably on an adjacent hill known as the Colle Vignale, though the population soon spread onto the site of the present town as well. The many decorative terracottas found on the Colle Vignale are now in the Museum of the Villa Giulia in Rome (33). Two temples on this hill date from at least *c.* 500 B.C. The temple of Lo Scasato near the town has been called the Temple of Apollo, from a statue of the god found here. The temple in the area called Sassi Caduti (Fallen Stones), on the left bank of the river Maggiore, is thought to be a Temple of Mercury from similar evidence.

On the left bank of the river Maggiore, north of the Colle Vignale, a temple was found at Celle, of about the same date, but in the precincts there were many votive offerings from the Bronze Age. Archaeologists therefore think that this was the Temple of Juno Curitis, traditionally the protectress of the city. This deity gave her name to the new colony of Falerii Novi (Colonia Junonia) after the capture of Falerii Veteres by the Romans in 241 B.C. The similarity of the cult of Juno Curitis, or Curritis, with that of Argive Hera is extremely interesting and perhaps is the basis of the tradition that Falerii was a colony of Argos. Ovid (*Amores*, III, 13) also describes the festival of the goddess which he attended with his wife who was a native of Falerii. In his book *Samnium and the Samnites* E. T. Salmon discusses the identity of this goddess, *Kerres*, with *Ceres*, the goddess of the corn-crops. He points out that the Samnites in common with all primitive races, appear to have had this goddess from the earliest times. I have also noticed that feature about the native religions throughout southern Italy. In spite of the superimposition of the Greek Olympian hierarchy, the religion of peasant Italy remained tied to the soil. The shepherd, and more so the farmer, had no use for poetic, or philosophical ideas of the gods; they needed assistance in down-to-earth matters like the fertility of their herds and fields.

This whole area was very much a border territory. It was also the home of the Aequi, who lived along the banks of the rivers Anio,

Tollenus and Himelia. Numerous other Etruscan and Faliscan sites are known in this region, such as Vignanella, Corchiano (Fescennium?), Narce and many more, all connected by the ancient road system. The Etruscan road running south from Corchiano is particularly spectacular.

From Civita Castellana the Via Flaminia descends into the valley to cross the Tiber and make the steep ascent of the opposite side to run along the crest of the ridge. There are very fine views into the valley of the Tiber on the left and over the foothills of the Apennines on the right.

Otriculi (Roman Ocriculum) is now only a small village. Strabo mentions it in connection with river-borne trade on the river Nera and another that he calls the Larolon, the identification of which is not yet known. It would seem that Ocriculum was the market centre for this trade.

Descend from Otriculi by a steep hill to the river Nera, and reach the crossroads where the Via Tiberina crosses the Via Flaminia and becomes Road 3.

Narni (Roman Narnia). Originally called Nequinum, the town changed its name to Narnia when it become a Roman colony in 299 B.C. It was the birthplace of the Emperor Nerva. There are the remains here of a splendid Augustan bridge which originally carried the Via Flaminia, which then had a slightly different route from that of today. The bridge is 128 m long and one of the arches is still intact (see Plate 23).

Terni (Roman Interamna). A town of Roman foundation on the banks of the river Nera, the full name being **Interamna Nahars.** Parts of the amphitheatre and long sections of the wall remain. Terni was the birthplace of Claudius Tacitus, Emperor in 275–6. The town was an important road centre in antiquity: the Via Tiberina crosses the Via Flaminia here. The town was also an important halt on the drove road used by transhumant flocks when they were taken up to the summer pastures in the Apennines. One route followed the river Nera into the Monti Sibillini, where now Road 209 winds through the forested valleys, eventually to Tolentino and Ancona. Others moved up the Velino to Rieti (Roman Reate) Antrodoco, L'Aquila and the Gran Sasso, the highest mountain in the Apennines.

From Terni it is possible to visit the famous *Cascata delle Marmore*, 8 km to the east on the road to Rieti. These waterfalls are about 200 m high; they are best visited on a Sunday when there is much more water in the falls, for during the week industrial pressures considerably lessen the flow. Curius Dentatus, who conquered the Sabines in 271 B.C., cut a channel to divert the Velino river over a precipice into the river Nera, to prevent floods in the plain of Rieti.

After leaving Terni, the Via Flaminia climbs steadily over the pass known as Valico della Somma, through rocky wooded scenery for 28 km to Spoleto.

Spoleto (Roman Spoletium) is situated on a hill at the foot of the *Kn* forest-covered Monte Lucco, at the southern extremity of the Umbrian plain. Spoletium was a 'Colonia Latina' founded in 240 B.C.

Plate 23. Narni: the Augustan bridge which carried the original Via Flaminia.

Roman remains include impressive sections of the wall, the theatre, the Arch of Drusus erected in A.D. 24, part of a 1st-century temple nearby, and a Roman house under the Palazzo Comunale said to be that of Vespasian's mother. The civic museum contains a good collection of local material. The lower courses of the wall date back in places to the 6th, 5th and 3rd centuries, Umbrian at the base overlaid by Roman. Down by the church of San Gregorio, near the offices of the Dazio or excise office, are the remains of a bridge built in about A.D. 200. It owes its present position to a diversion of the river at some time.

Air photography has revealed the Roman surveying and centuri-ation of the surrounding land, that is to say its division into a grid. Each square of the grid contained two hundred *jugera*, equivalent to 51 hectares (125 acres). A juger was the amount of land that could be ploughed in a day by a yoke of two oxen. The land was divided amongst the colonists, in lots from 2 to 100 jugera. The foundation of a colony was accompanied by the customary city-founding ceremony, after the colonists had marched to the site in military style. On arrival sacrifices were offered and the diviners took the augury. The Commissioner clad in ritual dress ran a bronze plough around the periphery of the new town where the wall was to be erected. At the position of the gates the plough was lifted free of the soil. Distribution of the allotments was actually by lot (*sortes*). This may have been to prevent any one section of the colonists forming a block to control the colony. In the early Citizen Colonies the allotment was usually only 2 jugera, but in the Latin Colonies it was much larger, and the size of the allotment depended upon the recipient's military rank, with centurions receiving more than troopers, and all military personnel getting more than any non-Roman citizens who might have enlisted in the scheme. Where the colony was established in hostile country, measures for its defence were probably undertaken by Rome until the colony was well established. The same applies to the first season's cropping, as some provision must have been made to tide the population over until the harvest. When surveying to make their grid, the Romans did not use the north as their cardinal point as we do, but the east. Maybe this was because the east was considered the most auspicious quarter whilst the north on the contrary was the home of the dead.

141 **The Springs of Clitumnus.** (Fonti del Clitunno, signposted on the left of the road.) (See Plate 24.) This beautiful spot apparently

Plate 24. The springs of Clitumnus near Spoleto.

remains substantially the same today as it did in Roman times, except that the villas and the bridge are gone. One therefore cannot do better than quote this letter that Pliny the Younger wrote to his friend, Romanus. 'Have you ever seen the fountain of Clitumnus? If you have not already seen it, and I presume you haven't or you would have told me, do see it. I did a few days ago; and how I regret not having seen it before.

'A hill of moderate height, with a shady grove of ancient cypresses; at its foot a spring bubbling from several mouths of diverse sizes, flowing away in a murmuring stream, widening into a large pool, so limpid and transparent that you can count the coins that visitors have thrown in amongst the shining pebbles. From the pool the waters flow, not because of the sloping ground, but by the fullness of their own abundance. The spring soon becomes an ample river, capable of carrying pleasure craft, which when rowed or poled with difficulty against the current, return quickly to their starting point, without any need of oars. This offers a delightful pastime for visitors to navigate the stream with work and repose alternately.

'The banks are lined with ash trees and poplars, which the limpid waters reflect as if they were in their depths. The coolness of the water and its freshness, rivals that of virgin snow. Nearby is the ancient temple and oracle of Clitumnus, with a standing statue of the god dressed in his *toga praetexta*, thus revealing the presence of the god himself, ready to give oracles. All round him are numerous statues of the gods of the minor springs, each with its own cult, and its own name, some their own particular spring, besides his, which is the father of all. But they all merge into the main stream where the bridge crosses, which divides the sacred area from the profane. Boating is allowed in the upper part only, but lower down one may swim. The people of Hispellum [Spello], to whom divine Augustus made a gift of this place, provide at the public expense not only baths but also hospitality. Beautiful villas are not lacking on the banks. In short there is nothing but pleasure to be obtained here. You can also educate yourself by reading the inscriptions the visitors have cut on the walls and columns to praise the fountain and the god. You will commend some of them, others will make you laugh, except that you are too good natured to laugh at anything. Addio.' (*Letters* VIII, 8.)

An early Christian church has superseded the Temple of Clitumnus a few hundred metres from the lovely pool that still recalls Pliny's picture.

158 **Foligno** (Roman Fulginia) lies on the eastern margin of the Umbrian plain at the entrance to the gorge of the river Topino. Fulginia seems to have opposed Rome in the Third Samnite War, when the Samnite general Gellius Egnatius succeeded in breaking through the Roman encircling cordon; he passed through the Marsic country to join with the Etruscans at Perugia and all Umbria was in revolt. The Senones (Gauls) were also allied with the Samnites. Fulginia was in a dominating position at the entrance to the Topino valley and at the same time commanded the routes to Ancona, via Camerino and Gualdo Tadino, and also over the Umbrian plain. 8 km away on Road 316 is *Bevagna* (see p. 175).

DIVERSION TO PERUGIA VIA ROAD 75

Spello (Roman Hispellum) situated at the base of Monte Subasio *Km*
(1290 m), a fine old walled town and a Roman *municipium* in the
days of Augustus. It must have had a fair-sized population as there
are the remains of an amphitheatre just outside the town on the
road to Perugia. The Porta Consulare (see Plate 25), the main gate
to the town, is of Augustan date and is still a fine example of a three-
arch gateway. The central arch is still in use, but the side arches are
blocked up. Two other gates, the Porta Venere and the Porta
Urbica, are also well preserved with their flanking defence towers
which have been restored. The Belvedere is the ancient acropolis.

   Assisi (Roman Asisium) reached by a winding approach road *Km*
climbing the flank of Monte Subasio. The town was a flourishing

Plate 25. Spello: the Porta Consulare, of Roman construction.

Roman *municipium* controlling the central Umbrian plain. It was the birthplace of St Francis and is always full of pilgrims and crowded with visitors from all over the world. The walls are medieval. The Roman town lay around the present Piazza del Comune, where there are the remains of the Augustan Temple of Minerva comprising some columns of the *pronaos* with their entablature, now incorporated in the church of Santa Maria. Behind the cathedral are the theatre and the amphitheatre, capable of seating several thousand spectators, which indicates that the town must have been the centre of a very well populated area. From the Museo Comunale (6) it is possible to visit the remains of the Roman forum.

21 **Perugia** (Roman Perusia) reached after crossing a fertile section of the Umbrian plain covered with farms and still cultivated with the same methods of husbandry as in Roman times, such as ploughing with yoked oxen. The river Tiber is crossed where the Via Tiberina (Road 3 *bis*) joins on the left. For the description of Perugia see below under Via Tiberina (p. 175).

RETURN TO THE VIA FLAMINIA AT FOLIGNO

DIVERSION TO ANCONA VIA CAMERINO (ROAD 77)

The road from Foligno to Ancona over the Apennines passes through some magnificent scenery and several places on the road are of

47 historical interest in the expansion of Rome over Italy. **Camerino** (Roman Camerinum) was an Umbrian city with which Rome concluded a treaty in 310 B.C., which effectively prevented the Etruscans giving the vital help needed in the Second Samnite War. In the Third Samnite War, the year 295 opened with a Samnite victory over Cornelius Scipio Barbatus at Camerinum, but for some unknown reason this was not followed up, and Rome was able to reinforce the local commander with two legions. With this combined force the two Consuls, Fabius Rullianus and Decius Mus, moved towards **Sentinum,** the capital city of the Samnite League. Here in the valley of the Sentino, the upper reaches of the river Esino, the decisive battle was fought and because the Etruscans and the Umbrians were not present at the battle, the Romans were easily victorious, but both Decius Mus and Gellius Egnatius, the Samnite leader, were killed. Though Rome owed the victory largely to the tactical brilliance of Fabius Rullianus, the popular hero was Decius Mus, who was said to have been killed in act of *devotio*: crowning by his personal sacrifice the sacrifice of the enemy to the infernal gods as well. As the surviving Samnites tried to reach their homes in the south, they passed through the country of the Paeligni who killed a great number of them. Before the year was over all Umbria had submitted to Rome, and Fabius Rullianus had defeated the Etruscans somewhere near Perugia. Sentinum was captured by Sulla in 82 B.C. in the Social War and depopulated. The ruins of the town are at Sassoferrato and are better reached from Osteria del Gatto by Road 76, or from Scheggia by Road 360 (see below).

Camerino is on the watershed between the Chienti and Potenza rivers, on the border of Umbria and Picenum (roughly speaking, the modern province of Marche). Animal husbandry seems to have decreased in importance during the Bronze Age here and by the end of the Bronze Age the pattern of settlement probably looked very much as it does today. Small farms dot the wide river valleys that run parallel down to the Adriatic while most of the villages and towns occupy the ridges in between. Information about the later archaeology of Marche is sadly lacking; it is about 161 km from Foligno to Ancona, but there are scarcely half a dozen Roman ruins of any consequence in that distance and indeed the prehistory of the area is much better documented (see Chapter 1). Perhaps large towns were in any case very rare; today the region is one of the most densely populated rural areas in Italy, on some of the richest agricultural land. Inland towns hardly exist; sheep farming is minimal and instead most of the lowland Marche carries thousands of small but prosperous farms cultivating cereals, olives and vines. Our evidence—or the lack of it—suggests that this was so in antiquity; certainly the population was dense in Roman times, when Pompey, whose estates were in Picenum, said that he had only to stamp his foot there to raise an army.

The junction of Road 78 from Ascoli Piceno with Road 77, below *Km* Macerata. 7 km down Road 78 to the south are the ruins of **Urbs Salvia** on the banks of the Fiastra, a tributary of the Chienti. The ruins lie on both sides of the road, rarely visited and peaceful; they are overgrown, lost in the olive groves that cover the river plain. There are remains of a theatre, some baths and a viaduct.

Macerata, a picturesque medieval town.   *Km*

The road winds north from the town down to the Potenza river. On
the left bank are the ruins of **Helvia Ricina**, a Roman town destroyed
by the Goths.

Road 77 then crosses over to the Musone river; turn left here for
Filottrano (see Chapter 1). It finally reaches Ancona at about
150 km from Foligno.

Ancona—capital of the Marche, the chief seaport between Venice
and Brindisi. It is said to have been founded *c.* 400 B.C. by Syracusan
exiles fleeing from the tyrant Dionysus. The name of the city,
literally an 'elbow', refers to the curved promontory that forms the

Plate 26. Ancona: the Arch of Trajan, built in A.D. 115.

harbour. The town was an important port during the Empire and
was particularly favoured by Trajan. On the old northern mole of
the harbour is the *Arch of Trajan*, a triumphal arch erected by the
architect Apollodorus in A.D. 115 in honour of Trajan (see Plate
26). (Compare the Arch of Trajan at Benevento in Campania.)
Traces of the Roman amphitheatre were excavated in recent years
to the left of the Palazzo del Senato above the Museum in the old
quarter of the town. The National Archaeological Museum of the
Marche (4) is housed in the Palazzo Ferretti, with a magnificent view
over the harbour. It contains a fine collection of prehistoric material,
including most of the material from the Marche sites discussed in

Chapter 1, in addition to material illustrating the history of Picenum
from the Early Iron Age until the arrival of Greeks, Gauls and
Romans.

RETURN TO FOLIGNO

From Foligno follow the Via Flaminia. At 4 km from the town the
road enters the narrow rocky valley of the river Topino, with pretty
wooded slopes and cliffs above the rushing river. Every 5 km or so,
as I mentioned in my Preface, there is a small hamlet that by its
very name displays its ancient foundation. All these hamlets are
probably ancient staging posts on the long journey from Rome by
mule, horse, donkey or on foot, or even in litters and ox-carts.

Nocera Umbra (Roman Nuceria Camellaria). Nocera stands upon *Km 1*
a bluff overlooking the valley of the Topino. Strabo says 'it is the
place where the wooden utensils are made' (V.2.10). The roofs of
ancient tiles and the splendid walls are so bleached by the sun and
wind that they are the same colour as the rocks they stand on.
Probably there was a spa here in Roman times because even today
there are important mineral water springs. There are no Roman
remains in the town.

From here Road 361 offers an alternative wild and scenic route
to Ancona over the Apennines and down the valley of the Potenza.

Gualdo Tadino (Roman Tadinum). After leaving Nocera Umbra *Km 1*
the Via Flaminia soon opens on to the Gaifana plateau. Gualdo
stands on the slopes of the foothills of the high mountains overlooking a very fertile area studded with farms, as doubtless it was
in antiquity. The interesting wooden wine barrel in Fig. 14 was found
at Gualdo. In 552 Narses routed the Goths and slew Totila here.

A crossroads, where the right branch (Road 76) goes to Ancona via *Km 2*
Fabriano and that on the left to Gubbio.

DIVERSION TO GUBBIO

Gubbio (Roman Iguvium) was a Roman *municipium* and there are considerable remains of a 1st-century A.D. theatre south of the town where classical plays are performed in summer. Famous finds have included seven bronze plates with long inscriptions. These are the Iguvine Tables with script in the Umbrian language, five in Etruscan and two in Latin characters, describing the rules of a college of priests, and now preserved in the museum in the Palazzo dei Consoli (14). The tablets were discovered in the 15th century A.D. and date probably to 250 to 150 B.C. They are engraved on both

Fig. 14. A wooden oil or wine barrel with bronze fittings, cut from a single piece of wood; from Gualdo Tadino and dated to the 6th century B.C.

sides. One of the ceremonies is similar to the modern English ceremony of 'Beating the bounds'.

The ceremonies were held in May and dedicated to Ceres. Every town and village celebrated this festival. A bull, a sheep and a pig were led in procession three times round the periphery of the fields, and were then sacrificed to the goddess. This ceremony was called the *Ambarvalia*. There was an additional ceremony performed at Rome, known as the *Ambarurbium*, when before being sacrificed the victim was led round the walls of the city to purify it. This rite seems to have fallen into disuse by the end of Republican times. The *Ambarvalia* survived at least until the time of Augustus as it is mentioned by Strabo, who says the priests offered sacrifices at certain special sites on the outskirts of the town. In Rome the sacrifices were made to Mars. After the annual ceremony fell into disuse it still survived when the Census was taken, and then there was a great procession of the population round the walls with the sacrifices taking place in the Campus Martius.

RETURN TO THE VIA FLAMINIA

Scheggia (Roman Silium?) is at the western end of the pass over Km 21
the Apennines. Here Road 360 on the right goes to Sassoferrato
near which, to the south-west, are the ruins of Sentinum (see
p. 167). See also Chapter 1 for Bronze Age sites near Sassoferrato
and in the Gola del Sentino.

After passing over a bridge over the extremely narrow gorge of
the Burano, the valley widens again at Cagli.

Aqualagna: still in the wide valley dotted with farms, but the road Km 24
soon enters the narrow gorge of the river Furlo (Gola del Furlo).
A few hundred metres into the gorge the road passes a prominent
cave at the height of the road, on the left bank: the *Grotta del
Grano* was the scene of early excavations, when a Bronze Age and
Iron Age deposit was found.

Here at the narrowest part, the vertical sides of the gorge are only Km 25
a few metres apart. Via Flaminia traverses a shelf cut in the rock
on the north side of the gorge, and at one point passes through a
tunnel which was constructed by the Emperor Vespasian in A.D. 76
(*Galleria del Furlo*).

Fossombrone (Roman Forum Sempronii) situated on the river Km 26
Metauro. There are scanty remains of the Roman town at San
Martino, 3 km downstream. It was somewhere near here that
Hannibal's brother Hasdrubal was intercepted by the Consuls M.
Livius Salinator and C. Claudius Nero. In the battle that followed
Hasdrubal was killed and his head was sent to be thrown into
Hannibal's camp in Apulia. This was, in fact, the decisive battle of
the Second Punic War, as ever after it was impossible for Hannibal
to obtain reinforcement, or even supplies, from Carthage. 2 km up-
stream from the town was a Roman bridge over the Metauro of the
3rd century A.D., but it was blown up in the last war.

Fano (Roman Fanum Fortunae). Situated on the Adriatic coast. Km 28
Augustus established a colony here in A.D. 9 and built the walls
round the town. The main gate, the Porta Augusta, and long
stretches of the wall still survive. There was a famous Temple of
Fortune here from a very early date. All along this little stretch
of coast between the mountains and the sea were Roman colonies
like Ariminum, Pisaurum, and Fanum, established to hold the Gauls
in check as this was one of the easiest highways into central and
southern Italy.

n 300
Pesaro (Roman Pisaurum). There is a small port at the mouth of the river Foglia which was probably in use in antiquity. All the indications point to Pesaro having been a market and *entrepot* for the trade from the Po Valley to Italy, the Balkans and the Aegean. This trade assumed importance after the Etruscans lost command of the western seas and were then obliged to divert this commerce to Adriatic ports. There are little or no remains from the past in the town but the Archaeological Museum (21) is worth a visit and the Museum of Majolica, which is and has long been the speciality of the town, is particularly famous.

VIA TIBERINA

Just outside Rome to the north, at Prima Porta, the Via Flaminia forks, and the Via Tiberina begins. At the fork an inscription commemorates the Battle of Saxa Rubra, when Constantine defeated Maxentius in A.D. 312. It was here that Constantine was converted to Christianity by the vision of a flaming cross. Between the roads are the ruins of the *Villa of Livia*, wife of Augustus: for the famous wall paintings from here see the National Museum of Rome (27). The path to the villa is signposted to the right beyond the houses. The Via Tiberina goes along the west or right bank of the river Tiber, at first following much the same route as the Autostrada del Sole.

18
When the Autostrada del Sole was being constructed at Scorano on the river Tiber in 1953 the site of *Lucas Feroniae* was discovered; the site is immediately by the Fiano Romano or Roma Nord exit of the Autostrada. This place was probably both a religious centre and market for the products of Latins, Etruscans, Sabines and Faliscan tribes as early as the 7th century. The rites of the cult were remarkable; Strabo (V.2.4) describes them: 'For those who are possessed of the goddess walk with bare feet through a great pile of embers without suffering, and a multitude of people come together at the same time for the sake, not only of attending the ceremonies of the Festival which is held every year, but also of seeing the aforesaid sight.' Feronia was a native agricultural deity, and was also the patroness of slaves and freedmen. Her principal shrine was at Anxur, or Terracina, in Latium. Lucus Feroniae was sacked by Hannibal in 211 B.C. For further information, see G. D. B. Jones in the *Papers of the British*

School at Rome, 1962, pp. 116–207. The Via Tiberina now passes the *Ager Capenas* to the south of Monte Soracte, the area between the Tiberina and the Flaminia. Once again there is a wilderness of deep ravines running from the mountain south-eastwards to the Tiber. Turn left just before Scorano, for *Capena* (5 km). Perched on Castellaccio Hill, a precipitous bluff that is surrounded on three sides by streams running in ravines, Capena lay at the north-eastern end of a depression called Lago Vecchio. To reach the ruins, go past the modern village for 2 km and take the path that leads north as the road bends sharply west. Capena was founded in the 8th century, legend says by emigrants from Veii under provisions of the *Ver Sacrum*. This was a widespread practice in central Italy, according to the tradition, but there is no archaeological evidence. Children born at a certain time were obliged to emigrate when they grew up. Strabo tells how the Sabini vowed their children to *Mamers* (Mars). In due course they were sent out as colonists, led by a bull. The bull 'lay down to rest in the land of the Opici', and the local inhabitants were driven out of their villages which were then settled by the new colonists (V.4.12). This story of the foundation of Capena is not supported by archaeological evidence, which shows connections with Falerii and not with Veii. A number of inscriptions in the Faliscan dialect, closely akin to old Latin, have been found in the Ager Capenas. The early burials were in *pozzo* and *fossa* graves (see Figs. 7 and 8) and contain only local pottery. From the chamber tombs which came into use in the 6th century, some imported vases of Proto-Corinthian type were found, but (unlike at Falerii) Attic vases were very rare. There was also a bronze and pottery industry, but of a rather crude local type. Some traces of the defence wall of cyclopean masonry, and a lower rampart can still be seen. Again, for further details see G. D. B. Jones in the *Papers of the British School at Rome*, 1962, pp. 116–207.

The Via Tiberina continues along the Tiber valley, more or less parallel to the Via Flaminia and more or less on the same line as the old road though it is generally lower towards the river than the Roman one, as far as Nazzano. Here the modern road crosses over to the east (left) bank of the Tiber. It follows the river upstream as far as Magliano Sabina, where it joins the Via Flaminia as far as Narni. **Narni Scalo.** The fine Roman bridge of Augustan date (see Plate *Km 8*23) suggests that this was the original route of the Via Flaminia, from the bottom of the hill at Otriculi. The bridge gives some idea of the heavy traffic the roads carried, and Strabo calls attention to river-borne trade as well.

n 89
S.3
Road 205 branches off to the left for Orvieto via Amelia, continuing to the west coast as one of the Etruscan cross country roads.

n 102
San Gemini and Roman Carsulae about 4 km to the north. The town has sometimes been called the Pompeii of Umbria; it was totally destroyed by the Goths in the 6th century A.D. The North Gate is intact, from which a cobbled road runs down to the main ruins; grooves from chariot wheels can still be seen in the road, which is remarkably preserved. There are extensive remains of the amphitheatre and theatre, lawcourts, baths and the forum. Pliny's mother-in-law had a farm here.

1 110
Acquasparta. Road 418 on the right goes to Spoleto.

1 112
Here Road 316 on the right goes to **Bevagna** (Roman Mevania) following what may have been the ancient Via Flaminia to Hispellum.

4 129
Todi, the Umbrian city of Tuder, on the river Tiber. It was probably an Etruscan foundation. There is a small civic museum with a local collection of Etruscan and Roman material including coins (36). In the Mercato Vecchio, the Old Market, there are four columns of the Roman basilica. The walls of the town are medieval but with a Roman gate. After leaving Todi the Via Tiberina runs along the Tiber valley to the foot of the hill on which Perugia stands.

1 176
Perugia, Roman Perusia. The Etruscan name is not known. The city stands on a hill 500 m high, and 100 m above the Tiber valley, with a panorama all round of splendid scenery. The walls of the Etruscan city have a circumference of about 3 km; much of them survive, together with the five gates that are still in use. Inside the city, owing to continuous occupation, there are few remains of Etruscan or Roman work. Uni was the protecting deity of the city; her temple would have been on the highest hill on the acropolis of Monte Sole. Traces of four or five temples in all are known, dating from about the 5th to the 1st centuries. More than a dozen large cemeteries are in the vicinity of Perugia with hundreds of graves, and there are several fine examples of isolated family mausolea. One of the main industries was the production of travertine cinerary urns carved with scenes from Greek mythology, the chase, battles and so on. Terracotta vases and pots for domestic use were also made in quantity. An artistic and industrial bronze industry was active round the city, especially at **Bettona** (Roman Vettona), 12 km south-east of Perugia, where the great number of swords, spears,

and other warlike items suggest a constant state of military readiness to deal with raids from over the frontier, or a large exporting industry in weapons. Extensive Etruscan walls can be seen at Bettona. Little is known of the history of Etruscan Perugia: a long inscription, the *Cippus Perusinus*, contains 46 lines of Etruscan script, which so far defies all efforts to decipher it. It is thought to be a conveyance of property. Perusia was one of the twelve cities of the Etruscan Confederation (see Map 4), and submitted to the Romans in 310 B.C. During the struggle for power following the assassination of Julius Caesar, Perugia was one of Mark Antony's strongholds. Lucius Antonius who was Antony's brother and consul in 41 B.C., joined with Fulvia, the wife of Antony, to attack Octavian. The leaders of the legions stationed at Teanum Sidicinum endeavoured to effect a reconciliation and fighting began when these efforts failed. Both parties wrote to Antony in Greece, but the letter took so long to arrive that the affair was then out of hand. Lucius and Fulvia were pursued by Octavian's generals, Salvidionus, Rufus and Agrippa, and they shut themselves in Perugia. The town standing on its high hill with thick defence walls was impregnable to assault but easy to blockade. Soon hunger drove Lucius to desperation. On New Year's Eve, after an attempted sortie, many of his supporters deserted and at the end of February he surrendered. Octavian could not afford to quarrel with Antony at that stage, so Lucius and Fulvia were allowed to join Antony in Greece. Perugia itself was given over to plunder by the soldiery, looted and burnt. The populace was allowed to go free, but the Senators and other Antonians who were taken prisoner were all executed by Octavian.

The road from Perugia winds down to the plain. Just before the level-crossing at the foot of the hill, there is the so-called *Ipogeo dei Volumni* on the left, one of the finest Etruscan tombs known. It was discovered in 1840 and dates from the second half of the 2nd century B.C., or perhaps as late as 100 B.C. Shaped like a Roman house, it is richly decorated with stucco and reliefs. Nine travertine urns in the central chamber contain the ashes of the Volumni family.

PART IV

Samnium and the Italic Tribes

6. VIA SALARIA (S.S.4), VIA SABINA (S.S.17), VIA CAECILIA (S.S.80)
(See Map 5)

With the consolidation of the territory in the immediate vicinity of the city, Rome was ready to expand her frontiers in the direction of the Apennines. The problems of conquest were very different from those in more open country, where large towns controlled a wide agricultural region, and a communications network already existed. In the Apennines the topography presents a jumble of high mountain ranges, elevated plateaux and valleys closed at both ends by high saddles. There are no economic minerals in this limestone and even the potter's clay is only second-rate. In such a terrain much of the population of tough mountaineers has always led a pastoral life. In the winter they occupy semi-permanent villages on the plains or in the valleys, and in the summer, take their flocks and herds up to the mountain pastures.

Originally all the Italic tribes sprang for the greater part from one indigenous stock (see Chapter 1). In the course of time and by infiltration of fresh immigrants, tribal evolution took place until the Adriatic slopes of the Apennines were peopled by about a dozen separate units in the area covered by this Guide (see Map 2). All of them spoke very similar dialects that were akin to Latin. In central Italy important lines of communication were the 'drovers' trails', or *tratturi*, which in one form or another must have existed from earliest times. One of the most famous traverses Samnium from north-west to south-east, to Apulia. By this well-marked trail Hannibal advanced into Apulia. The problem facing the Romans was to prevent these sparsely distributed units from forming effective military concentrations. They managed by establishing colonies at strategic points along the tribal frontiers, often a very long distance from local population centres.

The roads leading from Rome to the Adriatic coast are the connecting links between the capital and these colonies. It speaks eloquently of the sparse indigenous population when one considers that the average colony comprised but a few hundred veteran legionaries. Some had their families, others married local girls. Such small units could establish themselves in two or three years in the normal way. In a hostile district, where the building of a walled town was necessary, it only took a year or so longer. The word *colonia* does not mean colony in the modern sense, neither does it imply a large subject territory. The modern Italian word *colono* is the equivalent of 'peasant' or 'farmer', which is exactly the Roman meaning of the word *colonus*.

Rome quickly learned that the most efficient way of consolidating her conquered territories both in Italy and abroad, was by peopling them with Roman colonists. If prospective colonists were not available at any time, the conquered land under state ownership was leased out for grazing purposes. 'Colonization' was an official proceeding by the state, and not the result of enterprising pioneering by private persons.

The procedure was of two types. In the one case the intending settlers received a gift of a certain area of land chosen by lot from the surveyed areas. The settlement was not organized into a self-administering unit, but remained under state control. In the more important case the settlers received their gifts of land, but were also organized into a self-governing *colonia*, with their own communal centre for civic administration. The decision as to which type would be launched was dependent on the military situation. In a hostile region where the colonists would be exposed to raids and reprisals by the local displaced inhabitants, the colony consisted of a well-fortified town with a good local defence organization that could mobilize the defending forces at very short notice.

So in effect the foundation of the Roman colonies meant the foundation of new Roman city states in the conquered territories, sited along the frontiers between the tribal units, or at a pass or river ford, or some equally strategic point. The formation of the colonies served two purposes. First it removed a large number of landless poor from the population of Rome and made them liable for military service. Secondly the system established bases for further expansion into new regions.

In the period before the end of the Second Punic War, all the colonies outside the immediate territory of Rome were *Latin colonies*, that is to say the inhabitants did not have the rights of Roman citizens. They varied greatly in size. Ostia was originally only five acres, whilst others covered several hundreds. Each colonist received a parcel of land, which varied from two *jugera* ($\frac{1}{2}$ hectare) to 200 *jugera* (51 hectares), the allocation being made according to military rank and by drawing lots.

At the beginning of the 4th century B.C. Rome was sacked by a band of raiding Gauls. They were driven back and Rome made a treaty with Samnium for mutual defence against a repetition of the disaster. The treaty enabled Rome to establish colonies along the Adriatic coast at Pisaurum, Firmum, Hadria, Sena Gallica and other places not only as a deterrent against the Gauls from Cisalpine Gaul, but effectively controlling any action by the local Italic tribes as well. These colonies were linked to Rome by the roads that are the subject of Chapters 5, 6 and 7.

VIA SALARIA (S.S.4)

This was the adaptation of a very ancient track along which tribes living in the interior carried salt from the marshes at the mouth of the Tiber, hence the name Via Salaria. Originally it probably went to Cures but was extended to Asculum (Ascoli Piceno) and the Adriatic coast at Porto d'Ascoli by Augustus in 17–16 B.C. The road leaves Rome from Piazza Fiume on the site of the vanished Porta Salaria, and runs along the wide valley of the river Tiber.

12 **Fidenae.** The site is below Castel Giubileo, a medieval fortlet on the hill that overlooks a ford over the river. Little can be seen of the ancient town, which was a formidable obstacle to early Roman expansion. Fidenae was a colony of Veii and controlled the Cremera river on the opposite bank of the Tiber, where the whole Fabian *gens* or clan except for one youth was destroyed in a battle with the army of Veii. The town was occupied by the Romans, traditionally by Mamercus Aemilius in 440 B.C. The capture of Fidenae opened the way to Veii for Rome.

15 **Settebagni,** the entrance to the Autostrada del Sole from the Via Salaria. Here, near the hamlet of Marcigliana, was the site of the disastrous defeat of the Romans by the Gauls at the Battle of the Allia in 390 B.C.

23 Turn right from the Salaria on to the Via Nomentana to Monterotondo (3 km) and Mentana (a further 2 km). Mentana is on the approximate site of the ancient town of Nomentum.

35 **Passo Corese** (Roman Cures) was formerly a large city but by the

1st century it had declined to a small village. It was supposed to have been the home of the Roman kings Titius Tatius and Numa Pompilius. Via Salaria now begins to climb the foothills of the Sabine Mountains, and Road 313 forks to the left for Terni on the Via Flaminia.

Turn right to **Poggio Moiano** (6 m) on Road 314. This road goes *Km 5* to **Vicovaro** on the Via Tiburtina past Horace's farm at **Licenza,** about 10 km before Vicovaro. For the description of the villa, see Chapter 7, p. 195, for the villa is more accessible from the Via Tiburtina.

Rieti (Roman Reate) was the principal city of the Sabines at the *Km 8* foot of Monte Terminillo on the banks of the river Velino. In the Social War in 91 B.C. the following tribes along the Via Salaria were in revolt: the Marsi, Paeligni, Vestini, Marrucini and Picentes Asculani. The Romans placed their armies to prevent the junction of these tribes with the Samnites to the south. The XII Legion under Q. Servilius Caepio was based on Reate, with other commanders along the length of the road going eastwards towards the Adriatic coast. Early in the campaign the Marsi and the Picentes, aided by the Vestini, prevented the capture of Asculum and forced the Romans under Pompeius Strabo to retire towards Firmum, where they were besieged. Reate was also the birthplace of the antiquarian M. Terentius Varro (116–27 B.C.) and of the emperor Vespasian. The only Roman remains of note in Reate are part of an arch of the 3rd century A.D. There is a small Roman collection in the local museum, in the Palazzo Comunale in the central square. In ancient times Reate was also famous for its breed of mules. From here Road 79 follows the valley of the river Velino to Terni (40 km). There is also a good third class road to Avezzano along the valley of the river Salto, which may have been an ancient drove road on the route to Monte Velino.

Terme di Cotilia, 6 km east of Cittaducale. Here Vespasian died *Km 1* in A.D. 79. The spring of the Peschiera on the other side of the Velino here is the second most copious source in Italy (3,400 gallons per second). Little remains of the baths today, of which Pliny the Elder says 'those waters are drunk as a purgative' (N.H. 31.32), and Strabo adds 'the cold springs of Cotilia, where people cure their diseases, not only by drinking from the springs, but by sitting down in them'.

Antrodoco (Roman Interocrium). Here the road forks with the Via *Km 1*

Salaria continuing on the left through the very scenic Gorge of the Velino, whilst the road on the right becomes the modern road the Via Sabina or S.S.17 (see below). After several kilometres of the Gola del Velino, a gorge with vertical cliffs and narrow passages of surpassing beauty, the Via Salaria reaches Posta (125 km).

140 **Passo della Serra,** which is the watershed between the Tyrrhenian and Adriatic seas. Here the Via Salaria enters the valley of the river Tronto (Roman Truentus).

181 **Acquasanta.** Here in the thermal sulphur springs Caesar's and Augustus' friend Munatius Plancus was cured of rheumatism.

201 **Ascoli Piceno** (Roman Asculum) was the principal town of the Picentines. It stands on a hill 152 m above sea level at the confluence of the rivers Tronto and Castellano. There is a small museum in the Palazzo del Popolo. Asculum was captured by the Romans in 268 B.C. and the whole population forcibly transferred to Apulia far to the south. This left a largely Latin population, but it did not prevent the Picentines joining the rebels in 90 B.C.; the revolt was at first successful when Pompeius Strabo was driven into Firmum. Towards the end of the year 90 B.C., however, the tide turned and in its turn Asculum was besieged by Sextus Julius Caesar, and the morale of the besieged began to fall. This led to many executions by their leader, C. Videlicius, but did not save the city. It was captured on 17th November the following year and the inhabitants were sold into slavery. Those who escaped were later intercepted by the Romans as they tried to cross the high passes of the Gran Sasso and were either killed or frozen to death. This success ended all resistance in the north, but the revolt still continued from a new capital at Aesernia (Isernia) in Samnium. Of the Roman town there are remains of a theatre in the west, although the nearby Ponte di Cecco was destroyed in the war. A section of Roman wall survives and remains of a Roman Corinthian temple have been incorporated into the church of San Gregorio. Asculum is supposed to have been the site of Pyrrhus' victory over the Romans in 279 B.C.

226 **Porta d'Ascoli** is the site of Castrum Truentum and the end of the Via Salaria on the Adriatic coast where it joins the north-south coastal highway.

VIA SABINA (in part the ancient Via Caecilia)

on the Via Salaria from Rome. At this point, at Antrodoco, the *Km 1*
right fork of the road becomes the modern road S.S.17 called the
Via Sabina and the long climb up to the watershed along the Ravine
of Antrodoco begins.

Sella di Corno, 990 m above sea level. On the eastern side of the *Km 1*
pass the road now enters the valley of the river Aterno, which opens
out into a wide amphitheatre ringed by high mountains. In the
centre of the plain stands the town of Civitatomassa.

Just beyond Civitatomassa the road forks left to **San Vittorino** *Km 2*
(Amiternum), on the banks of the river Aternus and the birthplace
of Sallust. It was a Sabine town which joined the insurgents in
the Social War in 90 B.C. During the period of the initial successes
of the rebels, the Roman praetor, Q. Servilius Caepio, fell into an
ambush prepared by Pompaedius Silo and was killed. Silo now
marched on Rome with ten thousand men, but was eventually
stopped by Marius and Sextus Julius Caesar. In Imperial times the
city was very prosperous, both because of the fertility of the surrounding region and its siting on the important crossroads of the
Via Caecilia (Road 80) and the Via Claudia Nova (Road 5 *bis*). The
ruins of Amiternum are visible from the road at San Vittorino and
are clearly signposted. The Roman theatre and amphitheatre are well
preserved today.

The Via Caecilia was possibly built as an extension to the Salaria
in 284 B.C. from Cures to Rieti, Amiternum and **Teramo** (Interamnia
Praetuttiorum) to reach the coast at Giulianova. Teramo was a
Roman colony probably founded about 268 B.C., although this date
is disputed. The Via Claudia Nova was built by the Emperor
Claudius in A.D. 47. It was a strategic road but follows the route of
the drove road up onto Monte Velino and down to Alba Fucens,
where it joins the Via Valeria at 130 km from Rome.

L'Aquila. The city is of medieval foundation, but the interest in *Km 3*
this Guide is the museum (15) housed in the magnificent Castello,
a perfect moated castle. The archaeological collection on the ground
floor is particularly rich in material from Amiternum. Most of the
material of the archaeology of the Abruzzo, however, is housed in
the National Archaeological Museum of the province at Chieti.

After L'Aquila Road 17 continues through the country of the
Vestini to Popoli where it joins the Via Valeria. The former *tratturo*

or drove road to Foggia and Apulia can still be discerned 1 to 2 km south of the Via Sabina and running parallel to it from L'Aquila until km 62. By the side of the *tratturo* are the slight Roman ruins of Ansidonia, reached from the village of Castelnovo at km 58.

The section of Road 17 to the south of Popoli and Roads 82 and 83 are dealt with in Chapter 7.

7. VIA TIBURTINA, VIA VALERIA (S.S.5), AND ROADS 17, 82, 83
(See Map 6)

The region covered by these roads comprises the Apennines and the western foothills bordering the wide valley of the rivers Sacco and Liri. Further north were the tribes that formed the Italic League described in Chapter 6 (see Map 2). The numerous tribes were of a common stock and spoke proto-Latin dialects. The principal members of the group were the Samnites, whose territory extended north from the river Aufidus in the south, a long way outside the limits of this Guide (see *Southern Italy: An Archaeological Guide* by Margaret Guido). Their western frontier was the river Liris (Liri) and the foot of the lower Apennines. On the east were the Frentani and the Apuli. Space is not available here to follow their history, which is admirably dealt with by E. T. Salmon in his *Samnium and the Samnites*, also listed in the Bibliography.

As soon as Rome had consolidated her position by the annexation of the Latin tribes (which took place after the so-called Latin War of 340–338 B.C.), she controlled southern Etruria, Latium and Northern Campania. But the degree of control of individual tribes and towns varied considerably: some tribes were completely Romanized, others were allies who were independent but inextricably under Roman control. The remainder of Italy was still largely dominated by the Samnites, who actually controlled a larger territory than that of Rome, and a very prosperous region. The clash came in 345 B.C. and lasted until 290, when the Samnites were finally defeated and incorporated into the Roman state.

Rome had set up a colony at Fregellae near the junction of the rivers Sacco and Liri, on what was later to be the crossroads of the Via Latina and Road 82, the road into the Abruzzo. This was taken to be an act of war by the Samnites, and hostilities opened. In 321 came the disaster of the *Caudine Forks* (see p. 35). Nevertheless by 316 Rome was ready to fight again. For the first time a Roman army reached the Adriatic and turned south to seize Luceria on the borders of Samnium and Apulia. The decisive battle was fought near Terracina on the west coast in 314, but the war lingered on until 304 B.C. In about 307 B.C. the Romans extended the Via Valeria, and established two important colonies at Alba Fucens and Carseoli. These effectively split the Marsi, Paeligni, Hernici and the Aequi from the Umbrians and the Etruscans.

In 298 hostilities broke out again. The Third Samnite War began with a combination of Samnites, Gauls and Etruscans. But this coalition was defeated with a great victory at Sentinum in 295, followed by another defeat for the Samnites at Aquilonia (modern Montaquila ?) near Venafro in 290 and the war was ended. The next test the Romans had to face was the arrival of Pyrrhus who in 284–270 won a number of battles, but being unable to break down the resistance of the Roman colonies, eventually departed from Italy in disgust. The above short note summarizes the main history of the region, which was accompanied by the establishment of colonies at all strategic points. Then followed the connection of these to the capital by a series of military roads. As time went on northern Campania with its fertility became the attraction for Etruscans, Samnites and Romans. The large number of ancient sites clustered along its borders reflects the struggle for its domination.

VIA TIBURTINA (S.S.5)

The Via Tiburtina begins at the Porta San Lorenzo in Rome, and after crossing the ringroad continues to Tivoli, where it becomes the Via Valeria and extends to the Adriatic coast.

12 The river Aniene, the classical Anio, is crossed at Ponte Mammolo, the successor to the Pons Mammaeus, the Republican bridge.

21 Turn left to **Montecelio** (11 km), thought to be the site of the Latin town of Corniculum. Remains of a Roman temple have been built into the castle.

22 **Bagni di Tivoli,** or Acque Albule, a very smelly sulphuretted spring, which was a spa in Roman times. After a further 3 km, the river is crossed by the Ponte Lucano; this was a five-arched Roman bridge named after Lucanus Plautius, but it has been rebuilt several times. From the new road bridge it is possible to visit a prehistoric cave, the *Grotta Polesini*, which is situated upstream on the right bank of the river. For further details of this cave, which contained Palaeolithic and Bronze Age deposits, see page 64. A kilometre to the east of the

Map 6. Main modern roads and ancient sites east and
smaller lettering and where there is no Roman nam

ne. The modern Italian name of the site is given in
name only is given.

bridge, on the road to Tivoli, the road to *Hadrian's Villa* is prominently signposted on the right.

Hadrian's Villa. This great memorial to Roman grandeur stands *Km* at the base of the hill upon which **Tibur** (Tivoli) was built. It was designed by Hadrian himself in collaboration with his architect Apollonius of Damascus, whom the Emperor afterwards at first exiled then executed for his outspoken criticisms of the Emperor's ability as an architect. The villa took several years to build (A.D. 117– 135), and covers an area 1,000 m by 500 m. The various component buildings were named after the places that the Emperor had visited in the Empire. The dating of the building is very precise, owing to the Roman custom of stamping bricks with their factory of origin and the name of the reigning consul.

The visit requires at least three or four hours to do justice to the immense site (see Plan 12). It is open from 9 a.m. to one hour before sunset every day. From the entrance, cars proceed to an inner parking lot where there is a bar and a model of the villa. An official guide-book is on sale at the site. The earliest construction was the circular *Teatro Marittimo* dating from the first year of Hadrian's reign (see Plate 27a). Here the brick stamps reveal later additions and altera-tions to the original design. Much of the villa has been restored. There were luxurious apartments, guest rooms, a garden pavilion, dining-rooms, baths, a library, porticos, a gymnasium and the famous *Temple of Serapis*. Since 1870 the villa has been systemati-cally excavated, but the first 'excavations' began in 1535. Much of the villa is still unexcavated; nevertheless, all the museums in Rome are full of items from it.

Proceed to the *Stoa Poikile*, modelled on that of Athens, a vast rectangular cloister (232 m by 97 m); the fishpond in the centre has been restored. The short western side of the Stoa stands upon an understructure in which are the so-called *Cento Camerelle*, small rooms distributed over three or four floors, which may have been the barracks of the guard.

At the north-eastern angle of the Stoa, one enters the *Hall of the Philosophers*, a grandiose apsed room of rectangular plan. Pass through this to the *Teatro Marittimo*, surrounded by a cloister which is colonnaded with some of the columns still standing. South of the theatre are the ruins of the *Small Thermae*, made for sun-bathing and also surrounded by a cloister enclosing a *Frigidarium*. (In these baths there is an elliptical room with two baths in the

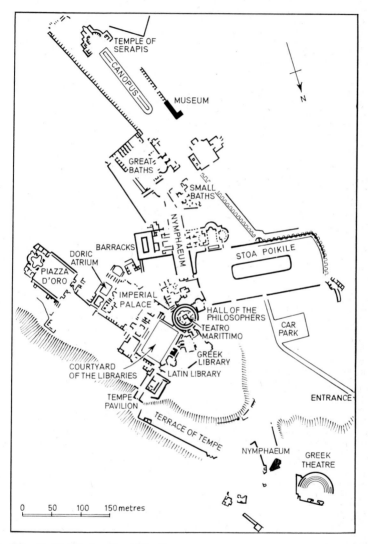

Plan 12. Hadrian's villa at Tivoli.

apses, a swimming pool, and an octagonal dining-room, and a circular *Caldarium*). Between the theatre and the baths is the valley of the *Nymphaeum*, on the east side of which is a curious building with a rectangular *atrium*, surrounded by three semicircular *esedra*. In the *Large Baths* there is a noteworthy apsed hall, with the roof partly collapsed in one apse, and in the other the roof is decorated with very beautiful stucco reliefs in the vault. The *Canopus* is an artificial valley, flanked on the east by a long wall, and on the west by a series of rooms on two floors. Running down the centre is a canal, or long narrow lake, on both banks of which are statue plinths and column bases (see Plate 27b). At the far end is the *Temple of Serapis*, a semicircular building with several rooms. One of the best views of the site is from here. To the south-east of the temple is the so-called *Accademia*, which some scholars believe was a second palace. The round hall is called the Temple of Apollo. 400 m to the southeast is the *Odeion* or Theatre, where the Imperial Box can still be seen. To the east of the theatre is a hollow cut out of the *tufo* rock, which leads into a semicircular hall, the entrance to *Hades*, a group of subterranean corridors. Hadrian wanted to reconstruct the Hades of the poets' imagination in brick and stone. (Return to *Nymphaeum*.)

The *Praetorium* is behind the Large Baths. It consists of a series of tall narrow arcades on three floors which are supposed to have been the barracks of the Praetorian Guard, or possibly store-rooms. From here walking through the olive groves to the east of the Small Baths, one reaches the *Imperial Palace*, a vast rectangular cloister with a large pool in the centre. This covers some 50,000 sq m and comprises four groups of halls and rooms surrounding the four cloisters. At the south-eastern end is the Piazza d'Oro with a splendid peristyle formed by sixty columns. One side is the annexe with four large niches from which statue fountains played onto the marble steps. Proceeding to the north, there is the *Doric Atrium* with fluted columns, and flanked by a *Nymphaeum*, and the barracks of the Vigiles (night watchmen or firemen). Then follows the *Great Cloister* (or Palace Cloister) with the form of a Basilica in plan, with three naves, a lavatory and a *cryptoporticus*. Finally there is the *Courtyard of the Libraries*, where there are two buildings with several floors, named respectively the *Greek Library* and the *Latin Library*. On the north side of this courtyard are two small rooms with mosaic pavements, which were probably guardrooms. Opening from these is the *Terrace of Tempe*, from which there is a very fine

Plate 27.
Hadrian's villa:
(a) the Teatro
Marittimo,
dating from
A.D. 117.
(b) the Canopus.

view in the shade of a delightful wood. At the south-eastern extremity
of the Terrace is the *Tempe Pavilion*, a kind of summerhouse viewpoint comprising a large hall with big windows looking out over the
Vale of Tempe, with an artificial cliff cut into the soft *tufo* in imita-
tion of the famous valley in Thessaly. On passing through the
Nymphaeum one reaches the *Greek Theatre*, near the Casino Fede,
which is the Antiquarium of the Villa. The *Little Theatre* is still
covered with a jungle of perfumed herbs and briars, but part of the
seating and of the stage can be seen.

The whole complex of the Villa is an amazing extravagance, and
not occupied by Hadrian for long, as he was always travelling abroad
until his last years.

RETURN TO THE MAIN ROAD WHICH NOW CLIMBS THE STEEP
HILL TO TIVOLI

Tivoli (Roman Tibur). Tibur was a very ancient Latin town which *Km 3*
was a *civitas foederata* of Rome, that is to say, a fully self-governing
ally. The town stands on a high hill covered with olive groves, and
dominates the route to the east along the line of the Via Valeria.
Before it was subdued by Rome, the Roman armies during the
Samnite Wars had to make a detour through Rieti. Tibur did not
receive full Roman citizenship until 87 B.C. It was a favourite resort
of patricians, and there are many remains of their sumptuous villas.
Marius, Sallust, Cassius, Catullus, Maecenas and Quintilius Varus
all had villas here. Near the Villa Gregoriana is the *Temple of Vesta*,
a small circular Republican temple on the edge of the cliff, converted
into the church of Santa Maria della Rotonda; nearby is the
rectangular *Temple of the Sibyl*. Tibur had the duty of housing and
guarding Roman state prisoners. One of these was Queen Zenobia
of Palmyra. She had assassinated her husband and then, whilst
acting as regent for her son, had endeavoured to create a wide
empire consisting of Syria, Egypt and all Asia Minor. This naturally
led to war with Rome. Zenobia was defeated and led in triumph to
Rome, but her life was spared. She was given a villa at Tibur and
allowed to spend the remainder of her days there. The cascades and
fountains in the gardens of the Villa d'Este at Tivoli are well worth
a visit. There are several remains around the town. Take the Via
Quintilio Varo from the Porta Sant'Angelo. This passes the ruined

arches of the *Acqua Marcia*, an aqueduct built in 144 B.C. from the Via Valeria to Rome. By the church of Santa Maria di Quintiliolo are the ruins of a Roman villa, said to be that of Quintilius Varus. The Via Valeria now climbs up the valley of the Aniene to Vicovaro.

n 45   **Vicovaro** (Roman Varia). Here Road 314 goes to Licenza (8 km), where the poet Horace had his farm, given to him by Maecenas in 32 B.C. Horace tells of its peace and beautiful setting. The villa which is thought to be the poet's is signposted (*Villa di Orazio*) on the left of the road at the bottom of the hill up to Licenza. Excavations are still being carried out on the periphery of the villa, which is compact and well preserved—in places up to about a metre above ground level. The situation is charming: the villa is on a low

Plate 28. Excavations at Horace's villa at Licenza.

hill above the road surrounded by woodland, with glorious views of the Sabine hills around. There are the foundations of a score of rooms and several mosaic pavements (see Plate 28). A spring further up the valley may be the *Fons Bandusiae* of Horace's immortal ode (Odes III.13). The road eventually joins the Via Salaria at Poggio Moiano.

Road 411 on the right goes to Subiaco, and eventually to Frosinone.   Km 57 Near Subiaco an artificial lake was formed by a dam on the River Aniene and Nero built a villa there. The ruins of the villa can still be seen 15 km beyond Subiaco.

Carsoli (Roman Carseoli). This place was a key point in antiquity   Km 71 (see Map 2). It was a settlement of the Aequi, who fought against Rome in the concluding stages of the Second Samnite War. In 303 B.C. Junius Brutus overwhelmed the Aequi in less than a week. Their territory around Lake Fucens and to the west of it was taken from them, and they disappeared as a nation. The Romans then established two colonies, one at Carseoli and the other at Alba Fucens. These two colonies effectively controlled all movement across the western side of the central Apennine watershed, thus preventing any junction between the Samnites and potential allies to the north. In the Marsic phase of the Social War in 91 B.C., the Italiote tribes had their capital at Corfinium (see p. 199), which had recently been built. To counteract the rebellion, the consul Rutilius Lupus had his head-quarters at Carseoli with Legions III and IV. Legion XII was at Reate and Legion XV by the Fucine Lake. The insurgents attacked each Roman general in turn, and finally on 11th June 90 B.C. the consul himself was defeated and killed and Carseoli was plundered. But the tide soon turned, when Rome was able to bring up reinforce-ments. By the following year the new capital at Corfinium was captured and the rebels transferred their headquarters to Bovianum further south. The remainder of the Social War was fought on the Samnite front, largely outside the limits of this Guide.

During the Second Punic War, Hannibal failed to take Carseoli but the constant demand for soldiers by Rome, especially after the battle of Cannae, forced the colony to announce that they could supply no more. Nevertheless the loyalty of these communities and Hannibal's inability to capture them as he had no siege train, were the main factors in his final defeat. The ancient town was further down the valley near Oricola-Pereto station, at km 66.

The long climb up to the Passo del Bove (1,111 m) begins after

Carseoli; the Via Valeria then descends to Tagliacozzo (km 97) in the valley of the river Imele, on the Adriatic side of the watershed. Avezzano. In ancient times the Via Valeria did not run through Avezzano, but through **Alba Fucens** (see Plan 13) about 10 km to the north. Avezzano stands on the northern rim of the former Fucine Lake (Lacus Fucinus), which was drained in 1875. The archaeological interest of the area is two-fold; around the shores of the former lake there are many caves and rock-shelters which were occupied in prehistory (see Chapter 1) and Alba Fucens was the principal city of the Aequi, which, as noted above, was destroyed in the Social War. It became a Roman colony of 6,000 citizens in 304 B.C., and in Republican days it was a state prison for many notable prisoners, like Syphax captured at the battle of Zama, Perseus king of Macedonia, and Bituitus king of the Averni. The fortifications dating from 300 B.C. are still well preserved. The site lies between the snow-capped peaks of Monte Velino and the bed of the lake. The town was built on three hills, San Nicola, San Pietro and Pettorino. On San Pietro stands a 12th-century church dedicated to the Saint, and built partly over the *Temple of Apollo. The Theatre* is carved out of the Pettorino Hill. These hills were of great strategic importance, and the Romans surrounded them with massive defence walls no less than 5 km in circumference, reinforced by a kind of advanced wall, or earthwork on the north-west side. The town is a perfect example of Roman town-planning, with *cardines* and *decumani* at right-angles to each other, and four gates. At the south is the Porta Maxima on a cardo, the Porta Fellonica was on the north of the town, the Porta di Massa on the saddle between the hills of San Nicola and Pettorino, and the Porta S. Massimo on the west. The town stood at the foot of the three hills, the streets following the declivities of the terrain. Renewed building operations at the end of the Republican period and in the 1st century A.D. added more public buildings whilst leaving intact the plan of the town. The *Amphitheatre* of elliptical plan lies inside the walls below the hill of San Pietro. The *Forum* is between the Via Valeria and the theatre in the centre of the city. It contains the principal public buildings: the *Basilica* flanked by a large covered portico, a circular market and the *Thermae*. The shops are along the Via dei Pilastri, so-called from the arcades in front of the shops. Alba Fucens was the market for a wide agricultural area, and also for a fishing industry in the Lake. Graffitti of boats can be seen on the walls of the *Temple of Apollo.*

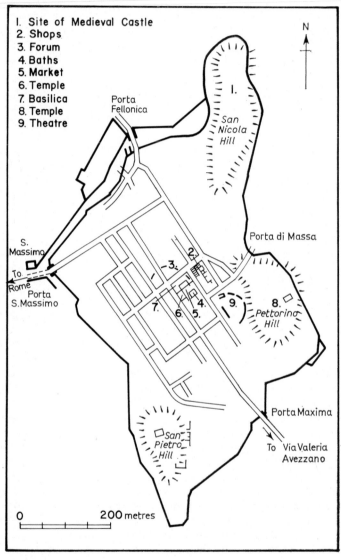

1. Site of Medieval Castle
2. Shops
3. Forum
4. Baths
5. Market
6. Temple
7. Basilica
8. Temple
9. Theatre

N

Porta Fellonica

1.

San Nicola Hill

Porta di Massa

S. Massimo

To Rome

Porta S.Massimo

2.

3.

7.

6. 5. 4.

9.

8.

Pettorino Hill

Porta Maxima

To Via Valeria Avezzano

San Pietro Hill

0   200 metres

Plan 13. Alba Fucens.

The Lake was 60 km in circumference and 36 m deep. Because it flooded so often the Emperor Claudius constructed an *emissarium* in A.D. 52 to carry the floodwaters into the river Liris. The tunnel was 5 km long with 40 light-shafts. It took 30,000 men eleven years to build. The ruin of the construction can be seen 5 km south of Avezzano, at the foot of the hills on the western edge of the plain. The Emperor Claudius staged a *Naumachia* or naval combat on the lake in which no fewer than one hundred ships and ten thousand men took part. They fought to the death until one side was completely annihilated, and entirely for the amusement of the holiday crowds. Near the ruins of Claudius' tunnel is the prehistoric cave, the Grotta di Ciccio Felice. Following the Lake basin round to the other side, one can visit other caves on the south-eastern shore near Ortucchio: the Grotta Maritza, Grotta La Punta, and the Grotta Ortucchio. Still further round on the same road north of the village of Venere, are the Grotta Clemente Tronci and the Riparo Maurizio. These prehistoric sites are discussed in Chapter 1. San Benedetto dei Marsi is on the ruins of *Marruvium,* the capital of the Marsi. From Avezzano Road 82 follows the line of a drovers' trail traversing the Sabine country to the coast: it passes down the Liris valley from Alba Fucens to Formia on the west coast. It also went northwards to L'Aquila.

RETURN TO THE VIA VALERIA

This was probably extended by Claudius in A.D. 47–9 to Chieti and the coast.

132 **Cerchio.** Here Road 83 forks off on the right (on another drove road route) to pass through the Abruzzi National Park, to join Road 17 at **Aufidena** on the river Sangro (see p. 201).

169 **Raiano.** The Via Valeria emerges from the Gorge of San Venanzio into the Sulmona basin.

175 The Via Valeria joins Road 17 and makes common run into the town of **Popoli.** Near the junction of the roads are the ruins of **Corfinium,** the chief town of the Paeligni; it was the capital set up by the Italic League in the Social War. The town was re-named *Italia,* but its glory was short-lived as it was destroyed after only two years of war. Later, under the Romans, it became an important crossroads and market. The museum (10) is worth a visit.

Popoli. A small town at the entrance to the gorge of the river *Km 1* Pescara. Here Road 17 forks to the left to continue to L'Aquila. There is little of archaeological interest in the town. 2 km beyond Popoli, the new road to L'Aquila leaves on the left. The road skirts the village of Capestrano and a sign on the road (*Zona Archeologica*) marks the area of the discovery of the *Warrior of Capestrano* (see Plate 4) described in Chapter 1.

Chieti (Roman Teate Marrucinorum). The chief town of the *Km 2* Province today, just as it was also the capital of the Marrucini in antiquity. The town is situated high above the valley of the Pescara with a magnificent view of the Maiella mountain. There are Roman remains of considerable interest. Three small temples have recently been discovered behind the Post Office. A large cistern in the Strada Marrucina is very well preserved—it comprises no fewer than nine subterranean compartments intercommunicating by means of arcades. It is excavated in the rock of the hillside, and supplied water to the thermae situated below. The principal attraction of Chieti is its museum (8), where the *Warrior of Capestrano* (Plate 4) can be seen. There is a prehistoric section, with the material from the caves and open sites of the Abruzzo, and Roman material from Alba Fucens and also from the Temple of Lucius Storax.

Pescara (Roman Aternum) on the Adriatic coast. Little remains of *Km 2* the Roman town, which lay at the southern end of modern Pescara.

ROAD 17 (S.S.)

In Roman times this was paved and may have been the Via Minucia, built by Q. Minucius Rufus between 125 and 120 B.C. But long before that it was probably the major drove road running south from the summer pastures above Amiternum by Corfinium, Sulmo, Aesernia, Bovianum to Beneventum and down to the winter pastures on the Tavioliere plain (Foggia) (see Map 2).

At the junction with the Via Valeria 6 km west of Popoli, take the *Km 1* road on the right to Sulmona. This is Road 17 and distances will be measured from this point.

Turn left to the Abbey of Santo Spirito or Badia Morronese, a *Km 6* hermitage built on the edge of the basin. By the hermitage are the ruins of the so-called *Villa di Ovidio*. It is rather a pity, but the ruins have been identified as a Temple of Hercules and the poet's home has yet to be found. The ruins are on the steep flanks of Monte Morrone and command a superb view over the Sulmona basin. On clear days it is possible to see the Gran Sasso in the distance to the north-west.

14 **Sulmona** (Roman Sulmo) situated in a wide cup-valley on the river Gizio. On a relief found at Sulmona is the picture of a flock moving along the drovers' trail. Sulmona was a Sabine city and was famous for its ironworks. Above all, it was the birthplace of the poet Ovid. There are several Roman remains in the town but none of outstanding importance. The Cathedral is built on the ruins of a Roman temple.

50 **Roccaraso.** All this region was the very heart of the Samnite country. Archaeological exploration is being carried out only now, and many places that before have been only names mentioned by the ancient writers are being found and identified. The Cinquemila plateau between Sulmona and Roccaraso has always been one of the main summer pastures for the transhumant flocks.

61 **Castel del Sangro,** in the valley of the river Sangro. There are many sporadic remains of Samnite settlement here, but owing to lack of epigraphical evidence, the site remains unidentified. About 5 km south of the town the road forks, the branch on the right leading to **Alfedena,** about 5 km away. On the opposite side of the river are the cyclopean walls of the Samnite town of **Aufidena.** Road 17 continues south through the main Samnite area.

98 **Isernia** (Roman Aesernia) became a Roman colony in 263 B.C. and was the centre of much fighting during the Samnite Wars. It is situated on a hill at the confluence of the Carpino and Sordo rivers. In the tower of the Duomo are four Roman statues. In other parts of the town there are some Republican and Imperial remains, and one of the Roman bridges is intact. There is also a small civic museum.

126 **Boiano** (Roman Bovianum) has been identified as the chief town of the Pentri; traces of the ancient walls can still be seen.

136 **Sepino** (Roman Saepinum). The ruins of the ancient town are 3 km north of modern Sepino at **Altilia,** where excavations are now in progress. There are long sections of the walls, a theatre, baths, temples, private villas, a forum and long stretches of paved road.

160 At the top of the pass, Road 87 forks to the right via Telese to **Caiazzo** and **Capua.** Telese is near the ruins of the Samnite town of Telesia; Caiazzo was Roman Caiatia and was a town of the Falerni. A cistern under the market place is still in use.

Benevento (Samnite Malaventum, Roman Beneventum) was the *Km 1* chief town of the Hirpini, a Samnite tribe. It became a Roman colony in 268 B.C. There are many Roman remains in the town, notably the *Arch of Trajan* (erected between 114 and 117), the 1st-century A.D. *Roman Theatre*, and a large, as yet unexcavated, area round the Theatre. There is a fine little museum (the Museo del Sannio) in the medieval cloister of Santa Sophia, with Greek and Roman items from the surrounding region.

The continuation of Road 17 to Brindisi is outside the area of this Guide.

ROAD 83 (S.S.)

Perhaps this was another of the drover's trails. The modern road starts at the eastern shore of the Fucine Lake at the junction with the Via Valeria, and passes through the territory of the Marsi and the modern Abruzzi National Park to join Road 17 at Alfedena. Road 83 then continues down the valley of the river Volturno passing through Venafro to join the Via Casilina at Vairano Scalo. At Venafro the cyclopean walls and the remains of an amphitheatre have survived. Along its route through very beautiful limestone mountain valleys are occasional settlements, testifying to their existence by the massive polygonal walls still standing on the hilltops. Archaeological research of this hinterland has only begun in recent years, and is best summarized in E. T. Salmon's admirable survey of Samnium and its history.

ROAD 82 (S.S.)

This was an extremely important highway from very early times connecting the Via Salaria at Rieti with the Via Valeria at Alba Fucens; from here it now traverses the valley of the river Liris (which was the frontier between Rome and Samnium) as far as Interamna near the confluence of the rivers Liris and Sacco. From here the road passes over the Aurunci mountains to Itri, and Formia on the west coast. The distances are given as from Avezzano.

Sora. From Avezzano the road traverses the long narrow valley of *Km 5* the river Liris, the Val Roveto. This was the country of the Marsi, but very sparsely inhabited, with no identifiable sites until one reaches Sora. Here the river makes a bend to the west and enters the former territory of the Volsci, in much more open country. This is, in fact, the easiest route from Latium into Samnium and was the scene of much fighting in the Samnite Wars.

84 **Frosinone** (Roman Frusino) (see Chapter 8). From here Road 82 continues via Pico and Itri to Formia, by a long climb up to the pass over the Aurunci mountains to the sea. Along the roadside small groups of farms are dotted, which have experienced negligible change since the days of Republican Rome, and whose peasant life and economy are rooted in the prehistoric past.

PART V

Latium, Campania and Roman Colonization

8.VIA PRENESTINA, VIA CASILINA (S.S.6), VIA TUSCOLANA (S.S.215), VIA LATINA (S.S.215)

It is difficult to decide which of the regions of Italy is the most rewarding to the general visitor and student of archaeology. The specialist knows what he wants to see, but the amateur and first-time visitor may well be overcome by the beauties of the countryside, especially in the usual holiday seasons of spring and summer, and the wealth of antique material offered for his appreciation. I know the feeling well after twelve years of residence; trying to link hilltop villages with their ancestral Etruscan and Samnite fortresses, or motoring along the Via Latina, I am constantly reminded of the quotation from the Latin historian Livy with which I began this Guide. Livy knew his early Rome and Latium so well. His writings not only tell of the legendary stories of Rome's foundation, and the beginnings of her rise to power, but are full of true appreciation of the ancient religious beliefs on the interventions of the gods into human affairs, without which 'all is vanity'. The whole complex of the Alban Hills, an enormous ancient volcano, now extinct, was the mysterious home of some of these gods, especially of *Diana the Huntress*, and of *Virbius*, the god of the woods. Emperors had their villas here, and today the Pope has his summer residence at Alba Longa (Castel Gondolfo), the traditional home of the Latin race founded by Aeneas, and the inspiration of Virgil's epic poem.

Latium has the advantage today, as it had in antiquity, of having a good road service with Rome. This allows the visitor to base himself on Rome and explore Latium in day trips (see Maps 5 and 6). If he has to rely on public transport, naturally only the principal places can be visited in this way. But car owners have another splendid field to explore, and can make memorable discoveries off the beaten track—hill-top villages like Cori with fine remains of the so-called Temple of Hercules and Roman walls; and dozens of others with Roman, Latin, Etruscan or Samnite defence walls. All of which will help to recreate the history of the region—of raiding bands of cattle rustlers, pirates, night attacks across the tribal frontiers, for ambuscades and incessant warfare were often the lot of the inhabitants of these beautiful valleys and their bordering mountain heights.

Several Roman roads served the region, the Via Praenestina, the Via Labicana (now Casilina), the Via Tusculana, the Via Latina and the Via Appia (see next Chapter), all based on older tracks. Modern traffic needs have altered the relative values of these roads. The Via Praenestina (now Prenestina) has declined from its original position as a major highway to the lowly status of a tourist third class scenic drive to the ancient towns of Latium. The autostrada runs parallel with and in close proximity to both the Via Prenestina and the Via Casilina; a very good thing from the tourist point of view, as it takes the industrial load off the picturesque country roads. The section of the ancient Via Praenestina from Rome to Palestrina (Praeneste) is today just a local road though not always exactly the same route, for stretches of the old road can be seen alongside the present road. The fastest route for car owners is by way of the Via Casilina to the junction after San Cesareo, then left to Palestrina by Road 155. The Via Prenestina skirts the foothills of the Hernician mountains connecting various Latin cities and finally reaches Frosinone. On the other hand the Roman military highway, the Via Latina, follows the most direct route (as the modern Via Casilina) down the middle of the valley of the river Sacco to Frosinone, and beyond.

The early history of Rome was written in this region. First the city's foundation by a group of marauding adventurers from the Alban Hills, then the slow consolidation of the new settlement and its immediate surroundings; this process took two centuries or more, before the new city reached complete independence from Etruscan dominance and was ready to embark on the subjugation of Italy.

By 500 B.C. the Etruscan power was declining and the Latins had revolted and expelled the Etruscan king from Rome. The First Samnite War was in 343–341 B.C. and resulted in the specification of the respective spheres of interest of the two protagonists, by which the river Liris was made the general frontier between Rome and Samnium. This left the western Volsci, Aurunci and the Campani in the Roman sphere (see Map 2). Consequently these tribes naturally expected a Roman attack. The Latin War broke out in 340–338 B.C. and all Latium and a further area round Rome became *Latium Adjectum* which can be translated as 'The enlarged Roman territory'. It is this area which is served by the roads described in this chapter and the next (see Map 6).

VIA PRENESTINA (the ancient Via Praenestina)

Though the Via Latina was probably the oldest of the Roman roads in the area, the Via Prenestina must, during the formative period outlined above, have played a very important part. A glance at the map shows the wide, open valley running from the north-west to the south-east between the Monti Lepini and Aurunci along the coast and the Monti Hernici in the east. The massif of the Alban Hills stands as a bastion at the northern end. The Via Prenestina traverses the valley to the east of the Alban Hills, and then skirts the foothills of the Hernici Mountains to join Road 156 eventually at Frosinone. Road 156 continues into the Monti Lepini, passing through the towns of Priverno (Privernum), Sezze (Setia), Norma (Norba), Cori (Cora), and Segni (Signia), thus completing a ring of defences against the Samnites and their allies.

The Via Prenestina begins at the Porta Maggiore in Rome together with the Via Casilina. The latter road is at this point the Via Labicana of antiquity, which ran from Rome to Labicum and then joined the Via Latina at Ad Biviam, 48 km from Rome. Today it is the main highway from Rome (S.S.6) to Frosinone and Cassino, with the exception of the autostrada. (Perhaps we should add here that *all* cars with foreign licence plates pay the lowest toll on the autostrada south of Rome, irrespective of engine size.)

19   **Gabii,** ruins of. Gabii was one of the earliest Latin towns, and a cult centre second only to that of Praeneste or Lucus Feroniae. Traditionally it is said to have been founded by colonists from Alba Longa. In fact little is known of its early history, but it must have been an important place. Remains include a *Temple of Juno*, dating from the late 3rd century B.C. Although it declined into insignificance during the whole of the Republican times, it flourished again under Hadrian. The fashion of wearing the toga called '*cinctus Gabinus*' apparently originated here. There are stone quarries nearby that supplied material for many of the public buildings in Rome. Further on, to the right, there is a long stretch of Roman pavement. The ruins of Gabii stand between the dried-up lakes of Castiglione and Regillus. Lake Regillus was the scene of a battle in 496 B.C. when the Romans defeated the army of the Latins led by the Tarquins and put paid to the Tarquins' attempt to recover their throne in Rome. The Romans are said to have been divinely aided by the Dioscuri, Castor and Pollux.

Palestrina (Roman Praeneste). The 'cool Praeneste' of Horace, a *Km 3*
favourite summer retreat for Roman patricians. This is the site of
the *Temple of Fortune*, one of the greatest monuments that has come
down to us. The city was famous for its roses and its walnuts and
has a magnificent setting on an isolated hill. The foundation dates
either from the 8th or the 7th century. Following a long series of
wars with Rome, it did not become an ally until the Social War,
after which the citizens received the Roman franchise. In 82 B.C.,
when Marius Junior had taken refuge in the town, it was besieged
by Sulla. After the capture of the city, Praeneste was destroyed by
the troops, but Sulla then proceeded to establish a new *colonia* of
veterans and either to build or restore the great shrine of Fortuna.
Revealed by bombing during the last war, the original plan has now
been recovered, and so well restored that today the Temple is clear
to view. A visit here is perhaps more rewarding than any other place
in Latium.

The Shrine takes the form of a huge triangular hill-side structure
(containing the whole of the medieval town) culminating in the
Temple at the top. In 1958 the lower area was cleared. The retaining
wall and the ramped entrances can be visited from the Piazza
Regina Margherita (the former Forum) where the Cathedral is also
built upon an ancient building. From the Piazza, by the gate on the
left of the Seminario, one enters the *Sacred Area*, a vast courtyard
divided into four naves by five lines of columns, of which the bases
remain with some fragments. At the end of the courtyard, there is
a grand apsed hall, with a rectangular plan. The façade of the
Cathedral was removed, and behind it was found a lofty Roman
temple, with an arched entrance, the *cella* being in the nave of the
Cathedral. North-west of this temple was a cave known as the
Antro delle Sorti, doubtless where oracles were given. Here are
remains of a wonderful 1st-century mosaic, representing the bottom
of the sea off Alexandria in Egypt. The floor is sloped slightly, and
it was sprayed continually with a film of running water from a
fountain to brighten the colours. Also depicted on the mosaic are
some architectural items in the Second Pompeian style which confirm
the dating. At the opposite side of the Sacred Area is the *Apsidal
Hall*, a rectangular room in *opus incertum* (see Fig. 15), from where
the beautiful Barberini mosaic was recovered, a Hellenistic copy of
an Egyptian mosaic of early Ptolemaic date. It has been completely
restored and is now displayed in the museum at the site, the Palazzo

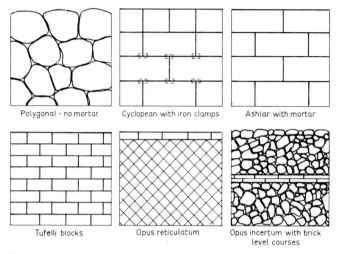

| Polygonal - no mortar | Cyclopean with iron clamps | Ashlar with mortar |
| Tufelli blocks | Opus reticulatum | Opus incertum with brick level courses |

Fig. 15. Types of masonry used in the ancient world.

Colonna Barberini on the site of the rotunda of the temple. The mosaic depicts the Nile from the source to the Delta, with animals, both real and imaginary, all labelled with their Greek names. There are hunting and fishing scenes, farms, palaces, temples, ships under sail, boats and luxury barges. It is a whole anthology of life in the Nile valley, from Ethiopian savages to the sophisticated Greeks of the Delta cities. This is by far the greatest masterpiece of mosaic that has ever been recovered. The influence of Egyptian art was considerable during the declining years of the Republic. There are also examples in the Naples Museum from the Temple of Isis at Pompeii, and the paintings on the walls at Baiae, where Cleopatra may have been in residence on and off for four years prior to the assassination of Julius Caesar.

An inscription gives the name of the founder of the Sullan colony, M. Lucullus, the brother of the general and gourmet who has passed into history for his extravagant dinner parties. The inscription was found associated with the long retaining wall in *opus incertum*, on an epistyle (marble connection between two columns). This, with the double row of column bases still extant, has enabled the restoration of the two-storied Basilica to be made. The Basilica is at a higher level than the temple in the Cathedral, as is shown by the position of the two sets of column bases on the south-west side of the Basilica, where the lowest columns are below the level of the floor. The lower level comprises the Treasury of the Shrine and was built in tuff blocks (*tufelli*—see Fig. 15), in front of which was a colonnade of Doric columns.

Above this lower level was a terrace, covered with shops before an aerial bombardment in the last war. When the site was cleared it was noted that there was a two-level terrace, with a long polygonal retaining wall 98 m in length. The wall-top forms the architectural level for the main complex of the Temple, now known as the *Upper Sanctuary* with its fine approach ramps, *Hemicycle Terrace*, *Terrace of the Arches*, with half-columns, and the *Cortina Terrace*, all leading upwards to the *Shrine of the Lady Fortune* at the summit. The Italian architects who were responsible for the reconstruction were Fasolo and Gulini. They found the approach ramps were supported on concrete vaults, concealed by walling of *opus incertum*, with the exception of the central vault, which was a fountain. The terrace is paved with large polygonal blocks. A room at the foot of the ramp is decorated in the Pompeian First Style, again suggesting construction by Sulla. One interesting feature of the construction of this ramp is the inclination of the tops of the columns. A study of the other indications along the roadway leading up to the ramp finally revealed that the outer half of the road was built with a blank wall obscuring the view over the countryside. A pitched roof and this line of columns with the inclined tops formed a peristyle opening inwards towards the uncovered half of the ramp. The approach ramps open out on to the *Hemicycle Terrace*, which is paved with bricks set in herring-bone pattern, and in the centre is a great stairway leading up to the *Terrace of the Arches* with half-columns. This Hemicycle Terrace, as with the whole of the Upper Sanctuary, is asymmetrical about the central axis. A triple set of stairways on the axis leads up from terrace to terrace, to the Round Temple at the summit.

At the side of the stairway there were fountains, and fountains everywhere throughout the Sanctuary. Water must have played an important part in the rituals. Behind the stairway is a wide vaulted corridor which is supported on Ionic columns. On either wing of this corridor are the *Hemicycles*, which apparently were fitted with wooden seats for the spectators at some performance. The pavement is similar to that in the hall at the base of the ramp, thus suggesting that this whole section was of one constructional date. At either side of the Hemicycle Terrace were other approach ramps extending far out beyond the general ensemble of the Temple. In front of the eastern Hemicycle, there was a well, probably a wishing well, judging from the number of coins that were found in it. Note the present day custom at the Fountain of Trevi in Rome, and Pliny's account of the Fountain of Clitumnus given in Chapter 5.

The *Central Stairway* from the Hemicycle Terrace ascends to the Terrace of the Arches with half-columns, where there are nine arches on either side of the axis. P. McKendrick suggests that these may have been the stalls of the various Guilds: wine merchants, cooks, waggoners, weavers, garland makers, secondhand dealers, and money changers; who, as we know from inscriptions, made dedications to Fortune and had a financial interest in her Sanctuary. The even numbered arches are closed with a decorated wall, whilst the odd numbers are open and decorated with stuccoed walls and mosaic floors.

In the centre a second stairway rises to the Fourth Terrace, the *Cortina Terrace*; this was once a great square, nearly 150 m on each side, with an open colonnade to the south. On the east and west sides were porticos with three lines of columns. At the far side is a stairway ascending to a gallery upon which was the *Exedra*. Underneath the stair was a *crypto porticus*, separating the Cortina from the semicircular Terrace. Today this stair has been replaced by the double approach stair to the 17th-century Palazzo Barberini which has been adapted as the Museum. This occupies the site of the Semicircular Terrace, on which was built the Rotunda, the *Round Temple* with the cult of the Goddess. The draped Torso in blue Rhodian marble found in the vicinity, may possibly be of the Lady Fortune herself.

In appreciation of this great monument the author was reminded of the eternal sanctity that attaches to these cult sites. Once a place like Bethlehem, Jerusalem, Mecca, Paestum, Mount Ida acquires a sacred aura, it never loses it. Gods may change, new religious rites are performed in temples and churches built in or over their predecessors; protecting divinities are given new names but the site remains holy. So it was at Palestrina. The Temple of Fortune built by Sulla shows signs of being superimposed on a much earlier shrine, centred about the wishing well on the Hemicycle Terrace. But it should be emphasized that what is now visible is unquestionably a Roman masterpiece, incorporating much Hellenistic technique, especially in the use of ascending terraces drawing the eyes and thoughts of the faithful ever upwards to the culmination—the Round Temple of the Goddess.

After the wonders of the Sanctuary of Fortune, the quite interesting remains of Hadrian's villa at the foot of the hill are liable to pass unnoticed. They are just at the junction of the road from Valmontone with the Via Prenestina. A large vault and other remains with stucco decoration are still visible.

Cave. A pleasant and quiet place to have lunch after the visit to *Km 42* Praeneste, away from the tourist crowds, but with excellent food and even better wine made from grapes grown on the local hills. There are three restaurants close together in the village, all with good home cooking.

Turn left on the mountain road to Piglio (2 km) and the Altipiani *Km 60* di Arcinazzo (11 km); here turn left at the junction for Subiaco (17 km). There are the remains of a Roman villa, *Villa di Nerone*, on the right after 3 km from the junction, on the mountain plateau.

Fiuggi. A famous spa town, with curative springs. *Km 77*

Here Road 411 from the Via Valeria joins with the Via Prenestina *Km 88* which makes a sharp turn to the south.

Alatri. The Aletrium of the Hernici, a charming medieval town *Km 94* enclosed within the famous cyclopean walls. These are the most perfect example of pre-Roman walling in Italy. The citadel of the town, built of huge polygonal blocks (see Fig. 15), is also perfectly preserved. There is a small museum (2).

Frosinone (Roman Frusino), see p. 218. *Km 10*

VIA CASILINA, VIA TUSCOLANA, VIA LATINA

Judging from its name the Via Latina would appear to have been the oldest of all the Roman roads. The date of its construction is not known but it was probably early in the 4th century. Its route at any rate suggests a highway of great antiquity, as a means of communication from the thickly populated and prosperous northern Campania with the valley of the Liris, and the Etruscan territories to the north of Rome. The scenery is fine and constantly varying. The Via Latina like the Via Appia originally began from the Porta Capena, between the Colosseum and the Baths of Caracalla, and went to Frusino (Frosinone), Aquinum (Aquino), and Casinum

(Cassino), to join the Appia just north of Capua. A short branch ran as the Via Tusculana to Tusculum, to the east of the modern town of Frascati in the Alban Hills. Tusculum was a favourite holiday resort of the Roman patricians; the traditional 'dolce vita' still remains in Frascati and some of the best food and wine in all Italy is to be had in the delightful restaurants in the town. Today the Via Tuscolana (S.S.215) forks left from the Via Appia Nuova, just after the Porta San Giovanni; the Via Latina then forks right from the Via Tuscolana at the ring road (Raccordo Anulare).

To see the old Via Latina and its tombs go out on the Appia Nuova (S.S.7) leaving Rome at the Porta San Giovanni. The ancient Via Tusculana probably branched from the ancient Via Latina up to Tusculum. In a few kilometres the modern Via Tuscolana climbs up to Frascati while the Via Latina continues along the easier route through the Alban Hills to Grottaferrata, south of both Frascati and the ancient site of Tusculum. As the Via Tuscolana (S.S.215) leaves Rome after the Porta San Giovanni, the long lines of the arches of the aqueducts converging on the city are the feature of the landscape, but soon the green grass and vine-covered rolling hills of Latium, with occasional farmsteads and small shady plantations, give a vivid impression of the unchanging nature of this historic countryside (see Fig. 13). The lack of towns and villages on the plains speaks eloquently of troubled times in antiquity and the Middle Ages. All the ancient villages chose inaccessible hill-tops or a craggy bluff for their sites, a refuge to which the shepherds and cowherds could retreat with their animals when bandits and raiders crossed the tribal borders. After the First Samnite War, the Via Latina probably extended as far as the new colony of **Fregellae** (modern Ceprano), the foundation of which led to the Second Samnite War. All the country west of the river Liris, including Casinum, was Samnite territory at this time by treaty with Rome, and Fregellae was founded on the west bank of the Liris. The Samnites had their fortress at Teanum Sidicinum, where the valley opened onto the Ager Falernus of northern Campania. To counter this, the Romans founded a colony at Cales in 334 B.C. but they could only reach it by a roundabout route on the coast along the Via Appia and then inland from Sinuessa. It was possible to found Cales because the population of the new colony was Auruncan, whereas that of Teanum was Samnite, although their distance apart is only a few kilometres with a low ridge and small stream marking their frontier. The close proximity of Cales to Teanum shows very clearly the difficulties of communication when two hostile cities could exist within a few kilometres of each other. The colony at Fregellae not only controlled the Via Latina route, but also the pass over the Auruncan mountains served today by Road 82.

This was the situation in 328 B.C.; for the next five years or so, what fighting there was seems to have been along the middle Liris Valley; when the Third Samnite War began in 316 the Volsci also revolted. The Samnites attacked along the Liris valley then over the pass to modern Itri where, on the Lautulae Pass leading from Itri to Fondi, they inflicted a crushing defeat on the Romans whose general Aulius Cerretanus was killed. The Samnites then advanced as far north as Ardea, but the Romans had another experienced general in C. Sulpicius Longus, who attacked the Samnite lines of communication at Terracina. He won a decisive victory, and then proceeded to mete out such harsh punishment to the rebellious Aurunci that they ceased to exist as a nation. By 312 the danger was over and the Romans were masters of the situation on the middle Liris and in northern Campania. About this time the Via Appia was built from Rome to Capua along the coastal route and at the same time the Via Latina was also extended to Capua. The actual routes of the roads in northern Campania are a problem now being studied by the author.

The Historical Note will show that this area was a constant battlefield in the early expansion of Rome. It was a bitter struggle by the pastoral mountaineers to control the winter pastures on the plains, on the edge of which the lowland villages lay. This is one of the most interesting and at the same time scenic areas to visit and study. So much Roman and earlier material remains, the country is so beautiful and it is very easy to picture some of those events that made history 2,300 years ago. Very little exploration work has been done and much can be accomplished by walking over the ground identifying places and roads.

To see the main towns of the ancient Via Latina take the following route.

Leave Rome by the Porta Maggiore and take the Via Casilina (S.S.6).

Finocchio lies in a deep wooded valley. It was an important cross- *Km 18* roads, the left arm connecting with the Via Praenestina, and on the right one road goes into the Alban Hills and **Tusculum** (and today also to Monte Porzio and the autostrada). The ruins of **Tusculum** are at the top of the hill above the Villa Rufinella or Tuscolana, 5 km east of Frascati (from where the ruins are clearly signposted). On the path up the remains of the amphitheatre can be seen, then the so-called Villa of Cicero, the ruins of the forum on the left and of the theatre beyond. Traces of the citadel have survived on the summit, now marked by a cross. The view from here is magnificent.

30 San Cesareo. Just after the village the road forks, that on the left goes to Palestrina in 8 km. This, incidentally, is the best route by car from Rome to Palestrina.

38 **Labico** (Roman Labicum), the original destination of the Via Labicana.

41 **Valmontone** (Roman Vitellia). The town was an ancient foundation of which part of the walls remain.

48 **Colleferro.** Turn right to **Segni** (5 km) the ancient Signia founded by Tarquinius Priscus. The town has over 2 km of its ancient walls preserved, including the Porta Saracena. There are also a few traces of the Temple of Jupiter Urius, for which the town was noted in antiquity.

64 **Anagni** (Roman Anagnia); here in ancient times the road made a slight detour to reach the town, the chief town of the Hernici. There is a small museum (1) next door to the Duomo, which contains local material. Long sections of the Roman wall remain in the Via Piscina and in the Via Dante. Some 3 km south of the town is the *Circus Maritimus* where the Council of the Hernici used to meet. In the Second Samnite War the Romans won a battle here.

72 **Ferentino** (Roman Ferentinum) was a city of the Hernici, and was colonized by the Romans in the Second Punic War. It is situated on a hill that dominates the valley of the river Sacco. The acropolis has pre-Roman defence walls which were replaced by Sulla. In the Via Don Moresini was the market with a large hall and five shops covered with a vaulted roof. There was a triple wall to the town, dating from the 5th to the 6th centuries, with towers and gates added in the Middle Ages. The best preserved is the Porta Sanguinaria near the theatre (of Hadrianic date); nearby is the Porta Casamari, on the far side of which is sculptured in the rock the will of Aulus Quintilius, who, in the reign of Trajan, left his estate to the town. 2 km on the road to Frosinone on the left are the *Thermae Pompeianae*, where there was a spa in Roman times.

Frosinone (Roman Frusino) was also in a dominating position in *Km*
the valley of the Sacco. Frusino was a town of the Hernici and in
387 B.C., at the outbreak of the Second Samnite War, joined the
Samnites with Anagnia. Most of the old town is still buried under
the Piazzale Vittorio, where the public buildings are; only fragments
of the walls and traces of the amphitheatre have survived. Road 156
from the Latin towns of Antium (Anzio), Setia (Sezze) and
Privernum (Priverno), crosses the Via Latina at Frosinone and goes
into the mountains to the east as Road 214 to Isola di Liri and
Sora, then as Road 82 to Alba Fucens. Strabo says that nearby was
Torrica 'past which the River Trerus (Sacco) flows', and it is clear
from the historians that there were several towns of the Hernici in
the valley, such as Anagni, Alatri and Veroli, as well as others whose
identification has yet to be made.

Ceprano, possibly Fregellae already mentioned as the Roman *Km*
colony that was the *casus belli* of the Second Samnite War. In 125 B.C.
the city rose in revolt having expected a grant of Roman citizenship
and the Romans destroyed it. Also near here was **Interamna
Lirenas,** probably near the lake at the confluence of the Liris and *Km
the Sacco.

Arce. Turn left for the mountain road to **Arpino** (19 km), or take
the main road to Sora and turn right after 10 km on a less tortuous
road. Arpino occupies the site of Arpinum, the birthplace of Gaius
Marius and of Cicero. The hill-top town is surrounded by polygonal
walls of pre-Roman date, with one massive pre-Roman and one
Roman gate surviving.

Aquino (Roman Aquinum). After leaving Ceprano the route of the *Km
ancient Via Latina is doubtful. It may have gone slightly west
through Interamna, or slightly to the east to Murata as it does
today. With the disturbances caused by incessant warfare along this
border, anything was possible. Aquinum was probably a Volscian
town, but it is not mentioned until the Second Punic War. It
probably became Roman in 304 B.C. Aquinum was the birthplace
of Juvenal (*c.* A.D. 55); the ruins of the colony extend into the vine-
yards beyond the modern village. The Roman Porta San Lorenzo
still stands; beyond this are the ruins of an amphitheatre and a
basilica, while two churches, Santa Maria Maddalena and San
Pietro, incorporate the remains of temples of Diana and Ceres.
In the town the church of Santa Maria della Libera is on the
foundations of a Temple of Hercules.

140 Cassino (Roman Casinum). The whole region was much damaged in the last war. The archaeological zone is on the foothills and to the south-east of the town along the Via Casilina, as the Via Latina has become today. There is a 1st century amphitheatre of almost circular plan; the *Tomb of Ummidia Quadratilla* of cruciform plan, now a church; a semicircular *theatre* more than 50 m in diameter; several sections of the Roman road and of the Roman walls. The site was originally Volscian. Strabo says 'this too, is a noteworthy city, which is the last of the Latins, for what is called Teanum Sidicinum, which is situated next in order after Casinum, shows clearly from the title that it belongs to the Sidicini, and these people were Osci, a tribe of Campania that has disappeared.'

150 San Cataldo is about 5 km inside the boundary of Campania. At this point, the original Via Latina made a loop to reach Venafrum, but later it was continued to modern Vairano Scalo, where Road 85 was the ancient loop.

159 Vairano Scalo (Roman Rufrae?) which was a Samnite town, possibly of the Sidicini.

167 Teano (Roman Teanum Sidicinum) a Samnite town of the Sidicini as its name implies. According to Strabo 'it is the largest city on the Latin Way'. Throughout the Samnite Wars it was a fortress effectively controlling the Roman movements in northern Campania (see Map 2). A colony was established by the Romans at Auruncan Cales, just a stone's throw away over the ridge to counteract the Teanum threat. When Teanum became Roman, it was developed as the principal base for the Legion watching the frontier along the Mons Trebulanus and the valley of the river Volturnus leading into the heart of Samnium. There are considerable relics of the Roman occupation: the amphitheatre, the theatre and sections of the walls.

The Samnite and Sabellian tribes were a crude hardy folk, used to a life of toil in the open air, without any culture or desire to live in urban stability (see Plate 29). Strabo records that their incursion into Campania led to the barbarization of the area which was predominantly Greek. The pastoral way of life with no social and little political unity, was the factor which enabled a small but better equipped and organized minority of Etruscans to control the Campania, and eventually exercise a loose suzerainty over the indigenous tribes. This raises the question of whence the Etruscans came to Campania and by what route.

Many have supposed that, as they had command of the sea, the

Plate 29. Terracotta head of Samnite origin from Triflisco. The head was found in 1955 during dredging operations of the right bank of the river Volturno at Triflisco and is now in the museum at Santa Maria di Capua Vetere. It may be a divinity, and is certainly a unique example of this kind of Samnite art. It has been tentatively dated by M. Napoli to the late 5th or early 4th century B.C.

Etruscans would have come down the coast supported by their fleet; others have suggested that they came overland, following the route of the Via Latina. As in all similar cases there is support for both views. All these early migrations seem to have been peaceful penetrations into a new country, which suggests a loosely organized pastoral population who, provided they were not molested, would accept the strangers who perhaps offered exciting trade goods and who in any case came to cultivate the plains (see Fig. 13). In this way, the minority could easily establish themselves and rapidly become the ruling class. E. T. Salmon in his book *Samnium and the Samnites* suggests that one of the underlying causes of the Samnite wars was the conflict between the growing number of agricultural villages on the plains of Campania and the Samnite hill tribes, who found themselves gradually losing control of the traditional winter pastures on the coasts and the drove roads to them. The Etruscan hut-urns (see Plates 1 and 15 and Figs. 12a and b) give us some idea of the type of house that must once have dotted the coastal plains of Etruria. There is some evidence to suggest that the overland route would have been easier to an Etruscan force. The town of Sinuessa near Mondragone was a Greek trading station (formerly called

Plate 30. Cales: black terracotta oil-lamp from Cales. Diameter 9.2 cm. Now in Jatta Collection at Ruvo.

Sinope) founded in the 8th century, so it would hardly have been a friendly port to an Etruscan fleet.

E. T. Salmon also suggests that gladiatorial games probably had their origin amongst the Samnites. It is possible that in the first instance they formed part of the funeral rites and were not prolonged to the death. Later prisoners were used and the winner of the contest was promised that his life would be spared, so the games became public spectacles. In support of his theory Salmon recalls that the amphitheatres at Capua and Puteoli were the largest in Italy until the Colosseum was built in Rome some three centuries later.

Calvi Vecchia (Roman Cales). A town of the Aurunci that became a Roman colony in 334 B.C. It lies only about 7 km from Teanum Sidicinum, with just a low ridge of rough limestone and a small stream to keep two hostile cities apart, for Teanum was a Samnite dependency until the end of the Third Samnite War in 290 B.C. The colony was originally founded with 2,500 veteran legionaries, and rapidly became the most important military base in northern Campania. During the Second Punic War, it was the Roman base for operations against Hannibal, who was wintering in Capua. The advanced headquarters were at Casilinum (modern Capua) situated on the bank of the river Volturnus. Later Cales was the Roman capital of the whole of Campania for a while.

Cales owed its great prosperity to its potteries, which for four centuries produced some of the finest work in Italy (see Plate 30). The principal ware was a black-glazed type on a red clay base, with the surface either painted or with relief scenes from the Greek mythology. Beautiful examples are preserved in the Capua Museum. Industrial and domestic ceramics such as bricks, tiles, antefixes and 'loom weights' (see Fig. 16) were also produced. Figs. 1a and 1b illustrates some of the domestic bronze-work of the site.

The Cathedral is built upon the site of a former temple. The Custodian will show visitors over the vast area of the town, which

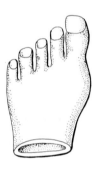

Fig. 16. Ancient loom weights from Liternum, Paestum, Cales and Sinuessa. Weights from left to right: 250, 375, 150 and 250 grammes. The first two are pink terracotta, the third red and the fourth yellow.

Fig. 17. Terracotta model of a gouty foot from Cales, used in magical cures.

occupied an isolated plateau formed by the river Rio dei Lanzi. Little exploratory work has so far been undertaken, but there are *thermae*, a theatre, three kilometres of tombs and numerous spoil heaps of the potteries, which all promise rich rewards when the excavation is finally undertaken.

One product of the Cales potteries throws light upon the medical beliefs of the period. Models of the diseased part of the body were made in light terracotta. The sufferer took the model to the Temple of the God of Healing, Apollo or Aesculapius, and threw it at the statue of the god; as it broke, so the disease would be cured (see Fig. 17).

Crossroads with the modern Via Appia. *Km*

Capua (Roman Casilinum). There are practically no Roman remains *Km* in the town. The Civic Museum contains a magnificent collection of Greek, Etruscan and Campanian pottery. In the basement there is a splendid collection of archaic Campanian/Greek statues made of *tufo*, of Hera as Goddess of Fertility holding babies in her arms—in some cases as many as eighteen.

This is the southern limit of this Guide. For details of the antiquities in the Naples area, see *Southern Italy: An Archaeological Guide*.

9 . VIA APPIA (S.S.7)

Between the Tiber and the Albani, Lepini and Ausoni mountains there is a wide coastal plain, with extensive waterlogged areas later known as the Pontine Marshes and now in greater part reclaimed. The Via Appia ran across the coastal plain to the sea at Terracina, then round the Gaeta headland into Campania (see Map 6). It was built in sections as the sphere of Roman domination extended southwards, and the need for a military line of communication with Campania became urgent. There are many problems about its original route that are still unsolved.

The Via Appia left Rome at the Porta Capena, and was constructed by the censor Appius Claudius Caecus in 312 B.C. to consolidate the subjugation of the Samnite territories to the south of Rome, and to provide a military communication with Campania. It ended originally at Capua, that is at Santa Maria di Capua Vetere; and was 211 km long. It was extended to Beneventum (Benevento), Venusia (Venosa) and Tarentum (Taranto) in the early 3rd century B.C. and finally to Brundisium (Brindisi) soon after 248 B.C. At first it had only a gravelled surface. In 298 B.C. a paved footway was laid as far as the Temple of Mars, about $1\frac{1}{2}$ km from the Porta Capena. In 295 B.C. the carriage-way was paved from the Temple of Mars to Bovillae, and in 191 the next few kilometres were also paved. It was not until the reigns of Nerva and Trajan, however, that the 30 km across the Pontine Marshes from the *Forum Appii* (see p. 228) 70 km south-east of Rome were paved, and the bridges over the streams and drains of the marshes repaired. A canal was dug alongside the road in an attempt to drain the marshes and to provide an alternative means of travel, by barge drawn by a mule at night across the flooded mosquito-ridden area. The section of the Via Appia that comes within the scope of this Guide is that from Rome to Capua. Visitors proceeding beyond Capua should provide themselves with Margaret Guido's companion Guide to Southern Italy.

Though the original purpose of the road was purely military, the Via Appia quickly became the main communicating link between the capital and Campania, Apulia and Magna Graecia.

Modern Capua was Roman Casilinum on the bank of the river Volturnus some 5 km to the north of the ancient Capua (now Santa Maria di Capua Vetere). Here also was the end of the Via Latina (see Chapter 8), which followed the valley of the rivers Sacco and Liri to the east of the ranges of the Lepini, Ausoni and Aurunci mountains. By contrast, the Via Appia followed the coast, except in the marshy coastal plains to the south of Terracina, where it followed the foot of the hills round the mountains to join with Road 82, the great Samnite highway from Alba Fucens, at Formia on the coast. From Formia it probably followed the modern road to Minturnae at the mouth of the river Liris, or Garigliano as it is now called, where there was another sacred locality, seemingly in the river itself. Here the road crossed the river by a bridge and ran inland to avoid the marshes and to reach Sessa Aurunca. From there it went to Casilinum and Capua, but the route is very uncertain.

19 The first 19 km of the Via Appia were described in Chapter 2. The new Appian Way has been made alongside the Via Appia Antica as far as Frattocchie, where they join. Here Road 207 forks right from the Appia, to Aprilia and Anzio. Various turnings off this road lead to the coast and the following places of great interest:

(1) *Lavinium* is reached by turning off right after 5 km to Pomezia, straight on for 2 km and right again, when the ruins are on the right. Grave robbing is not a modern invention, for it is on record that Hadrian found three pounds of gold and two hundred and six pounds of silver in a ruined temple at Lavinium. In the foundation legend of Rome, according to Virgil, Aeneas,

> '. . . Troiae qui primus ab oris
> Italiam fato profugus Lavinaque venit
> litora,'
>
> (*Aeneid* 1.1–3)

first founded Lavinium; his son Ascanius ruled at Lavinium for 30 years and then transferred his rule to the city of Alba Longa (Aeneid I, 1–3 and 267–71). In 1959 a line of thirteen altars was found here, dating from the 6th century. They are thought to be the altars of the Penates and perhaps also of Vesta. As soon as the great officials of Rome, consuls, praetors and dictators, were elected they went to Lavinium to sacrifice to these gods. In pre-Roman days there was a shrine to *Frutis* (Aphrodite). A dedication to Castor and Pollux in archaic Latin on a bronze plate was found near the altars. The lettering is the same as that on the Lapis Niger (Tomb of Romulus) in the Forum at Rome. There was also a bronze dedication inscription to *Ceres*. So all in all, it is difficult to say to which god or gods, the Sanctuary is sacred. The medieval castle occupies the site of the ancient town.

(2) To visit *Pliny the Younger's Villa*, carry on from Pomezia to the sea (7 km) and turn right along the coast road for 12 km. Turn right here for the ruins of *Laurentum* (500 m), then left at the ruins along the Viale di Plinio for 500 m to the Villa (on the left of the road).

(3) **Anzio** (Roman Antium) the destination of Road 207. Antium was one of the chief towns of the Volsci; its captains were notorious pirates. Coriolanus fled to Antium when he was banished from Rome in 491 B.C. When the town was subdued in 338 B.C. the ships were seized and the prows or beaks sent to adorn the Rostra, or Speakers' Platform in the Roman Forum. It later became a favourite summer resort for Roman patricians. The Roman town was to the north-east of present-day Anzio on the higher ground. Near the promontory of Arco Muto are the ruins of *Nero's Villa*, built of *opus reticulatum* (see Fig. 15); the *Apollo Belvedere* (now in the Vatican), the *Borghese Gladiator* (now in the Louvre) and the *Maiden of Anzio* (National Museum at Rome) were all found here. The town today is a pleasant fishing village; the sea food in the fish restaurants is superb.

RETURN TO THE VIA APPIA (S.S.7)

Albano Laziale, on the slopes of the Alban Hills. The town is of *Km* very ancient foundation, but little remains of its Etruscan or Latin origin. It is, however, rich in Roman material. The town was a part of the *Castra Albana*, a series of military stations constructed in the 2nd and 3rd centuries A.D. by Septimius Severus. The Castra occupied the whole of the site occupied by the present town. Many of the splendid ruins were first brought to light by allied bombing in 1944. *Porta Praetoria* was the principal entry; it is 30 m wide and had three openings flanked by two towers. The Church of Santa

Maria della Rotonda was formerly the Nymphaeum of the Villa of Domitian. It is circular in plan with three side chapels. The *Cisternone* (at 86 Via Aurelio Saffi) is a large underground cistern (capacity 10,000 cubic metres), constructed by Septimius Severus for the supply to the troops. It is entirely constructed in the rock; the roof is supported on five lines of pilasters. The Amphitheatre is just outside and above the town on the road leading to the lake. It was built in the 3rd century A.D. and has a seating capacity of 15,000. There is a small Etruscan sepulchre known as the Tomb of the Horatii and Curiatii, or Tomb of Aruns (son of Tarquinius Superbus), but is in fact, of late Republican date. There are some remains of the Temple of Aesculapius; the cathedral stands on a temple dating to the time of Constantine; the church of San Pietro stands on the *thermae* of the Roman camp.

m 26   **Ariccia** is in a beautiful woodland setting. The modern town is reached by the Via Appia crossing a viaduct over 300 m long and over 59 m high, with three arches. In this valley (an old volcanic crater) was the old town of Aricia of the Latins. In the grounds of the Palazzo Chigi is a section of the *Roman Way* which led up to the top of Monte Cavo. Aricia was the scene of the battle *c.* 524 B.C. between the Cumaeans and Etruscans in which the Etruscans were routed, and after a Latin rising were expelled from Rome. Aricia was later captured by C. Maenius in 338 B.C. and soon after received the Roman franchise. It was famous in antiquity for its wines and vegetables and above all for the cult of Diana. The rites demanded human sacrifice, and the High Priest obtained his office by killing his predecessor. Consequently he always went armed with a sword to defend himself. The holder of the office was usually a slave. The Sanctuary of Diana was on the shore of Lake Nemi, where the goddess was worshipped with a local god, *Virbius*, god of the woods.

m 29   **Genzano di Roma.** This is the site of the Temple of Diana and there an ancient Festival called *Feriae Latinae* was held on the top of the hill in the *Temple of Jupiter Latiaris*, to which all the Latin states sent representatives; a white heifer was sacrificed and feasting followed. During the Festival peace reigned throughout Latium. Today another Festival is held, the Infiorata: on the Sunday after Corpus Domini the streets of Genzano are carpeted with flowers, and the Procession of the Infiorata is held. At nearby Nemi there is a museum in which there are models of two ceremonial barges found in the Lake; the ships themselves were built by Caligula to convey visitors across the lake for the Festival of Diana and were destroyed by the Germans in 1944. Near the lake in the *Giardino* are the ruins of the Temple of Diana Nemorensis, excavated in 1885 and 1924–8.

Velletri (Roman Velitrae) a town of very ancient lineage, but little   *Km 40* or nothing remains to tell of its past grandeur; the Cathedral stands on the remains of a Roman basilica. A country road descends on the right leaving the town, to the village of Lanuvio (Roman Lanuvium). The village is built on a bluff at the base of the Alban Hills; part of the Roman walls and the podium of the Temple of Hercules remain in the town. On the outskirts, on Colle di San Lorenzo, are the ruins of the *Temple of Juno Sospita* for which the town was famous.

From Velletri the Via Appia descends to the Pontine plain, a very marshy district which defied all efforts at reclamation until recent times.

Cisterna Latina, where a road forks right for Latina. These are   *Km 55* modern towns built under Mussolini. Shortly after leaving the town, the Via Appia runs over the longest straight stretch of road in all Italy—40 km known as *la fettuccia*—the ribbon. Turn left in Cisterna for Cori (10 km)—Roman Cora; the town was traditionally founded by Dardanus of Troy or Coras, brother of Tibertus. At the top of the Via Pelasga is the so-called Temple of Hercules—probably a temple of Jupiter, Juno and Minerva. Remains of a cistern, a *piscina* and Roman walls survive near the Piazza San Salvatore, where there are two columns of a temple of Castor and Pollux. Sulla is said to have built the Ponte della Catena outside the town. Just before reaching Tor Tre Ponti there is a cross roads. On the   *Km 60* left is a good country road that goes towards the Lepini mountains and the imposing ruins of the Volscian city of **Norba** (now Norma), surrounded by cyclopean walls. Near here was *Forum Appii*, the crossroads where the brethren met St Paul (Acts XXVIII. 15). Travellers from Rome could change here to a canal boat on the journey to Anxur (Terracina).

Borgo Faiti. Turn left on Road 156 to Sezze (Roman Setia) and   *Km 74* Priverno, thence to Frosinone. There are cyclopean walls at Sezze.

From the history of the Samnite Wars it is clear that there must have been good communications along the coast from Ardea to Terracina and Formia, for at the opening of the Second Samnite War the Samnite forces succeeded in penetrating to Ardea along

Plate 31. The portico in the Temple of Jupiter Anxur at Terracina; late 2nd–early 1st century B.C.

this route. Augustus was very fond of the wines from Setia which he preferred to the Falernian.

Terracina (Volscian Anxur, Roman Tarracina) lies right on the coast at the foot of a high hill upon which is the *Temple of Jupiter Anxur*. There are many interesting remains but so far little excavation has been done. The Cathedral is built upon the *Temple of Roma and Augustus*, a part of which can be seen at the side; considerable remains of the pavement have survived. Near the Piazza del Municipio bombing revealed a number of Roman wall footings.

n 103

At the end of the Salita dell'Annunciata there is a Triumphal Arch
with one opening. Also near the Cathedral is the *Templum
Capitolinum*, probably of the 1st century A.D., with three cells and
walls faced with *opus reticulatum*. 3 km away by a good road on the
top of the cliff above the city is the acropolis surrounded by massive
walls built by Sulla. Within these is the *Temple of Jupiter Anxur*
erected in the 1st century. All that remains is the podium and the
base of the *platea* formed of impressive arches making a *cryptoporticus*, some 60 m long (see Plate 31). The view from the temple
is magnificent over the Pontine marshes with the massif of Monte
Circeo in the distance. (See the Palaeolithic section in Chapter 1.)
Just to the south of the town is the Pisco Montano, a fine example
of Roman road engineering, where a vertical clean-cut section of
cliff 34 m high is exposed; here a rocky promontory was removed
to permit the construction of the Via Appia at its base. There is
also a Triumphal Arch at the base, surmounted by medieval
additions. This work was carried out by Trajan when he repaved the
Via Appia and extended it to Brundisium by a shortened route (the
Via Traiana).

DIVERSION TO GAETA

About 5 km to the south of Terracina the road forks, and the Via
Appia on the left continues to Fondi. (Watch the signposting as
the road to Fondi actually leaves the Via Appia on the right and
passes under a tunnel.) The road to Gaeta was the Via Flacca
(Road 213), traces of which can still be seen cut into the rock face
near the modern coast road. At km 125 is **Sperlonga,** which is
recorded by Tacitus as a favourite resort of the Emperor Tiberius.
Just beyond the town on the right is the *Grotta di Tiberio,* the famous
cave in which Tiberius installed a wonderful collection of statuary
now in the splendid little museum above the cave. One day the roof
of the cave fell in and the Emperor was only saved by the bravery of
Sejanus, the Captain of the Guard. Excavation of the cave by G.
Jacopini has enabled partial reconstruction. In the centre of the pool
in the cave is a pedestal, on which the excavator supposes that the
original Greek statuary group of Laocoon being devoured by a
serpent stood; all others, including the statue in the Vatican, were
copies.

The cave was also a prehistoric shelter (see Chapter 1). Between Sperlonga and Gaeta, there are two other caves producing evidence of Stone Age occupation. About 3 km on towards Gaeta, a path is signposted on the right leading down to the *Grotta dei Moscerini*, a few metres above the modern beach. Again at another 3 km on the left is the *Grotta di Sant'Agostino* (see Chapter 1 for further details). At km 135 is **Gaeta**, standing on a high promontory overlooking the sea. It is said to have been named after the nurse of Aeneas. On the *Monte d'Orlando* is the splendid tomb of Lucius Munatius Plancus, the friend of Julius Caesar, Cicero and Horace and the founder of Lyons. It is a circular tower surrounded by a corridor.

The Via Appia may be joined by taking Road 7 *bis* to Formia, about 8 km away.

Return to Terracina and take the left fork, signposted to Napoli and Fondi and follow the Via Appia across the marshy plain skirting the base of the hills, to reach Fondi (17 km).

n 121   **Fondi** (Roman Fundi). This is a fascinating little town, as yet unspoiled by modern buildings. The area of the built-up section within the space of the ancient walls retains the Roman grid pattern. The Via Appia goes into the town straight to the Piazza that was the Roman forum. To reach it take the left road at the petrol filling station as you enter the town. At this point also there is an excellent little restaurant, the Albergo Appia. At the Piazza turn sharp right and in about 100 m on the right is a magnificent length of *polygonal wall* at least 100 m long and 10 m high, perfectly preserved and forming the wall of a building (see Plate 32). Continuing along the road from the Forum for about 200 m the Cathedral is on the left. The podium is Roman with the ancient steps in *selce* blocks still in place and used. There are many Roman fragments in the Cathedral suggesting that this was the site of the Capitolium. At the end of the street, on both sides of which are the narrow *cardines* of the Roman plan, is a fine medieval castle. Fondi repays a visit; it is the Fundi of Horace's Satires, one of the towns producing the famed Caecuban wine.

n 135   **Itri.** Leaving Fondi the Via Appia soon begins to climb into the Auruncan mountains by the ancient Pass of Lautulae. The route through the valley to the pass is most interesting as the modern Via Appia is on one side of the torrent with its hairpin bends to reduce gradient, whilst on the other side is the ancient road, now a country track, running in a perfect straight line up the valley. The

Plate 32. Fondi: a splendid example of polygonal walling.

high-power electric pylons are erected all along it, adopting its direct route to the summit of the pass. Here in 315 B.C. at the outbreak of the Second Samnite War the Roman army was defeated. Just before entering Itri there is a section of the paved Appian Way still to be seen and in use. At Itri the Via Appia joins with Road 82 which has been mentioned many times as the highway from Alba Fucens to the west coast. Along the route through the mountains are little groups of cottages inhabited by shepherds just as they were in antiquity. The inhabitants of these mountains were the Ausoni and the Aurunci who rebelled against Rome under pressure from the Samnites in 315 B.C. But after the Romans were victorious they meted such punishment to the rebels that 'they ceased to be a nation' according to Strabo. This pass and the narrow gap between the hills at Teanum Sidicinum may be considered the Gateways to Campania, and the Romans took care to secure them for the future.

m 143 **Formia** (Roman Formiae or Hormiae, probably from the Greek name for an anchorage). In Republican days Formia was one of the principal resorts of the Roman patricians and many well-known names are identified with remains of villas there. One of these was Cicero, who perhaps is buried there. Certainly he was killed at the town in 43 B.C.

There are many well-preserved remains in the town, notably in the Piazza della Vittoria and the Villa Comunale, both of which stand on Roman constructions. Along the beach are the ruins of swimming pools and beach houses. Further down the coast in the Bay of Naples was Baiae, where there is nothing left of the Roman beach; therefore this area at Formia is of great value in reconstructing the holiday scene. In the Villa Rubino there are the remains of a villa which local opinion attributes to Cicero. About 2 km on the Via Appia towards Rome there is a fine mausoleum comprising a conical superstructure on a square base, which is said to be Cicero's tomb (although it may be asked whether he would have had a tomb, as a proscribed and executed criminal). Formia must have been the principal market for the wines of the Caecuban plain, the *Ager Caecubus*, which extends from Formia to Sinuessa on the coast, and as far inland as the hills.

Formia during the First Samnite War seems to have had the status of *civitas sine suffragio* (probably Fundi was also in this category), which made it a Roman community whilst still retaining some municipal self-government. In the Second Samnite War the Samnites tried hard to get these towns to revolt, but without success, so they were overrun when the thrust to Ardea took place. Then the Samnites were driven back and defeated near Terracina. During the next ten years Rome greatly increased her power in this region. By 316 B.C. even Teanum had come to an understanding. In the Third Samnite War, the Samnites plundered all the *Ager Falernus* and the Auruncan territory as far as Formia, as the colonies at Sinuessa and Minturnae were too weak to offer any resistance. Our sources tell us that the invaders were driven back by Appius Claudius Caecus, the builder of the Appian Way. Finally Formia and Fundi were granted full Roman citizenship in 188 B.C.

m 153 **Scauri.** Here was another sea resort for the Roman patricians. Today the ruins of the villa of M. Aemilius Scaurus, consul in 115 B.C., can be seen.

m 157 **Minturnae** at the mouth of the river Liris (modern Garigliano).

Strabo says 'the river Liris formerly called Clanis, empties into a sacred precinct that is much revered by the people of Minturnae'. A few years ago a large number of coins were found by divers in the river (the coins are now in the American Academy in Rome). It is possible that these were coins offered by the pilgrims. This ritual of offering coins was widespread in antiquity. At Minturnae there is a magnificent second century aqueduct bringing water from the hills to the town (see Plate 33). Excavations have been in progress on and off for several years, but I am afraid conservation is at a minimum and much of the fine mosaic flooring found in the excavations has been lost due to neglect. Amongst their most important results was the discovery of numerous inscriptions of the religious guild of the freedmen and slaves, showing that in the last century of the Roman Republic, at Minturnae at least, there was already a

Plate 33. Minturnae: the Augustan aqueduct.

considerable industrial slave population. There is a theatre of the
2nd or 3rd century A.D. which has been restored for performances.
The town lies only about 2 m under the surface of the fields and
about 4 hectares have been cleared. Nothing has been published,
but it was clearly a town of Auruncan origin, with a temple whose
columns were made from the *tufo* from Roccamonfina, which rings
with a musical note when struck. There are many examples of the
use of this *tufo*—for example, at Cumae the columns of the portico
round the Forum, whose capital was carved with representations of
Sabellian warriors. So far about 500 m of the old Via Appia, which
passed through the town on the east side of the Forum, have been
excavated. There are some fine arches of the *thermae* still standing.
Along the Via Appia was a colonnaded arcade. The bridge over the
river Liris no longer exists. Minturnae stands in the heart of the
Caecuban plain, of which Strabo says 'although it is marshy, it
supports the vine that produced the best of wines, I mean the tree
vine'. This vine is still cultivated there and can be seen twining up
the trunks of the poplars with which it tends to cohabit.

The problems of ancient road communications both here and in
the *Ager Falernus* are most interesting, as they reflect the steady
development of the region. The difficulties of identification are
increased by the existence of the wedge of Samnite territory at
Teano until the 3rd century, which effectively separated the Roman
colonies and allies along the Via Latina from the Campania and the
Auruncan allies. The author is at present engaged on this problem.
The whole area seems to have been at all times, from the very
ancient days, mainly in the hands of very wealthy aristocrats,
possibly also absentee landlords. Pottery in the Capua museum
testifies to the presence of Greek traders in the 8th or beginning of
the 7th century B.C., by which time the Etruscans had established
many settlements. Strabo mentions quite a number of Italic tribes
living in the region, Sidicini (at Teano), Caleni (at Cales), Aurunci
(at Sessa), also Opici, Ausones, Osci, and Samniti. These were
subdued by the Etruscans, probably by peaceful infiltration, who
took over their cities and became the local aristocracy. From the
fertile plains came wine and wheat, spelt, rice, millet and all kinds
of vegetables. Horses bred and raised here were also famous in
antiquity. Some authorities think that the aristocratic cavalry from
here serving in the Roman armies, was the origin of the Equestrian
Order in the Roman social system. The area became prominent in

the Second Punic Wars, when Hannibal wintered his army at Capua (Santa Maria Capua Vetere) in 216 B.C. Perhaps the luxury and life of debauchery led by the troops was one reason why Hannibal never again won a battle against the Roman armies!

From Minturnae, after crossing the river Liris, the Via Appia again turns towards the hills, possibly to avoid marshes and mosquitoes. Horace writes of the Pons Campanus in an amusing story of a trip from Rome to Brindisi in thirteen stages. (Sat.1.5.) He says 'We stopped overnight in the city of the Mamurras (Formia), where Murena gave us lodging and Capito dinner. Next day at Sinuessa we met Plotius, Varius and Vergil. No better men than these inhabit the earth, and I am very greatly attached to them. What embraces, what effusions of joy there were—nothing, in my opinion, can equal a true friend. The little inn at the *Pons Campanus* gave us lodgings, and the locals provided wood and salt.'

Strabo tells us 'the only cities on the coast that the Via Appia touches are Terracina, Formia and Sinuessa'. This seems to make it clear that in the late 1st century B.C. the modern route of the Via Appia over the saddle between Monte Massico and Monte Lupara was not in general use. As in the case of the stretch from Terracina to Fundi, it followed the contour of the hills, on which the great villa farms stood, to the coast at Sinuessa, where it again turned inland, close along the hill-side.

From Minturnae the Via Appia ran along the Rio Travata to reach   *Km 1* this milestone, where there was a 'T' when the road was first built. The left road ran down to the stream, which it crossed by a long bridge, the fine *Pons Auruncus* (today the *Ponte degli Aurunci*), 500 m downstream from the modern road bridge (see Plate 34).

Sessa Aurunca (Roman Suessa) capital of the Aurunci and a town   *Km 1* of very ancient foundation, standing on a bluff overlooking the plain. The walls of the acropolis are probably Auruncan at the base, with Roman and medieval supercourses. In the town are numerous Roman remains built into the houses. No archaeological research has been done in this field. Suessa was an important place in Republican days, as there are the remains of an amphitheatre in a field below the acropolis along the approach road. Traces of the Baths can also be seen. A branch of the Via Appia serving the town continued to Teano as a paved road, and there joined the Via Latina which continued to Capua and Santa Maria Capua Vetere. The question of when this road was built is still under investigation, as

Plate 34. The Pons Auruncus at Sessa Aurunca on the Appian Way.

until 290 B.C. Teanum Sidicinum was Samnite, whilst Suessa was friendly towards Rome. There is a road from Teano to **Carinola** (Roman Forum Propilii) which was the chief town of the Ager Falernus. Carinola was also reached by the road from Sinuessa.

161 At this milestone also, the right road turns west towards the hill passing the modern village of Carano to reach **Piedimonte Massicano,** where there are considerable Roman remains including many fragments of marble columns, indicating some large buildings. It was probably a market town for the region. The Via Domitiana is about 10 km from here. It was built by the Emperor Domitian in A.D. 95 as a more direct route to Baiae and Neapolis. The new road was built from Minturnae along the coast to Sinuessa, following from there a previous road to **Castel Volturno** built about 212 B.C., when the Roman fortress (Roman Castrum Volturnum) was established as part of a ring of defences against Hannibal, who was about

Plate 35. The Via Appia at Castel Starza in the Ager Falernus.

to make Capua his main headquarters, and where he wintered in 216 B.C. The castle, which is medieval, stands on the bank of the river Volturno, at the site of the Roman bridge over the river. The walls of the fortress are still traceable and the grid plan of the ancient town with its narrow streets at right-angles to the castle walls is still there. A curious little church with the altar at the west end lies within the grid and seems to be a survival of the Roman temple of the fortress. As would be expected, the fields of the colonists were on the north bank of the river, as the south bank towards Capua was enemy territory. The Roman centuriation all along the Via Domitiana and parallel to it, extends for nearly

4 km to the north, with a width of almost 5 km. There are no fields on the south bank, nor was there any road connection with Capua (as there is today) until about 200 B.C. when the Punic War had ended. Here is the southern limit of this Guide.

The problems of the roads in the Ager Falernus discussed above are now being studied by the author. Near the Via Domitiana at km 13 is a warm water sulphur spring, that may be the one cited by Strabo as being able to cure 'barrenness in women and insanity in men'.

Livy refers to a battle fought near here, which was the decisive victory of the Romans in the Latin War. The site was 'at the foot of a mountain, not far from Capua'. Livy also says it was very close to Veseris, but we do not know for certain if Veseris was a mountain, a town, a river, or what. M. W. Frederiksen suggests it was probably the town of Vescia, the ruins of whose polygonal walls are on the top of Monte Massico, reached by a path from Falciano.

So, on these questioning notes, it is time to close the discussion of the routing of the roads round the Ager Falernus. When it is known where the roads went the reward will be more villa farms and Roman centuriated fields and a better picture of country life in antiquity in this fascinating land.

GLOSSARY

Acropolis	Usually a hill upon which the temples of a city were built. It was fortified as a refuge.
Ager	Literally a field, but also farming area, or grazing land, or simply 'territory'.
Ambarvalia	A religious procession around the fields to ensure fertility.
Ara Pacis	The Altar of Peace erected by Augustus in Rome to mark the end of the wars following the death of Julius Caesar.
Atrium	A room in a house provided with a central opening in the roof which sloped inwards to permit collection of the rainwater which was stored in a tank for use.
Caldarium	The hot room of the *thermae*.
Capitolium	The temple in the *forum* in Roman towns with the statues of Jupiter, Juno and Minerva.
Cardines	The north/south streets of the Etrusco-Roman town plan.
Cella	The place in the temple occupied by the statue of the god.
Centuriation	The Roman survey of the fields for the colonies. The area was divided into rectangles each containing 100 jugera. The east point was their reference, not the north as used today.
Cippus Perusinus	A tablet containing 46 lines of Etruscan script, believed to be a transfer of property.
Circus	The arena where horse and chariot races were held.
Civitas Foederata	An independent ally of Rome.
Civitas sine suffragio	A community of Roman citizens with all rights except the Roman vote, but self-administered.

Colonia	Foundations of agricultural communities usually of veteran soldiers, but also of ordinary citizens, planted at strategic points. The colonists inter-married with the natives and thus formed a strong Roman base in conquered territory.
Corn dolly	A plaited doll made from ears of corn, and placed at the ends of the lines of stooks in the fields to protect the corn during drying from damage by earth spirits.
Corvus	The boarding-brow of a ship, hinged to drop on the deck of an enemy ship and provided with a spike to dig into the deck and lock the ships together whilst boarders passed along it.
Cryptoporticus	An underground arched passage.
Curia	The meeting place of the Senate in Rome, and town councils elsewhere.
Decumanus	The east/west streets of the Roman town plan.
Exedra	A hall or arcade with recesses and seats.
Fasces	The bundle of rods and an axe carried before the consuls.
Forum	The main square of the town, market place and centre of communal activity.
Frigidarium	The cold room of the *thermae*.
Harpax	The secret weapon of Agrippa, a harpoon that could be catapulted into an enemy ship which was then hauled alongside by means of the attached cable, so that boarders could get to work.
Inhumation	Burial of the dead in the ground.
Jugerum	Roman measure of land equivalent to five-eighths of an acre.
Latium Adjectum	The enlargement of the Roman territory by the inclusion of Latium.
Libertus	A freed slave.
Miliarium Aureum	The point in Rome from which all road distances were measured, 'The Golden Milestone'.
Municipium	A self-administering Roman city with full Roman franchise.
Obsidian	Volcanic glass found only at certain places in the Mediterranean area, widely traded in prehistoric times.

Opus incertum	The ordinary rough masonry walling (see Fig. 15).
Opus reticulatum	The diamond shaped masonry in walls. It was in use from the 1st century B.C. to the end of the 1st century A.D. (see Fig. 15).
Peristyle	Row of columns surrounding temple or court.
Piscina	A swimming-pool or a fishpond.
Porta	A gate or door.
Porticus	A cloister.
Portus	A seaport.
Pronaos	Space in front of body of temple, enclosed by portico and projecting side walls.
Quinquereme	A ship with one bank of oars and five men to each oar.
Rostra	The orators' podium in Rome decorated with the beaks (rostra) of enemy ships captured in battle.
Selce	The dictionary gives 'flint' as the translation of this word, but it has come to mean the Roman road paving stone of lava, sandstone, flint or other hard stone.
Situla	A pottery or bronze bucket or cauldron, often lavishly decorated.
Sortes	The method of land distribution in the colonies by lot.
Tabularium	The archive in Rome where some state documents were preserved.
Tepidarium	The tepid room in the *thermae*.
Thermae	The public baths.
Tinia	The chief Etruscan god.
Triclinium	The dining-room of the Roman house.
Trireme	A ship, with three banks of oars with one man to each oar.
Tufelli	Rectangular building blocks cut from *tufo*, usually about the size of a modern brick (see Fig. 15).
Tufo	A volcanic rock, both solid and in sandy form. It has the property of hardening on exposure to the air, hence its great value as a building stone. Roman cement was also made from it.
Tumulus	A mound built over a grave.
Turan	The Etruscan Venus.
Uni	The Etruscan goddess, the equivalent of Juno.

Vasa Arretina	A special type of pottery made at Arretium.
Ver Sacrum	A sacred year when all humans and animals born during the year were forced to emigrate on reaching maturity. It seems to have been a Samnite or Italiote custom.
Zilath	The Etruscan equivalent of the Roman consul, or chief magistrate.

ADDRESSES OF THE SUPERINTENDENTS OF ANTIQUITIES (SOPRINTENDENTI ALLE ANTICHITÀ) IN CENTRAL ITALY

Soprintendente alle Antichità dell'Etruria
  Via della Pergola 65, FLORENCE
Soprintendente alle Antichità delle Marche
  Museo Archeologico Nazionale delle Marche, ANCONA
Soprintendente alle Antichità dell'Umbria
  Museo Archeologico Nazionale, PERUGIA
Soprintendente alle Antichità di Roma
  Foro Romano, ROME
Soprintendente alle Antichità del Lazio
  Piazza della Finanze 1, ROME
Soprintendente alle Antichità dell'Etruria Meridionale
  Museo della Villa Giulia, ROME
Soprintendente alle Antichità di Ostia
  Scavi di Ostia, OSTIA ANTICA
Soprintendente alle Antichità dell'Abruzzo e del Molise
  Museo Archeologico Nazionale, CHIETI
Soprintendente alle Antichità della Provincia di Napoli e di Caserta
  Museo Archeologico Nazionale, NAPLES

Italy, outside the big towns, is still a country of *contadini* or peasant farmers. This is the secret behind the welcome offered by the small inns along the roadside, deep in the mountain valleys or in the hill-top villages. The cooking is the pride of the housewife, and the *padrone* grows his own vegetables under the terraced vines. Each region has its special dish, *fettucini alla Bolognese, ricotta Romana, fritto misto, tartufi al burro*. I suggest you wait until you get to Italy to find out what these delicacies are, and what they can do to complete a perfect day and to stimulate discussion on your discoveries at the local sites. *Bistecche* and *costate all'osso* are slices of beef which are fried, grilled, fried with tomato sauce, or with piquant sauce, cooked in wine or made into cutlets. Omelettes are plain, or filled with vege-tables, cheese or jam. Vegetables . . . and what vegetables, new potatoes all the year round; peas, beans, peppers, asparagus, fennel and egg plant in season, fried or served as a dish by themselves. Cheeses with strange appetising names: Cacciotta, Bel Paese, Gorgonzola, Pecorino (made with sheep's milk), to eat with salads of *ruta*, lettuce, radishes or spring onions.

But the traditional dish, especially on the coast, is not meat but fish. The Romans in particular were especially fond of fish. The monumental repast that must have graced the tables of the Caesars is *zuppa di pesce*, in which three kinds of Mediterranean fish and a small squid are cooked in a rich sauce, baked in the oven and served in the dish in which they are cooked. Every Italian cook prides himself on his version of this masterpiece. There are also red mullet, scampi and octopus to mention only a few others. In every case, be sure and ask for the local speciality and the local wine. Any 'foreign' product will be expensive and probably not nearly so good as the fresh local produce. Warmed up left-overs are unknown, all dishes are indi-vidually cooked for each customer. This makes the time for the meal a rather long affair, but it affords a good opportunity to sample the local wines and discuss the day's results. Take the advice of the *padrone* on the wine, some years are better than others for the white or for the red. Wines grown on volcanic soils are the best; some, like Chianti, Orvieto and Falernian, have been famous since Roman days.

The categories of the restaurants follow an established scheme: *ristorante, trattoria, osteria*. In the restaurant prices are naturally higher than in the humble local *osteria*, but sometimes the cooking is better in the small inn as it is real 'home cooking' and not mass production. Prices also vary but a good meal can still be obtained in the smaller establishments for about a thousand lire a head.

Before beginning to eat or when greeting friends sitting at another table, it is correct and appropriate to say 'Buon appetito'. It is likely some diners will say 'Favorite' which is a formal invitation to share their meal, but the reply is still 'Buon appetito' and *not* acceptance of the invitation. These old-world courtesies are much respected in Italy and visitors who enquire after the family health, admire the latest baby, comment on the daughter's beauty and on father's elegant new suit, will never fail in popularity.

BIBLIOGRAPHY

A short serviceable list of works relevant to Central Italy.

Alföldi, A., *Early Rome and the Latins*, Ann Arbor, 1963.
Ashby, T., *The Roman Campagna in Classical Times*, 2nd edn., London, 1970.
Beloch, K. J., *Campanien*, 2nd edn., Breslau, 1890.
Cambridge Ancient History, Cambridge, 1923–47.
Cary, M., *History of Rome down to the Reign of Constantine*, 2nd edn., London, 1954.
Cicero, see Grant, 1969.
Conway, R. S., *The Italic Dialects*, Cambridge, 1897.
Conway, R. S., *Ancient Italy and Modern Religion*, Cambridge, 1933.
Cook, A. B., *Zeus: A Study in Ancient Religion*, 3 vols., Cambridge, 1914–40.
Frederiksen, M. W., 'Republican Capua: A Social and Economic Study', *Papers of the British School at Rome*, XIV, 1959, pp. 80–130.
Grant, M., *The World of Rome*, London, 1960.
Grant, M., *Roman History from Coins*, Cambridge, 1968.
Grant, M., *Selected Political Speeches of Cicero*, transl., with an introduction, London, 1969. (Penguin Classics Series.)
Grant, M., *The Annals of Imperial Rome, by Tacitus*, transl., with an introduction, London, 1971. (Penguin Classics Series.)
Jones, H. L., *The 'Geography' of Strabo*, text and English translation, London, 1917. (Loeb Classical Library.)
Livy, see de Sélincourt, 1965.
MacKay, A., *Naples and Campania*, The Vergilian Society of America, 1962.
MacKendrick, P. L., *The Mute Stones Speak*, London, 1962.
Meiggs, R., *Roman Ostia*, Oxford, 1960.
Momigliano, A., 'An Interim Report on the Origins of Rome', *Journal of Roman Studies*, LIII, 1963, pp. 95–121.

Nilsson, N. M. P., *Imperial Rome*, London, 1926.

Ogilvie, R. M., *The Romans and their Gods in the Age of Augustus*, London, 1969.

Paget, R. F., *In the Footsteps of Orpheus*, London, 1967.

Paget, R. F., 'The Naval Battle off Cumae in 39 B.C.', *Latomus*, XXIX, 2, 1970, pp. 363–9.

Paget, R. F., *The Waters of Cumae*, The Vergilian Society of America, 1972.

Pallottino, M., *The Art of the Etruscans*, London, 1955.

Salmon, E. T., *Samnium and the Samnites*, Cambridge, 1967.

Salmon, E. T., *Roman Colonization under the Republic*, London, 1969.

Scullard, H. H., *The Etruscan Cities and Rome*, London, 1967.

Scullard, H. H., *From the Gracchi to Nero*, 3rd edn., London, 1970.

de Sélincourt, A., *The 'History of Rome' of Livy, Books XXI-XXX*, trans., with an introduction by B. Radice, London, 1965. (Penguin Classics Series.)

Strabo, see Jones, 1917.

Strong, E., *Art in Ancient Rome*, 2 vols., London, 1929.

Tacitus, see Grant, 1971.

Torr, C., *Ancient Ships*, Cambridge, 1894.

Ward-Perkins, J. B., 'Etruscan and Roman Roads in Southern Etruria', *Journal of Roman Studies*, XLVII, 1957, pp. 139–43.

Ward-Perkins, J. B., *Landscape and History in Central Italy*, J. L. Myres Memorial Lecture, Oxford, 1964.

Warrington, J., *Everyman's Classical Dictionary*, London, 1961.

Webster, G., *The Roman Imperial Army of the First and Second Centuries, A.D.*, London, 1969.

INDEX

Acheulean axes, 26, 61
Acquapendente, 147
Acquasanta, 183
Acque Albule—*see* Bagni di Tivoli
Aequi, 160, 196, 197
Aesernia—*see* Isernia
Agrippina seated (statue), 48
Agylla—*see* Cerveteri
Alatri (Aletrium), 214
Alba Fucens, 43, 197
Albano Laziale, 226
Alfedena (Aufidena), 201
Alsium—*see* Palo
Altilia, 201
Amazon on horseback with Galatian (sculpture), 51
Amelia, 151
Amendola, Tripod of, 42; Amendola Sarcophagus, 47
Amiterno, 43
Amiternum—*see* San Vittorino
Anagni (Anagnia), 217
Ancona, 42, 169
Anxur—*see* Terracina
Anzio (Antium), 226
'Apennine' Bronze Age, 30, 69
Apollo (statue), 54
Apollo Apollini (sculpture), 44
Apollo Belvedere (sculpture), 52, 226
Apollo del Tevere (sculpture), 50
Apollo Milani (sculpture), 44
Apollo of Veii (terracotta), 142
Apollo Sauroctonus (sculpture), 52
Apoxyomenos, 52
Apulia, 28
Aqua Marcia, 195
Aquino (Aquinum), 218
Aricia, 227
Arpino (Arpinum), 218
Arretium (Arezzo), 33, 155
Artemis Laphria (sculpture), 44
Ascoli Piceno (Asculum), 183
Assisi (Asisium), 166

Aternum—*see* Pescara
Avezzano, 65

Bagni di Tivoli (Acque Albule), 187
Banditaccia necropolis, 114
Basilica di San Pelino, 44
baths, 78—*see also* Rome
Belverde, 59, 70
Benevento (Malaventum, Beneventum), 202
Bettona (Vettona), 175
Bisenzio, 54
Boiano (Bovianum), 201
Bolsena, 144
Boxer (bronze), 51
Boy with a Thorn in his Foot (bronze), 48
Boy with Goose (sculpture), 47
Breda, 140
brick-stamps, 98, 190
Bronze Age, 29, 65, 69, 71, 120—*see also* 'Apennine' Bronze Age
bronze work, 23, 45, 175
burins, 27, 64
bus services, 19, 23

Caere—*see* Cerveteri
Caiazzo (Caiatia), 201
Calvi Vecchia (Cales), 221, 235
Camerino (Camerinum), 167
Campania, 220
Capena, 174
Capestrano, 72, 73, 200
Capitoline Venus (sculpture), 48
Capua (Casilinum), 225
Capua (Santa Maria di Capua Vetere), 221
Caracalla (bust), 52
Carinola (Forum Propilii), 237
Carsoli (Carseoli), 196
Carsulae—*see* San Gemini
Carthaginians, 117
Cascata delle Marmore, 161
'cassa' tombs, 121

Cassino (Casinum), 219
Castel Bellino, 42
Castel d'Asso, 140
Castel del Sangro, 201
Castelluccio di Pienza, 154
Castel Starza, 238
Castel Volturno (Castrum Voltur-
    num), 237
Castra Albana, 226
Castro, 54
cave art, 64
Caverna di Frasassi—*see* caves
caves:
    Caverna di Frasassi, 71
    Grotta a Male, 59, 70
    Grotta Clemente Tronci, 65
    Grotta dei Baffoni, 72
    Grotta dei Moscerini, 62, 63, 231
    Grotta dei Piccioni, 59, 68, 70
    Grotta del Fossellone, 62
    Grotta del Grano, 172
    Grotta delle Capre, 63
    Grotta del Leone, 59, 67, 70
    Grotta dell'Orso, 59, 67, 68, 70
    Grotta del Mezzogiorno, 72
    Grotta di Ciccio Felice, 65
    Grotta di Gosto, 63, 70
    Grotta di Ortucchio (Grotta dei
        Porci), 66
    Grotta di Sant'Agostino (Grotta
        delle Marmotte), 62, 231
    Grotta di Tiberio, 62, 230
    Grotta Guattari, 62
    Grotta la Punta, 65
    Grotta Lattaia, 59, 68, 70
    Grotta Maritza, 65, 70
    Grotta Patrizi, 59, 67, 68
    Grotta Polesini, 27, 64, 70, 187
    Riparo Maurizio, 65
    la Romita di Asciano, 59, 67, 70
    le Tane del Diavolo, 59, 64, 70
Celle, 160
cemeteries, 68, 114, 121, 126, 133,
    136, 146, 153, 174—*see also*
    cremation cemeteries
centuriation, 150
Ceprano—*see* Fregellae
Cerveteri (Caere, Agylla, Cisra or
    Chaire), 33, 49, 52, 54, 111, 121
chamber tombs, 121
Chieti (Teate Marrucinorum), 200
Child Hercules (statue), 48
Chimera (bronze), 45, 155, 156
Chiusi (Cevsin, Camars, Clusium),
    45, 152

Cipus Perusinus (stele), 47
'circle graves', 131, 133
Circus Maritimus, 217
Civita Castellana (Falerii Veteres),
    159
Civitavecchia, 117
Clusium, 33, 44
coins, 133
colonies, Citizen, 163; Latin, 163,
    180
Commodus as Hercules (bust), 49
Conelle, 68
Corfinium, 199
copper, 29, 68
Copper Age—*see* Eneolithic Age
Cori (Cora), 207, 228
Cortona, 33, 155
Cosa, 109, 127, 128
cremation cemeteries, 30, 71, 121
Cumae, 127
cuniculi, 140, 142
Cures—*see* Passo Corese

Dancing Girl (sculpture), 50
Discobolus (sculpture), 50
Drunken Old Woman (sculpture),
    48
Dying Gaul (sculpture), 47

Elogia Tarquiniensia, 121
Eneolithic Age, 29, 65, 68
Eros and Psyche (sculpture), 47
Eros of Centocelle (statue), 52
Esquiline Hill, 48
Esquiline Venus (sculpture), 48
Etruria, 29
Etruscan League, 33
Etruscans, 31, 33, 44, 109, 187, 219

Faesulae (Fiesole), 33, 150
Falerii Novi, 151, 160
Falerii Veteres—*see* Civita Castellana
Faliscans, 161, 174
Fano (Fanum Fortunae), 172
Fanum Fortunae—*see* Fano
Fanum Voltumnae, 144
Fasti Consulares, 48
Fasti Triumphales, 48
Faun with Dionysus as a Boy
    (sculpture), 49
Ferentinum (Ferentino), 143, 217
Fidenae, 181
Filottrano, 42
Florence, 17, 148
Foligno (Fulginia), 165

Fondi (Fundi), 231, 232
Fonti del Clitunno—*see* Springs of Clitumnus
Formia (Formiae, Hormiae), 233
Forum Apfi, 224
Forum Propilii—*see* Carinola
'fossa' tombs, 114, 121, 133
Fossombrone (Forum Sempronii), 172
François Vase—*see* pottery
Fregellae (Ceprano), 215, 218
Fregenum, 111
frescoes, 51, 114, 122, 124
Frosinone (Frusino), 203, 213
Fucine Lake, 28, 65
Fuflona—*see* Populonia
Fullonica, 131

Gabii, 209
Galleria del Furlo, 172
Genzano di Roma, 227
Goddess with Child (statue), 54
Graviscae (Porto Clementino), 121
Gualdo Tadino (Tadinum), 19, 170
Gubbio (Iguvium), 171

Hadrian's Villa, 190
Head of Apollo (sculpture), 47
Head of a Priest (sculpture), 47
Head of a Youth (sculpture), 47
Head of Maryas (sculpture), 47
Head of Minerva (sculpture), 47
Helvia Ricina, 169
Hercules with the Stag (statue), 54
Hermes (sculpture), 50
Hispellum—*see* Spello
Hormiae—*see* Formia
Horta—*see* Orte

Ice Ages, 26
Idolino (bronze), 45
Iguvine Tables, 45, 171
Iguvium—*see* Gubbio
inhumation, 33, 121
Interamna Lirenas, 218
Interamna Nahars—*see* Terni
Interamnia Praetuttiorum, *see* Teramo
Ipogeo dei Volumni, 176
iron, 30, 133
Iron Age, 73—*see* 'Villanovan' Iron Age
Isernia (Aesernia), 201
Italic tribes, 196

Juno of the Palatine (sculpture), 50

Kore (statue), 50

Laocoon (sculpture), 52, 230
Last Glaciation—*see* Ice Age
Latium, 207ff.
Laughing Silenus (sculpture), 47
Laurentum, 226
Lavinium, 225
Lex de imperio Vespasiani (bronze tablet), 48
Licenza, 182, 195
Lucus Feroniae, 173
Lucca, 137
Ludovici Collection, 50
Luna, 122
Luni sul Mignone, 44, 70, 118

Magna Graecia, 33
Maiden of Anzio (sculpture), 51
Malaventum—*see* Benevento
Man and Wife (busts), 52
maps, 22
Marforius (statue), 47
Mars (bronze), 53
Mars and Venus (sculpture), 50
Marsi, 31
Marsiliana d' Albegna, 34
Massa Marittima, 132
masonry, 211
Meleager and his Dog (sculpture), 52
Mesolithic Age, 28, 63, 65
middens, 28, 59, 63
Middle Stone Age—*see* Mesolithic Age
Minerva of Velletri (sculpture), 48
Minerva or Athena (statue), 49
mines, 132
Minturnae, 233
Mirabella Eclano, 68
Montecelio, 187
Monte Circeo, 28
Monte d'Orlando, 231
Montefortino, 42
mosaic, 101, 106; Barberini mosaic, 210
Mother of the Gods on a Throne (statue), 44
Mousterian industries, 27, 61
museums:
　Agnani, 42, 217
　Alatri, 42
　Allumiere, 42
　Ancona (National Archaeological Museum of the Marche), 42, 71, 74, 169

Arezzo (Maecenate Archaeological Museum), 43
Assisi, 43
Avellino (Museo del Sannio), 74
Benevento, 202
Campobasso (Samnite Museum), 43
Capua, 223, 235
Castiglioncello, 137
Cetona, 70
Chieti (National Archaeological Museum of Abruzzo and Molise), 43, 65, 68, 72, 73, 74, 184, 200
Chiusi (Etruscan Museum), 43
Corfinio, 44
Cortona (Museum of the Etruscan Academy), 44
Florence (Museo Fiorentino di Preistoria), 73
Florence (National Archaeological Museum), 44, 73, 122, 131, 133, 136, 153, 155, 156
Grosseto, 45, 127
Gubbio, 45, 171
L'Aquila (National Museum of the Abruzzi), 45, 184
Naples, 45, 74
Nemi, 227
Orvieto, 46
Ostia Antica, 46
Palestrina (Archaeological Museum of Praeneste), 46
Perugia (National Archaeological Museum of Umbria), 46, 70, 73
Pesaro, 47
Rieti, 182
Rome (Baracco Museum), 47
Rome (Capitoline Museum), 47, 80
Rome (Chiaramonti Museum, Vatican), 52, 91
Rome (Etruscan Museum, Vatican), 53, 91
Rome (Forum Antiquarium), 49
Rome (Lateran Museum or Museo Profano), 49
Rome (Luigi Pigorini Prehistoric and Ethnographical Museum), 51, 61, 62, 64, 68, 74
Rome (Museo del Lazio)—see Rome (Luigi Pigorini . . .)
Rome (Museo di Roma), 84

Rome (Museum of Roman Civilization), 51
Rome (National Museum), 50, 173, 227
Rome (Palazzo dei Conservatori), 48, 80
Rome (Vatican Museum), 51, 91, 111, 114, 227
Rome (Villa Guilia Museum), 53, 111, 116, 122, 123, 156, 157, 160
Salerno, 74
Santa Maria di Capua, 220
Siena, 54
Spoleto, 163
Tarquinia, 55, 123
Todi, 55, 175
Viterbo, 55
Volterra (Guarnacci Museum), 55, 136

Naples, 17
Narce, 71, 120, 143
Narnia (Narni, Nequinum), 19, 161
Narni Scalo, 174
nenfro, 44
Neolithic Age, 28, 65, 67
Nepi (Nepet, Nepete), 151
Neptune driving his Chariot of Sea-horses (mosaic), 50
Nero's Villa, 226
New Stone Age—see Neolithic Age
Niobid (sculpture), 51
Nocera Umbra (Nuceria Camellaria), 19, 170
Norba (Norma), 228
Norchia, 140
Novillara, 47
Numana, 42, 43

obsidian, 69
Octavian (bust), 52
Old Centaur and the Young Centaur (sculpture), 48
Old Stone Age—see Palaeolithic Age
Orator (bronze), 45
Orte (Horta), 151
Orvieto, 44, 144, 146
Osimo, 42
Osteria del Gatto, 19
Ostia, 96
Otricoli (Ocriculum), 52, 161

Paeligni, 31, 199
Paestum, 126

Palaeolithic Age, 26, 61, 109
Palestrina (Praeneste), 210
Palo (Alsium), 111
Passo Corese (Cures), 181
Penelope (sculpture), 52
Perugia (Perusia), 33, 167, 175
Pesaro (Pisaurum), 47, 173
Pescara (Aternum), 200
Phoenicians, 117
Picentine tombs, 43
Piedmonte Massicano, 237
Pisa, 137
Pleistocene epoch, 26
Pliny the Younger's Villa, 226
Pontinian Mousterian industry, 61
Populonia (Fufluna or Pupluna), 33, 132
Porta d'Ascoli, 183
Portrait of L. Junius Brutus, 48
pottery, 28, 30, 142:
   Attic, 39, 45, 119, 133, 152
   biconical urns, 30
   black-figure, 39, 126, 152
   bucchero, 54, 142, 154
   Cales pottery, 222
   Campanian, 39
   'cardial ware', 28
   Corinthian, 39, 133
   Etrurian, 39
   François Vase, 45, 152
   geometric, 39
   hut-urns, 220
   Italiote, 39
   'milk-boiler' or 'strainer', 30
   orientalized, 39
   Pontic vases, 126
   proto-Attic, 39
   proto-Corinthian, 39, 119, 174
   proto-geometric, 39
   red-figure, 39, 152
   travertine cinerary urns, 175
   Vasa Arretina, 157
Pozzarello, 145
   'pozzo' ('pozzetto') tombs, 114, 121, 133
Prima Porta, 51
Punicum—see Santa Marinella
Puteoli (Pozzuoli), 97, 221
Pyrgi—see San Severa

Quercia, 19

Regolini-Galassi tomb, 111
Rieti (Reate), 182
Rignano, 159

Rinaldone, 29, 68
Riparo Maurizio—see caves
Ripoli, 28
roads, Etruscan, 138
roads, Roman, 17, 31, 40:
   Amerina, 40, 138, 150
   Appia, 41, 80, 93, 208, 216, 224
   Aurelia Nova, 40, 109
   Aurelia Vetus, 40, 109
   Caecilia, 41, 184
   Cassia, 40, 138
   Claudia Nova, 184
   Clivus Capitolinus, 84
   Clodia, 40, 138
   Domitiana, 237
   Flaminia, 19, 41, 158
   Labicana, 41, 208
   Latina, 41, 208, 214
   Minucia, 200
   Praenestina, 41, 208, 209
   Salaria, 41, 181
   Tiberina, 41, 161, 173
   Tusculana, 41, 208, 215
   Valeria, 41, 194
Romanellian industries, 63
Romans, 31, 77, 149
Rome, 17, 33, 77:
   Altar to the Unknown God, 89
   Ara Pacis, 81, 82
   Arch of Constantine, 83, 90
   Arch of Drusus, 93
   Arch of Septimus Severus, 87
   Arch of Titus, 88
   Basilica Aemelia, 86
   Basilica Argentaria, 90
   Basilica Julia, 83, 87
   Baths of Caracalla, 79, 82, 92
   Baths of Diocletian, 50, 79, 82, 91
   Baths of Septimus Severus, 83, 88
   Capitol, 80
   Castel Sant'Angelo, 91
   Catacombs, 93
   Circus Maxima, 92
   Circus of Maxentius, 94
   Cloaca Maxima, 92
   Colosseum, 83, 90
   Column of Marcus Aurelius, 80, 82
   Column of Phocas, 86
   Column of Trajan, 83, 89
   Domus Augustana, 83, 88
   Domus Aurea, 90
   Forum Boarium, 82, 90
   Forum of Augustus, 83, 90
   Forum of Nerva, 83, 90

Forum of Trajan, 83, 89
Fountain of Aesculapius, 91
House of Livia, 83, 88
House of the Vestal Virgins, 83, 87
Lapis Niger, 83, 86, 226
Mamertine prison (Tullianum), 86
Mausoleum of Augustus, 81, 82
museums—*see* museums
obelisk of Flaminius, 80
Paedagogium, 89
Palace of the Flavian Emperors, 88
Pantheon, 82, 84
Pons Cestius, 78
Pons Fabricius (Ponte dei Quattro
    Capi), 78
Pons Sublicius, 78
Porta Appia (Porta San Sebas-
    tiano), 82, 92
Porta Maggiore, 95
Porta Ostiensis (Porta San Paolo),
    82, 92
Porticus of the Temple of the Dei
    Consentes, 84
Pyramid of Gaius Cestius, 92
Regia, 88
Roman Forum, 82, 84, 85, 86
St Peter's Cathedral, 91
San Omobono, 73
Secretarium Senatus, 86
Septizonium, 89
Tabularium, 80, 83
Temple of Antonius and Faustina,
    86
Temple of Concord, 86
Temple of Cybele, 83, 88
Temple of Fortuna Virilis, 92
Temple of Jupiter, 95
Temple of Mars Ultor, 90
Temple of Minerva, 83, 90
Temple of Saturn, 83, 86
Temple of the Dioscuri, 86
Temple of Venus Genetrix, 83, 89
Temple of Vespasian, 86
Temple of Vesta, 83, 87, 92
Theatre of Marcellus, 82, 92
Tomb of Caecilia Metella, 94
Tomb of Romulus, 95
Tomb of Seneca, 95
Tomb of the Licinii, 95
Tomb of the Scipios, 82, 93
Tomb of the Sons of Sextus
    Pompeius Justus, 95
Torre del Milizie, 83, 89
Trajan Markets, 83, 89
Via Sacra, 83, 87

Rusellae, 33, 129

Saepinum—*see* Altilia
Samnites, 35, 160, 177, 182, 215
San Gemini (Carsulae), 175
San Genisto, 42
San Giovenale, 111
San Paolina di Filottrano, 71
San Severa (Pyrgi), 111, 116
San Severino Marche, 42
Santa Croce, 71
Santa Marinella (Punicum), 111,
    117
San Vincenzo, 134
San Vittorino (Amiternum), 184
Sarcophagus of Larthis Salaviti, 45
Sarcophagus of Ramia Uzenai, 45
Sarcophagus of the Married Couple,
    54, 116
Sarcophagus of the Muses, 50
Sarteano, 154
Scauri, 233
Scoppito, 43
Segni (Signia), 217
Sentinum, 167
'Servian wall', 78
Sessa Aurunca (Suessa), 235, 236
Settebagni, 181
Sezze (Setia), 228
She-Wolf (bronze), 48, 81
Siena, 148
Sleeping Ariadne (statue), 52
Sleeping Erinyes (sculpture), 50
Spello (Hispellum), 166
Sperlonga, 230
Spoleto (Spoletium), 162
Springs of Clitumnus (Fonti del
    Clitunno), 163
stelae, 47
Sulmona (Sulmo), 201
Sutri, 143

Tabula Iliaca, 48
Tadinum—*see* Gualdo Tadino
le Tane del Diavolo—*see* caves
Tarquinia (Tarquinii, Tarcauna or
    Tarchna), 33, 44, 120-4
Teate Marrucinorum—*see* Chieti
Teano (Teanum Sidicinum), 219,
    221, 235, 237
Telamon, 122
Telese (Telesia), 201
Teramo (Interamnia Praetuttiorum),
    184
Terme di Cotilia, 182

Terni (Interamna Nahars), 161
Terracina (Anxur, Tarracina), 229
terracotta, 23, 114, 142, 160, 175, 222
Tivoli (Tibur), 194
Todi (Tuder), 53, 175
Tomba di Nerone, 139
Torre in Pietra (Torrimpietra), 61,
    109
Torso of an athlete (bronze), 45
Torso of Hermes, 49
Torso of Peplophorus, 50
Trajan (bust), 52
tratturi ('drovers' trails'), 179
Triflisco, 220
Tuscania, 44
Tusculum, 215, 217

'urnfield' culture, 30
Urbs Salvia, 168

Vairano Scalo, 219
Valmontone (Vitellia), 217
Veii, 31, 33, 54, 140
Velletri (Velitrae), 228
Venafro, 202

'Venus figurines', 27
Venus of Cyrene (sculpture), 50
Vescia, 239
Vestini, 31
Vettona—see Bettona
Vetulonia (Vetluna or Vatluna), 33,
    44, 129, 131
Villa di Nerone, 214
Villa di Ovidio, 200
'Villanovan' Iron Age, 31, 117, 120,
    126, 129, 141
Villa of Livia, 173
Viterbo, 143
Volsinii, 33
Volterra (Velathri, Volaterrae), 33,
    134
Vulci, 33, 44, 53, 121, 124

Warrior of Capestrano (terracotta),
    43, 72, 73, 200
Winged Horses (terracotta), 121, 123

Young Girls from Antium (sculp-
    ture), 51
Youth leaning on a stick (bronze), 51

2/23/01 - 12